CAMPAIGNS AND HURRICANES

★ ★

CAMPAIGNS AND HURRICANES
A History of Presidential Visits to Mississippi
John M. Hilpert and Zachary M. Hilpert

★ ★

University Press of Mississippi / Jackson

www.upress.state.ms.us

The University Press of Mississippi is a member of
the Association of American University Presses.

First printing 2018
∞

Library of Congress Cataloging-in-Publication Data

Names: Hilpert, John M., author. | Hilpert, Zachary M., author.
Title: Campaigns and hurricanes : a history of presidential visits to Mississippi / John M.
Hilpert and Zachary M. Hilpert.
Description: Jackson : University Press of Mississippi, [2018] | Includes bibliographical
references and index. |
Identifiers: LCCN 2017038042 (print) | LCCN 2017040130 (ebook) | ISBN 9781496816474
(epub single) | ISBN 9781496816481 (epub institutional) | ISBN 9781496816498 (pdf
single) | ISBN 9781496816504 (pdf institutional) | ISBN 9781496816467 (cloth : alk. paper)
Subjects: LCSH: Presidents—Travel—Mississippi. | Presidents—United States.
Classification: LCC E176.1 (ebook) | LCC E176.1 .H555 2018 (print) | DDC973.09/9—dc23
LC record available at https://lccn.loc.gov/2017038042

British Library Cataloging-in-Publication Data available

Pat and Sandy

*Without your patience and support
this history would remain untold*

CONTENTS

INTRODUCTION

Prior to the twentieth century, no president of the United States visited Mississippi while in office. Several men who either would hold or had held the office traveled to or through the state during the 1800s. Zachary Taylor was the closest to a sitting president who visited during the early period; he stopped for a celebration at Vicksburg in 1849 as president-elect on the way to his inauguration. He and at least two other nineteenth-century presidents owned and frequented homes in Mississippi. Andrew Jackson reportedly camped in Hancock County on his way to the Battle of New Orleans in 1814. Legend has it that Abraham Lincoln walked the Natchez Trace in the 1820s. A list of more than forty fanciful or factual Mississippi connections with historical figures prior to or after the completion of their presidential terms—based on a variety of sources—comprises Appendix B following the final chapter.

However, the principal focus of this comprehensive guide is on known and verifiable visits to Mississippi by presidents of the United States during their years in office. William McKinley was the first to travel to the state while serving as president, arriving by train less than two months after his second inauguration in 1901 and making stops and speeches in a few communities. Theodore Roosevelt famously hunted—but never shot—bears in the Mississippi Delta the following year, thereby launching the teddy bear craze that persists to this day. William Taft and a flotilla of steamboats bearing hundreds of politicians, journalists, and other persons of renown stopped through in 1909. Woodrow Wilson and his wife spent a two-and-a-half-week 1913 Christmas and 1914 New Year holiday on the Mississippi Gulf Coast, earning him the distinction of making the longest presidential sojourn. (Prior to Harry Truman's presidency, he and his wife rented a cottage and vacationed on the coast for a stretch of six weeks.)

During the twentieth century and through 2016—the terminus for this accounting—thirteen of the nineteen US presidents visited Mississippi while in office. They are William McKinley, Theodore Roosevelt, William Taft, Woodrow Wilson, Franklin Roosevelt, Richard Nixon, Gerald Ford, Jimmy Carter, Ronald Reagan, George H. W. Bush, Bill Clinton, George W. Bush, and Barack Obama. Each of these earned a chapter in this book that provides details of his time in the state—who, when, where, why, and a summary or sampling of what he said. Four presidential addresses delivered in Mississippi had broader national significance, in the opinion of the coauthors of this book, and thus there are verbatim renderings of these four speeches in Appendix A.

By the numbers, George W. Bush is the unquestioned champion of presidential visits to the state, with nineteen during his eight years in office. However, when it comes to counting presidential visits, even a seemingly straightforward count requires interpretation. On November 1, 2003, for instance, President Bush made appearances in both Southaven and Gulfport on behalf of Haley Barbour's gubernatorial bid. Between those stops—the first in northern Mississippi and the second on the Gulf Coast—Air Force One flew the president on a round-trip to Kentucky for two campaign speeches in support of another Republican candidate. Thus a question arises: does the day represent one or two visits by Bush to Mississippi? The decision here was to consider it as one visit with two stops, but the reverse could be just as easily argued. Likewise, when Woodrow Wilson and his family vacationed for two weeks on the Gulf Coast, they were in residence at a home in Pass Christian. We credited that community with a presidential visit, but we did not sum as additional presidential visits Wilson's drives to nearby communities for golf outings, a worship service, or other day trips.

The George W. Bush illustration above also points clearly to the effects of the transportation revolution on the history of presidential travel. When Andrew Jackson camped in Hancock County in 1814—fifteen years prior to assuming the presidency—he was traveling from Mobile, Alabama, to New Orleans, Louisiana, a distance of roughly 130 miles. Days, not hours, were required for the trip. George W. Bush's one day of flying from Washington, DC, to Southaven, Mississippi; to Paducah, Kentucky; to London, Kentucky; to Gulfport, Mississippi; and back to the nation's capital covered a distance of more than 2,500 miles. The transportation factor alone accounts for much of the variance in the number of visits between earlier and later presidents. Other issues affecting decisions about presidential travel include cost, time, security, political considerations, national and international events, and the selection of impactful venues for promoting a president's policy preferences. The coauthors used these pages to discuss many of these factors as demonstrated by particular presidential visits to Mississippi.

Americans evidence endless fascination with the institution of the presidency, and they are generally anxious to see in the flesh any individual who has risen to the office. Even during periods of public disapproval, citizens will mass at rallies or overfill rooms for town hall–style discussions when a president comes to town. Seemingly embodied in one individual are the nation's hopes, dreams, expectations, and disappointments. How many jewelry boxes have one or more campaign pins tucked away from recent or long-forgotten elections? How many office or home walls have oversized portraits of the current president or of an admired predecessor in the White House? How many hundreds of thousands or millions of political arguments happen each day over coffee, as Americans assess the performance of the nation's chief executive? How many opinion pages in newspapers would be largely empty if there weren't a president to support or criticize?

Citizens of an area visited by a president have physical proof that they are valued participants in the life of the nation, important enough that the person considered the most powerful in the world has traveled to see them, to listen to them, and to seek their approval for policies, accomplishments, or candidates for office. Thus a presidential visit is nearly irresistible; it draws supporters, critics, and the merely curious. All states have histories of presidential visits, but for many states such events are relatively rare occurrences to be savored and recalled for years, even decades, into the future. More communities than not have never been visited by a sitting president of the United States, but still there will be those residents in town who entertain friends and neighbors with stories of their travel to larger population centers where they were so close to a president that they reached out for a handshake.

There are some presidential encounters that no town would desire, namely, those made in response to a disaster—hurricanes, tornadoes, floods, volcanic eruptions, earthquakes, and the like. Yet in those instances, a visit from the president offers comfort and assurance that the region's tragedy is recognized and that assistance from the highest levels of government is on the way. Mississippi has benefited from such presidential visits in the shadows of several disasters—Hurricanes Camille, Frederic, and Katrina to name a few.

Fortunately for most states, including Mississippi, presidential disaster visits are not the sole category. There are statewide and local candidates of the president's party to support. There are issues that are highlighted by the successes, problems, or voters of a particular location. There are awards to give, military installations to review, celebrations and commencements to attend, donors to thank, and on and on. Time is precious and travel is expensive. The purpose for each visit must be clear and meaningful.

Mississippi is not the most visited state by presidents of the United States, but neither is it the least visited. These days, Republican chief executives visit Mississippi much more frequently than Democrats, a predictable result of the fact that for sixty years only one presidential election in the state has gone the way of the Democratic candidate. This has resulted, in no small measure, from the success of the Republicans' Southern Strategy—described in the pages of this book—that has given the party a hold on the southeast region of the nation. Mississippi is a prime example of that success.

Despite the state's half-century history as a Republican stronghold, all eight presidents who served between Richard Nixon's oath of office in 1969 and Barack Obama's farewell in early 2017—five Republicans and three Democrats—made one or more visits apiece to Mississippi. Prior to the Nixon years, only five of the first thirty-six presidents visited while in office, and as recorded earlier in this introduction, there were no visitors before William McKinley in 1901. Including that first instance, there have been sixty-nine stops by US presidents in thirty-three Mississippi communities during forty-five separate trips to the state. Both Gulfport and Jackson have hosted one sitting president or another eleven times. Other communities with multiple visits are: Biloxi with eight; Bay St. Louis, Pascagoula, and Vicksburg with three apiece; Corinth, Meridian, and Pass Christian with two each.

Twenty-four Mississippi communities have hosted one visit. These are: Amory, Brookhaven, Camp Shelby (near Hattiesburg), Canton, Clarksdale, Columbus, Edwards, Gautier, Greenville, Long Beach, Lorman, Madison, McComb, Mound Bayou, Natchez, Poplarville, Smedes, Southaven, Starkville, Summit, Tupelo, Wesson, West Point, and Yazoo City.

Thirteen chapters comprise the main body of this book, and there are a conclusion and two appendices. Each of the chapters focuses on a single president, setting historical contexts both nationally and within the state for his visit(s) and describing in detail what occurred while he was in Mississippi. The conclusion is an essay considering the significance of presidential visits generally and seeking to understand how Mississippi's experiences with such events fit into this picture. As mentioned earlier, Appendix A is the verbatim presentation of four significant presidential addresses delivered in Mississippi, and Appendix B is a listing of prepresidential and postpresidential visits to the state by men who occupied the White House. As the notes on evidence caution, a few of the records of these latter visits are quite sketchy, suggesting that some stories might be more myth than fact. These reports are included, however, for those who may be curious, those who may have heard rumors, or those who may benefit from a launch point for further research.

It is likewise necessary that the coauthors offer this disclaimer: though they believe the information contained in this book represents a complete record of visits to Mississippi by sitting US presidents, it is possible the research for this book failed to uncover one or more presidential visits. No comprehensive list existed, just scraps, jottings, online mentions, and media accounts that the coauthors used to jump-start the project. The Mississippi Department of Archives and History maintained a file on the subject; it consisted of handwritten notes, clippings, and other loose sheets of paper offering glimpses of some visits. Still, this file proved to be a worthy, if incomplete, starting point. We are grateful to the archivists with that agency for stuffing items into the folder over many years and for providing them to us as a resource. If any presidential visit is missing from this comprehensive guide, the coauthors accept responsibility, beg the readers' forgiveness, and solicit the information for a future edition of the book.

Finally, the coauthors wish to acknowledge that a sad imbalance exists between the viewpoints of African American and white Mississippians in the early chapters that follow, one that grows out of the years of segregation and the suppression of black voices and votes throughout that history. The coauthors sought homegrown analyses of presidential visits by way of the many local newspapers published throughout the state. White, Democratic-leaning newspapers provided a wealth of information and analysis, but these same papers excluded the views of black citizens, who made up nearly 60 percent of the state's population at the beginning of the twentieth century. Working with far fewer resources than their white counterparts, African American journalists' valiant efforts kept Mississippians informed throughout the period via an extensive black-run press. Unfortunately, a tragically miniscule representation of their efforts survives today in archives; many of these newspapers, some that published for years, have vanished without a tangible trace. Researchers glimpse a few examples in the form of a handful in fragile condition that now are treasured by the same collections that assigned them no value only a few generations ago. Unfortunately, none of these few surviving editions discuss the presidential visits covered here. Interested readers will find an outstanding study of the state's expansive African American newspaper industry in Julius E. Thompson's 1994 book, *The Black Press in Mississippi, 1865–1985*, and the companion directory.

CAMPAIGNS AND HURRICANES

CHAPTER ONE

WILLIAM MCKINLEY

Twenty-Fifth President of the United States
Republican
Elected 1896 and 1900
Served March 4, 1897, to September 14, 1901

★ ★

Shortly after William McKinley's second inauguration on March 4, 1901, his office announced a plan for an extensive spring trip to the southern and western states with the stated goal of promoting public policies the president intended to emphasize over the next four years.[1] Traveling by rail, the nation's chief executive intended to make a number of stops on a two-day swing through Mississippi, along a path highlighted by an especially symbolic visit to the capital city. McKinley's presence marked the first visit to Mississippi by a sitting president, a bold move by a Republican politician at a time when an entrenched Democratic machine controlled the state.

A quarter-century before McKinley's arrival, Mississippi Democrats drove the last vestiges of the Reconstruction-era state government—a near-uniformly Republican body—from Jackson. The embers of the North-South divide that propelled the nation into civil war four decades earlier still smoldered throughout the state in 1901. John M. Stone, the last Confederate veteran to serve as governor of Mississippi, left the role only five years earlier, and the state was still home to some of the most strident antifederal attitudes in the country.

Mississippi was so much a Democratic state at the turn of the century, in fact, that the Republican Party did not even place a candidate on the ballot in the 1899 election for governor. That contest's winner, Democrat

Andrew H. Longino, defeated Rufus K. Prewitt of the Populist Party by a margin of greater than 8 to 1. McKinley himself did not carry a single county in Mississippi during the presidential election one year later, and the state was one of only two in which the incumbent president's share of the vote total was less than 10 percent.

Simply put, Mississippi was not McKinley territory.

When the administration announced the president's intention to visit the state, a version of southern hospitality prevailed. State newspapers encouraged an—albeit temporary—defusing of tensions in honor of the unprecedented visit. Some Mississippians even anticipated McKinley's arrival as an expression of national unity with the southern state. The *Greenville (MS) Times* of May 4, 1901, declared that McKinley's visit demonstrated "the softening and beneficial influence of personal contact between the scattered sections of this extensive commonwealth, and hence we believe that this trip can but make for good."[2]

Unity was an important theme for the president. McKinley's expansionist policies envisioned a rapidly industrializing and urbanizing nation that was fast becoming a major international player. Bitter sectionalism made no contribution to the goal of building a strong nation with an external role in the world that would rival the great European empires. Therefore, when the United States triumphed in the Spanish-American War of 1898, it was the American—rather than the Federal—army that citizens in both the North and the South cheered.

American military, political, and cultural influence around the globe was on the rise, and many in the nation celebrated eagerly. McKinley's visit, in fact, coincided with the opening of the Pan-American Exposition in Buffalo, New York, a world's fair organized to trumpet expanding US territorial and political strength throughout the Americas.

To drive home the theme of national unity, the administration scheduled a newsworthy and symbolic ceremony to take place in Jackson on May 1, the opening day of the exposition in Buffalo. During his stop in Mississippi's state capital, McKinley was to press a button that would open the Pan-American Exposition by sending electricity to the fairgrounds at a distance of 1,000 miles. The gesture meant to recognize the importance and centrality to the increasingly industrial, urban nation of even a state where over 90 percent of the population lived in rural areas.[3] With the push of a button, McKinley planned to acknowledge that the country's industrial might could only be built upon a strong agrarian foundation.

Politically, there was another objective for Republicans. While the McKinley and Roosevelt ticket made electoral gains for the party of Lincoln, the South remained a solid voting bloc for Democrats. Clearly, Republican leaders anticipated this outcome in the election of 1900. Vice-presidential candidate Theodore Roosevelt's extensive campaign by railcar through twenty-three states—480 communities—wasted neither time nor party resources on stops south of Missouri, Kentucky, and West Virginia.[4]

Thus McKinley, his wife, cabinet members and their spouses, and several journalists departed Washington, DC, on April 29, 1901, for the Pacific coast on a presidential train. Later in the tour, at the southernmost stop in El Paso, Texas, Mrs. McKinley became seriously ill, causing the president to alter his plans along the way. Eventually, the travelers left the West Coast, canceled the remaining stops, and returned to the nation's capital, where Mrs. McKinley recovered by early July.

Enthusiasm for the president and his entourage was obvious at the outset. Coverage occupied the front pages of newspapers across the nation. "With the cheers of 10,000 people ringing in his ears, the president started his westward tour this morning," wrote C. C. Carlton for the *San Francisco Call*. "The depot was thronged by a crowd eager to see and to bid him good-by and Godspeed. . . . The president and his wife bowed their acknowledgments to the enthusiastic cheers and hat wavings that testified to the esteem of the people."[5] Departure for the seven-week, 10,000-mile trip was at 10:30 a.m.

No president escapes public criticism, of course, and McKinley was subject to attacks for the extravagance of this trip. Journalists noted that the Pullman Company furnished transportation and consumables at an estimated total of $50,000, that the president traveled with twenty-seven official guests, and that there were six trunks of clothing loaded on the train for the chief executive and his wife. One wonderfully named newspaper, the *Kansas Agitator*—an organ of the People's Party, a short-lived populist group that endorsed William Jennings Bryan, McKinley's opponent in both the 1896 and 1900 elections—offered its opinion on the fifth day of the trip: "No king or potentate ever traveled in such style."[6]

Just as twenty-first-century presidents stay in constant communication and must be kept safe, so McKinley enjoyed the early twentieth-century version of those privileges. Telegraphers and messengers stood at the ready to serve communication needs throughout the trip, and a journalist reported that "every facility has been arranged to transact such business as is necessary."[7] All other trains—both passenger and freight—moved onto sidetracks, and, at times, a pilot train ran ahead of the president's special, as railroad officials took precautions to avoid mishaps.

On April 30, 1901, one day into the trip, the president traveled through northern Alabama and then visited Corinth, Mississippi. This day's final destination was a 4:30 p.m. arrival in Memphis, Tennessee, for a banquet and evening celebration. It became a lengthy event, and the weary travelers dragged themselves back to the train at 1:00 a.m. on the morning of May 1.

Following the festivities, McKinley and party departed Memphis at 1:30 a.m. for a journey of several hours to New Orleans. Stops along the way added time to the trip, as the president traveled through what journalists called "the valley of the Yazoo." McKinley appeared frequently on the train's rear platform to acknowledge crowds as he passed through small communities.[8] Vicksburg welcomed the president at 8:30 a.m. for a brief visit. His schedule set the next stop for Jackson at 10:00 a.m. There was a timetable that would take the party to New Orleans by 4:30 p.m.

April 30, 1901—Corinth

More than seventy-five years after McKinley's 1901 stop in Corinth, Mississippi, the community continued to enjoy the story of the event. On September 21, 1977, the *Daily Corinthian* recalled: "Tuesday, April 30, 1901, was a gala day for the Corinth area. That was the day President and Mrs. William McKinley came to town."[9]

On that day in 1901, newly elected US congressman Ezekiel S. Candler Jr., an attorney who practiced in Corinth's own Alcorn County, welcomed the president and Mrs. McKinley, as well as those accompanying them on the seven-car special train. Representative Candler spoke on behalf of the 4,500 persons who had assembled at the station for the occasion. As was the custom of the time for visits by dignitaries in many communities, factory whistles blew and an honor guard set off a cannon.

Candler assured the president that despite the deep resentments of the Civil War years, "in the present we stand shoulder-to-shoulder and heart-to-heart." Responding in kind, McKinley spoke of the courage of men on both sides of that conflict that was nearing four decades in the past, and he said, "There is but one side now."[10]

At the outset of his remarks, McKinley recognized that this stop was the first of a few planned for Mississippi, but that there were visits in other states preceding Corinth on this trip. He complimented his audience: "Of the many cordial receptions we have had upon our journey none have been warmer or more heartfelt" than the present one in what he termed an "interesting and progressive city." He nodded toward local history, observing that the "battle-fields about you attest the courage and valor and heroism of the American soldier on both sides of the line."

McKinley got quickly to his message of national unity by witnessing to the crowd that men of both the South and the North had subsequently and recently fought together in Cuba, Puerto Rico, the Philippines, and China. "When we are all on one side," he proclaimed, "we are unconquerable." Then, because there had been charges of militarism and imperialism in the election of 1900 by his Democratic opponents, the president assured, "We love peace better than war, and our swords never should be drawn except in a righteous cause."

Finally, McKinley took a moment to do what most presidents do as often as possible, namely, he proclaimed the positive results of his leadership: "I congratulate you, my fellow citizens, upon the prosperity of the country. We never were so well off as we are today. We never had so many happy homes. We never had such high credit, such good money, so much business as we have in the United States in the year 1901, and it is your business, for the public official is but the agent of the people. It is your business as well as mine to see to it that an industrial policy shall be pursued in the United States that shall open up the widest markets in every part of the world for the products of American soil and American manufacture."[11]

Altogether the McKinley stop in Corinth lasted about ten minutes.

May 1, 1901—Vicksburg, Edwards, Jackson, Wesson, Brookhaven, Summit, and McComb

Following the afternoon stop in Corinth and the longer evening celebration in Memphis, the McKinley entourage made a visit the next morning to Vicksburg. It was May 1, 1901.

Cheering crowds honored President and Mrs. McKinley as they rode through the streets of the community in a carriage especially decorated for the occasion. By doffing his hat to a Confederate flag and visiting the national cemetery, McKinley made a positive impression on his southern audience, and Mississippians responded in kind. The *Pascagoula Democrat-Star* of May 17 wrote that "the Confederate veterans of Vicksburg presented Mrs. McKinley with a souvenir spoon. In the bowl of the spoon were the words, 'Vicksburg, Miss.' On the handle was engraved a confederate and a union flag crossed; on the back of the bowl, 'To Mrs. McKinley from Camp 32 UCV [United Confederate Veterans].' The president could not miss the symbolism of the crossed flags, and he surely appreciated it in light of his campaign for unity. He spoke to an audience on the lawn of the Old Court House.[12] One source estimated that the size of the crowd was 15,000 people; they heard an address from the president that was "full of patriotic phrases."[13]

As elsewhere on his trip, the theme of prosperity-through-unity framed the president's brief remarks. "In the moment that I have to tarry with you," he said, "I can only make my acknowledgements and congratulate you one and all that you share in that universal prosperity and contentment so characteristic at this time in every part of our common country."[14]

Journalists recorded McKinley's addresses in Mississippi—generally as verbatim renditions abbreviated according to quickly scribbled notes—and they shared the president's thoughts with the public in both in-state and out-of-state newspapers. On this day in Vicksburg, for instance, they reported that he referred to the "historic city," and he informed his audience that he felt "at home" and that "nowhere in my native state of Ohio could I receive warmer or more sincere welcome than I have received at the hands and from the hearts of the people of Mississippi." He assured the people in the crowd that America "is the best country in the world."

Then the president continued with his themes of unity and congeniality between the South and the North: "It is the land we love; the land of possibilities and of opportunities to every child that dwells beneath the folds of our flag. I have been glad not only to be greeted by the veterans of the Grand Army of the Republic, but by the Confederate Veterans, by the people at large, but no welcome could be so sweet to me as that of the fresh young school children of the city of Vicksburg. To one and all I return my sincere and heartfelt thanks and leave with you the hope of your happiness and your prosperity."[15]

As the entourage steamed on, there were next a brief stop and crowd salute in Edwards and then a longer pause in Jackson, where the president was greeted by a welcoming party led by Mississippi's governor, Andrew Longino. The *Pascagoula Democrat-Star* reported that there was a large, diverse crowd when McKinley's train reached the city. "Acres of people, Democrats, Republicans, white and black had congregated at the depot and gave a royal welcome to Mississippi's capital."[16] Between this first visit to the city by a sitting president and the impending ceremonial button press that would send electricity to the Pan-American Exposition in Buffalo, Jackson's residents surely felt the pride that came along with the nation's attention. (In a strange turn of fate, not only did President McKinley switch on the lights on the exposition's first day, but in September 1901—just over four months later—he made his final speech and an assassin's bullet felled him on those same fairgrounds.)

Still, it did not take the president's approval to convince the citizenry of their rightful place on the national stage. McKinley's arrival in the city came at a time when Jackson was reaffirming its own centrality; the president's train rolled into town less than two months after the commencement of construction on the monumental new state capitol building, the gleaming Beaux Arts seat of government that would open its doors two years later.[17] Though the thoroughly modern and well-appointed structure had not yet begun to take form, Jacksonians' knowledge of its forthcoming completion was a constant reminder of the city's importance, as well as the citizens' ability to form a powerful state government.

As he had in Vicksburg, the site of so much Civil War history, President McKinley used his time at Jackson to express appreciation for the warm welcome in Mississippi: "I have received, in the course of my journey from the capital of this nation many hearty and generous receptions, but none more interesting or more memorable than the welcome extended by the governor of your state. . . . I thank your governor for announcing that I am president of all the country, all the states, and all the territories of this great country."

Though the Republican presidential ticket received less than 10 percent of Mississippi's votes in 1900, McKinley referred to himself in this peculiar way: "President by popular vote of every section of the union, by virtue of the forms and rules laid down by the legislation of the United States." His point was to convince the people of the South "that in our national sense of duty and of honor . . . we stand as one people. This country of ours has been growing in the past few years, growing whether we wanted it or not."

As in Vicksburg, the president had successes and national issues to report: "The war with Spain started us growing and we could not help it if we would. Our growth has made new problems, but the American people have faced them and will continue to face them."

Were there reasons to hope? McKinley proclaimed them: "We will have our differences, men always would, but we have more agreements than differences. We may differ as to politics, agree as to principles, but we keep in the home circles and settle our differences among ourselves, and, which is the grandest tribute in the world to the American people, we have settled matters of foreign policy in the past to our satisfaction, and will treat new ones in the fear of God."[18]

Regarding other stops on that day, it was during the centennial month of McKinley's tour that the *Clarion-Ledger* published this note in an article on presidential visits to Mississippi: "William McKinley made a short stop in Jackson in May of 1901 and then visited cotton mills in the state."[19] According to a handwritten note preserved in the files of the Mississippi Department of Archives and History, the president and his party visited Mississippi Mills in Wesson.[20] However, the most complete list of stops available today is from the May 11, 1901, *Macon (MS) Beacon*, where this sentence leads the brief report on McKinley's visit: "The presidential train made short stops at Corinth, Vicksburg, Edwards, Jackson, Wesson, Brookhaven, Summit, and McComb City."[21]

During his stop in Wesson, McKinley commented to the assembled crowd on his tour of the local manufacturing facility, and he drew lessons for the nation: "This was not on the programme, but it was desired that I might see not only this great plant but the happy and contented people it employs. This is a most interesting and gratifying incident of my trip, to see the working people from this great mill come out at a time when they are so busy, to join with others in giving me greeting as I journey through your state. The happiest people in the world are those who are best employed. Work means wages; wages mean contentment, and bring to the home opportunities of education for the children, and it is the boast of our civilization that every boy and girl in the land can aspire to the highest positions of trust and honor."[22]

Finally, from this busy day of visits, there is a record of the president's remarks in McComb. He mentioned, yet again, the general success of the unified nation and that, according to his observations, the people of the South were sharing in those blessings. He mentioned, "larger prosperity than ever before . . . higher national and individual credit . . . rates of interest are lower . . . money is easy and more plentiful."

As he prepared to leave McComb and the state of Mississippi, he put the nation's international opportunities before his hearers: "What we want in this country, now having reached a point of development where we can more than supply our own demands, is foreign market in distant lands. We want to send the products of our farms, our factories, and our mines into every market in the world, to make the foreign peoples familiar with our products, and the way to do that is to make them familiar with our flag."[23]

★ ★ ★

While Mississippians appreciated McKinley's visit in 1901, the *Pascagoula Democrat-Star* assured readers that southern hospitality should not be mistaken for a softening of sentiments toward Republicans. Writing after the president's entourage arrived in New Orleans, the paper stated: "Of the many thousands of freemen who greeted him with marked respect and a most dignified southern welcome, but few of them voted for him in the campaigns that twice made him chief magistrate of our country. They will not be lured into supporting his party in the future, because it is considered a class embodiment of the rich against the poor. Its principles are to make the rich richer and the poor poorer through a combination of aggressive ownership of all the vast wealth and resources of the republic. This monster of oppression is the mastodon of pelf whose species will become extinct when exterminated by the patriotism and vengeance of hungry and wronged mankind. We will vote the Democratic ticket again and again!—to keep the South solid for the precious sake of the good of the increasing unterrified majority.

"The president's trip is a triumph in proof of forbearance rather than an endorsement of either he or his party."[24]

Also providing coverage and commentary during the time President McKinley visited the state was a weekly newspaper, the *Macon Beacon*. That periodical regularly included a front page, two-column round-up of regional events under the banner "Mississippi Matters" written by J. L. Powers. Anyone who seeks to understand the sentiments of Mississippians in the early days of the twentieth century would do well to read the items collected by Powers. There was a report on the president's visit occupying one paragraph. However, leading "Mississippi Matters" on that day was a four-paragraph piece on a statewide meeting of the United Daughters of the Confederacy. Also prior to the McKinley report was a separate piece on Mississippians registering for a reunion of the United Confederate Veterans in Memphis, and just after the paragraph on the presidential visit was a plea for the submission of all funds collected by organizations in Mississippi for the erection of a monument in Richmond, Virginia, to Confederate president Jefferson Davis.[25]

CHAPTER TWO

THEODORE ROOSEVELT

Twenty-Sixth President of the United States
Republican
Elected 1904
Served September 14, 1901, to March 4, 1909

★ ★

Remembered today as an almost mythical figure and revered politician, Theodore Roosevelt elicited far less laudatory reactions from vocally Democratic Mississippians during his two visits to the state in the early twentieth century. Mississippi's white press largely despised the Republican president, due in no small part to his having invited African American educator and leader Booker T. Washington to dine at the White House on October 16, 1901, barely a month into Roosevelt's unexpected presidency upon the assassination of William McKinley. In a country where segregation both de facto and de jure shaped every public space and even private interaction, the slightest suggestion of racial equality—at the president's own dinner table, no less—was cause for vitriol among the majority of whites in the Deep South.

His critics—vocally and persistently mocking him in the press on issues ranging from race relations to injuries sustained in a September 1902 carriage-streetcar accident—had precious little hospitality to offer the president when he crossed the border into Mississippi a little over a year after his dinner with Booker T. Washington. Nevertheless, Roosevelt's first trip to the state produced one of the defining legends of his public life. During this visit—a hunting excursion following a particularly contentious autumn in Washington—a brief incident between the president and a hobbled bear became part of our national mythology thanks to popular retellings that glorified the quality of good sportsmanship in the face of extreme frustration. As media shaped the story, it burnished the president's more admired qualities as an outdoorsman and an adventurer. That it is so widely remembered owes not as much to the published newspaper accounts during the visit as to a political cartoon in the days following the event and a favorite children's toy that enterprising firms began selling shortly thereafter.

Roosevelt knew well the value of travel to advance his political fortunes. He submitted to whistle-stop tours of several weeks duration for his 1898 gubernatorial campaign in New York and his run in 1900 for the vice presidency.[1] Though recreational hunting was the announced intention of his 1902 trip to Mississippi, he almost surely planned to cadge political gain by accepting an invitation to a visible sporting event in this southern state. The South was solidly in the camp of the Democratic Party, and racist resentments in the long shadow of the Civil War remained high. When President Roosevelt used an interim appointment to name Dr. W. D. Crum, an African American physician, to the federal post of collector of customs in Charleston, South Carolina, many white southerners, including Mississippians, openly expressed their anger.[2]

These feelings of resentment remained for years. Mississippi was the only southern state that refused an invitation for Roosevelt to visit and make an address during a 1905 presidential tour of the region. Finally, when the president returned to the state in 1907 to champion an ambitious economic proposal for developing the Mississippi River, a boisterous reception appeared more positive, yet barely one year later more than 90 percent of the state's votes went to the Democratic candidate, William Jennings Bryan, in the election of 1908 rather than to Roosevelt's hand-picked Republican successor, William Howard Taft.

November 13 to 19, 1902—Smedes

Journalists throughout the country reported on Monday, November 10, 1902, that the president was going hunting. The trip was a much-needed vacation for a man both physically and mentally bruised after a tough few months. In early October Roosevelt had taken the unprecedented step of inserting himself into a contentious coal strike in eastern Pennsylvania that threatened to become a catastrophe as winter approached and furnaces began to starve for fuel. The risky move paid off as the strikers soon returned to work under better conditions, but public reaction to Roosevelt's incursion was mixed despite the favorable outcome. At the same time that negotiations were progressing, Roosevelt was recovering from injuries sustained in his vehicular accident of mid-September.[3] A week away from Washington traversing the wilds of the Mississippi Delta surely sounded like a fine break to the avid outdoorsman.

Roosevelt also likely desired to demonstrate to the public that, despite the accident, he remained as healthy and vigorous as ever. In that spirit, his administration made sure that information on his trip found its way to citizens across the country. On the front page of the November 10 *Indianapolis Journal*, for example, was this straightforward announcement of the unusual week ahead: "President Roosevelt, Secretary [of the Treasury George] Cortelyou, and President Stuveysant Fish of the Illinois Central Railroad will leave New York on a special train Tuesday. . . . [After several stops through Thursday] their train will go over the Yazoo Valley road where a camp has been established near Smead [*sic*] in Sharkey County, Mississippi."[4] According to the reports, the governors of Mississippi, Arkansas, and Louisiana had extended the invitation, and the party intended to remain in camp for most of an entire week.

Holt Collier, an African American resident of the Mississippi Delta known for owning the region's "most famous pack of dogs,"[5] agreed to lead the hunt. Despite requests that journalists respect the president's privacy, the trip and Roosevelt's lack of hunting success became national news.[6]

While the vacation fascinated readers, its focus on hunting and its rusticity were not surprises to anyone; Roosevelt's carefully crafted, ruggedly masculine persona outsized even the bears he hunted. In one of his many published works, a book written in 1893 and titled *Hunting the Grisly and Other Sketches*, Roosevelt described the very methods he and his party would employ a decade later in his visit to the lower Mississippi Delta: "In the southern states the planters living in the wilder regions have always . . . [kept] regular packs of bear hounds. . . . They follow the bear and bring him to bay but do not try to kill him, although there are dogs of the big fighting breeds which can readily master a black bear if loosed at him. . . . The [hunters] follow the hounds through the canebrakes, and also try to make cutoffs and station themselves at open points where they think the bear will pass, so that they may get a shot at him."[7]

Roosevelt's bear hunt drew front-page interest for days, as newspapers across the nation carried updates on the trip. Day by day the president's misfortunes became the story, as illustrated by this report that ran in St. Louis, Missouri, on November 16: "No fresh bear skin had been hung up today at the camp on the Little Sunflower up to 4:30 this afternoon. At that hour the president, Mr. McIlhenny, and Holt Collier were still out in pursuit of a bear ... but the remainder of the party had abandoned the chase and twenty of the twenty-eight dogs had straggled back to camp, completely tuckered out."[8] The president's hunting companion on this occasion, John Avery McIlhenny, was a native of Louisiana, the scion of the family that invented Tabasco sauce, and a decorated Rough Rider under Roosevelt's command in the war with Spain.[9]

Three days later, the party's luck was no better. Mississippians and their fellow citizens across the nation read that the hunting dogs followed fresh trails and the president trekked for miles on end, yet each time the party crossed fresh tracks, the bears eluded their pursuers.[10]

Ultimately, Roosevelt left Smedes without taking a shot. As the *New-York Tribune* reported on November 19, 1902, "The last day of the chase was simply a repetition of the three preceding days, so far as [Roosevelt's] luck was concerned. Try as the hunters would, they could not get a bear within range of the president's rifle."[11]

But while Roosevelt left the Delta without a trophy, an incident on the second day of the hunt quickly grew to become a popular part of the Roosevelt mystique. That morning, the president was following the dogs, when the pack detected the scent of a bear, and a chase of several hours duration began. Eventually the dogs cornered an old bear in a pond, and Holt Collier stunned the animal with a rifle blow to the head. While he awaited the arrival of the rest of the party, the guide tied the animal to a tree.

"When the president caught up with Collier, he came upon a horrific scene: a bloody bear ... [and] a crowd of hunters shouting, 'Let the president shoot the bear!' As Roosevelt entered the water ... he refused to draw his gun, believing such a kill would be unsportsmanlike."[12]

This seemingly insignificant incident continues to attract interest because of what happened next, as this copy from a 2013 tourist brochure by Mississippi's Lower Delta Partnership explains: "The press went wild with this story ... and it soon traveled across the country in news stories and cartoons. Morris Mitchom, a toy shop owner in New York, wrote the president asking if he could name the stuffed toy bears in his shop 'Teddy's Bears.' The president agreed and before long all stuffed bears were known as Teddy Bears."[13]

Clifford Berryman, cartoonist for the *Washington Post*, produced the memorable image: Roosevelt in Rough Rider attire with his back to a tethered bear, his hand in a gesture of refusal, and his rifle grounded. Below was the caption, "Drawing the line in Mississippi." The *Washington Post* published the cartoon in its Sunday edition on November 16, 1902.

The hunt continued with no better results for the president. As he searched in vain for a lively bear worthy of his deadly attention, and as news of his clemency for the wounded bruin made headlines around the country, sixty miles away from the president's camp a far less noble fight was brewing in Indianola, Mississippi. Several white residents of the small town conspired to remove Minnie Cox, the town's federally appointed African American postmaster. Congress confirmed Cox's appointment in 1891 during the administration of Benjamin Harrison, and she reportedly had an admirable record in the job. However, a newspaper editor in the Mississippi Delta—James K. Vardaman, who became the state's governor in 1904—convinced locals to seek her removal on the grounds that her race made her unworthy of the respected and lucrative position.[14] Roosevelt's response to the emergency influenced the state's perception of him for years to come.

While the president might have known of the situation during his visit to the Delta, it was not until December 30 that Roosevelt formally recognized the events in writing; by that time, the situation had reached a crisis state. Charles Fitzgerald, Mississippi's federal postal inspector, wrote in a report that "the people of this section of the state say the president is forcing Negro domination on them."[15] While Fitzgerald knew that such perceptions were more the product of racial paranoia than anything else, he recommended at least temporary closure for the post office in Indianola. Fearing for her life, Cox offered her resignation. Instead, Roosevelt elected to suspend postal operations in Indianola as of January 2, 1903, and he ordered the attorney general to prosecute the citizens of the community who threatened Cox. The post office remained closed until February of the following year, while Cox continued—at least on paper—serving as postmaster, thereby allowing her to continue to receive her federal salary.

Cox, whom the white Fitzgerald had regularly praised in his inspections of the Indianola office, left the town under duress shortly after Roosevelt's edict. When news of her departure spread through town, her thrilled agitators threatened to kill her if she ever returned to her office.[16] While the extent of Roosevelt's sympathy for Cox is not clear, his motivation behind the move was anything but murky: the president had no desire to grant a victory to citizens attempting to overthrow a duly appointed federal officer via threat of violence. Southern white newspaper editors, meanwhile, argued that his protection of Cox, along with his other appointment of an African American man to the position of collector of the Port of Charleston, South Carolina, was nothing less than a strategy to secure the support of black voters for his first race for the presidency in 1904.

Even as the controversy evolved, and while Roosevelt toted his rifle through the Mississippi wilds, the state's newspapers attacked the president as a party-first politician. The *Aberdeen Weekly* charged that he was trying to break national unity with the South: "Recent events and the antics of President Roosevelt clearly demonstrate the purpose of the Republican Party to revive the sectional hatred and prejudice that constituted the slogan of their party several years ago, and in the approaching campaign to 'waive the bloody shirt' as the banner around which loyal Republicans must assemble. In brief this is for the purpose of arousing the prejudices of the western and northern people against the South and to divert attention from the main issues—the trusts and the tariff."[17] These unfortunate attitudes toward Roosevelt persisted for years.

During October 1905 the president and his wife took a tour by train through the states of the Old South. On October 24 Roosevelt spoke in Birmingham, Alabama, and the following day he spoke in Little Rock, Arkansas, and in Memphis, Tennessee. Then, on October 26, he spoke in New Orleans. Thus the Roosevelts' train route took them in and out of Mississippi several times, but neither Governor James Vardaman nor any other officials issued an invitation to the president to visit or speak, making Mississippi the only southern state to ignore the president.[18] A popular political humor publication of the day, *Puck*, ran a cartoon on its cover dated October 18, 1905, depicting Roosevelt as a southern gentleman riding a horse through a field with a vulture—labeled "Vardaman"—glaring at him from a tree branch.

It was 1907 before Roosevelt returned to appear publicly in the state. In the only trip to Mississippi during which he made a formal public address, Roosevelt advocated for major changes to one of the state's defining geographical landmarks—the Mississippi River—as a way to increase commercial opportunities. The ambitious proposal, had it been carried out, would have dramatically affected issues ranging from transportation policy to river development and national commerce. The president's stops in Louisiana, Mississippi, and Tennessee pushed his emphases onto the pages of the nation's newspapers.

October 21, 1907—Vicksburg and Mound Bayou

Vicksburg's port on the nation's most important river system is an obvious stop for dignitaries visiting Mississippi, and its pivotal Civil War history meant that most voters of the early twentieth century recognized its significance. Roosevelt was in the South during October 1907 following a trip related to the work of the Inland Waterway Commission. He boarded a steamboat at Keokuk, Iowa, earlier in the month, and his ship joined a flotilla conveying hundreds of politicians, well-heeled businessmen, and other dignitaries to the annual convention of the Lakes-to-the-Gulf Deep Waterway Association in Memphis, Tennessee. This was an organization supporting the development of the Mississippi River as a more significant commercial thoroughfare. Roosevelt was the convention's keynote speaker, and as the *Greenville Times* reported, "Mississippi had an immense delegation of the most representative men of the state."[19]

Never one to miss an opportunity for adventure in the outdoors, the president scheduled another southern hunting adventure as part of his trip down the river. According to several reports, this attempt to shoot a bear in Louisiana was more successful than his earlier hunt in Mississippi: "[There is] news of the killing of a big black bear by President Roosevelt in the cane-brakes near Bear Lake, LA. . . . The president got his bear late Thursday."[20]

As part of his trip for the Inland Waterway Commission and following his sojourn for bear hunting, Roosevelt stopped in Vicksburg for four hours on Monday, October 21, 1907. He arrived on a steamboat named the *Belle of the Bends*, which he boarded just across the river at Delta, Louisiana. It was a ceremonial trip of barely three miles. A committee of 100 leading citizens of the Vicksburg area crossed the river to welcome and accompany the president, and a dozen smaller boats provided an escort.

"The bluffs overlooking the river were lined with people who gave the chief executive a hearty and noisy welcome. . . . Confederate and Union veterans joined to form an honor guard. . . . [He] rode in a carriage that led the parade through the main streets. . . . Thousands of people wore Roosevelt Day badges."[21]

On the lawn of the Old Court House, Mississippi congressman John Sharp Williams introduced the president, teasing with the assurance that Roosevelt had "tried to make as few mistakes as a Republican president could." In turn, the president praised southern valor in the Civil War and spoke warmly of Jefferson Davis. He promoted his positions on river development and reported progress on the Panama Canal construction.[22] Of particular interest to residents of the Mississippi Delta were his recognition of the potential for disastrous river floods and his expressed determination for the nation to construct a system of levees. Because of the significance of Roosevelt's address on this occasion, a verbatim presentation of the remarks in Vicksburg is available in Appendix A.

Following festivities that included a presidential tour of the national cemetery and military park, Roosevelt and his party left for a trip by rail to Nashville. In that Tennessee city, his schedule included a speaking engagement before he completed his return journey to Washington, DC, where a serious financial crisis, the Panic of 1907, required his attention.

However, there was one final, little reported presidential stop in Mississippi during the first leg of the trip home. Isaiah Thornton Montgomery, a prominent African American leader who founded Mound Bayou in 1887 as an all-black colony in the Mississippi Delta, was a delegate to the 1904 Republican National Convention, and he invited Roosevelt to visit his community. On the trip northward from Vicksburg, the president's train "made a stop of three minutes."[23] Roosevelt spoke briefly, congratulating the residents on both their prosperity and their refusal to permit saloons within the city limits. He encouraged the men and women alike to work hard and to educate their children. On November 27, 1908, Roosevelt referred to the "noteworthy record" of Mound Bayou, Mississippi, in a speech in Washington, DC. He commended to his listeners an article in the *Planters' Journal* of Memphis with the title, "The Most Remarkable Town in the South."[24]

★   ★   ★

When Theodore Roosevelt walked onto the larger stage of national politics as the Republican candidate for the vice presidency, he was a relatively young man who gained early recognition as an urban police commissioner determined to address corruption, a war hero who commanded the Rough Riders, and the governor of New York committed to battling a powerful political machine. Yet when he campaigned for the Republican ticket he shared in 1900 with William McKinley, the whistle-stop tour he took through twenty-three states included no communities in the Deep South among its 480 stops. Mississippi gave McKinley and Roosevelt less than 10 percent of its votes in 1900.

Thus, when Theodore Roosevelt became president of the United States upon the assassination of William McKinley in September 1901 and just over one year later decided to accept an invitation for a hunting trip in the Mississippi Delta, he had to know he was not entering friendly territory. As a Republican in the solidly Democratic South of the post–Civil War decades, he was already suspect, and the public perception of his more open approach to African Americans added to the distrust and anger in the racially charged atmosphere of Mississippi in the early twentieth century.

Perhaps the most remarkable episode of the Roosevelt story was the attitude he encountered during his visit to the state in 1907, when he stopped at Vicksburg, enjoyed warm greetings from a large crowd of Mississippians, and spoke affirmatively of soldiers from the state who fought for the Confederacy. It is fair to assume that the welcome had something to do with his reason for visiting, namely, to promote the development and control of the Mississippi River, issues important to Mississippians. Also, he had five additional years in the presidential role, time for his leadership and the nation's successes to win grudging tolerance, if not support, for him and his administration.

CHAPTER THREE

WILLIAM TAFT

Twenty-Seventh President of the United States
Republican
Elected 1908
Served March 4, 1909, to March 4, 1913

★ ★

In the days before modern airliners compressed the United States—and the world—to a manageable size in terms of the number of hours required for journeys across thousands of miles, President William Taft was a record-setting traveler. He averaged nearly 30,000 miles by train during each of his four years in office.[1]

This dedication to travel continued despite a bitter controversy in Congress regarding the sufficiency of the annual $25,000 budget for the president's over-the-road expenses. Taft exceeded the amount in his first fiscal year in office; as the *Aberdeen (MS) Weekly* grumbled exactly three months after Taft took office, "President Taft is rapidly winning for himself the name of 'Traveling Bill.' He has traveled more since he became president than most of his predecessors did during their entire terms in office."[2] Some in Washington insisted that the overage was his responsibility. Taft's fellow Republicans supported a second appropriation, while Democrats resisted on the basis that many of the trips were largely political. Insults flew back and forth, and there was even a point at which Democrats from the South were furious, as their southern hospitality was called into question. This issue of how much public funding should support presidential travel occupied Congress for decades.[3]

How many trips and how long they should be were not the only issues this traveling president faced: "Taft made not one but two pilgrimages to the west coast. The first, in 1909, lasted sixty days, traversed thirty-three states and territories, and resulted in 260 presidential speeches."[4] This trip began in mid-September with a stop in El Paso, Texas, where Taft became only the second president to touch foreign soil while in office, as he crossed the international bridge for a greeting and then a dinner with President Porfirio Diaz of Mexico. This border crossing also caused considerable consternation for the president's opponents and for traditionalists in general.[5]

It was on the last legs of this extensive journey that President Taft became the third chief executive of the United States to visit Mississippi while in office. He stopped in Vicksburg and Natchez during a five-day, late October riverboat excursion down the Mississippi River. After a few days in New Orleans, he boarded the presidential train for three additional Mississippi stops in early November—those in Jackson, West Point, and Columbus—as he made his way back to Washington, DC.

Calling Taft's trip down the Mississippi River an excursion actually suggests a greatly reduced image of its size and scope. "Two or three hundred congressmen and senators and governors of half the states of the union were aboard the dozen vessels, [along with] many other dignitaries, all bound for the Lakes-to-the-Gulf Deep Waterway Convention in New Orleans."[6]

As many people in Mississippi awaited a presidential visit, the *Columbus Commercial* had this to say: "President Taft, on one of the last laps of his record-breaking 13,000-miles tour, has had a busy time since last Monday afternoon when the prows of his gorgeously decorated fleet pointed away from St. Louis, headed for the Crescent City, where it reached port yesterday several hours late. It has been a week on the Mississippi, and never before in history has the Father of Waters born upon his bosom in one flotilla so much of the country's official greatness."[7] This last pronouncement was a bit overstated, of course, as President Theodore Roosevelt also made a grand journey on behalf of river development just two years earlier; Roosevelt similarly traveled with other dignitaries from Keokuk, Iowa, to Memphis, Tennessee, the site of the 1907 Lakes-to-the-Gulf Deep Waterway Association Convention (see chapter 2).

Corporations created these grand events to serve their lobbying interests. The schedule for Taft ran from October 25, 1909, the departure from East St. Louis, Illinois, to October 30, 1909, the arrival in New Orleans. "The personally conducted journey of President Taft down the Mississippi River [was] made to call the personal attention of the President of the United

States, members of Congress, army engineers, and levee engineers . . . to the commercial necessity and possibilities of deepening the Mississippi River."[8] Sponsoring organizations included the St. Louis Business Men's League and the Lakes-to-the-Gulf Deep Waterway Association. Both groups wanted several hundred million dollars in river system improvements to lower transportation costs for manufactured goods and agricultural products. Scheduled stops during the journey of Taft's flotilla were these river ports: Cape Girardeau, Missouri; Cairo, Illinois; Hickman, Kentucky; Memphis, Tennessee; Helena, Arkansas; Vicksburg, Mississippi; Natchez, Mississippi; and Baton Rouge, Louisiana.

Thus the context for Taft's visits to six Mississippi communities included his two-month train tour that had taken him to the nation's extreme southern and western borders. This extended journey finished with a flourish, as he and hundreds of dignitaries enjoyed their steamboat cruise. Journalists accompanying the traveling party reported not only the newsworthy incidents but also the human interest angles. Here is one example of the latter: "Half of New Orleans is drinking the Taft cocktail and the other half is waiting for the white aproned parties to mix them. In New Orleans, for ages it has been the custom to improvise a new drink and name it after distinguished citizens or visitors. . . . But the Taft cocktail, its proud inventor claims, is superior to them all in flavor, bouquette [sic], and soothing effects."[9] Unfortunately, there were no details reported about the concoction other than it being similar to a Cajun cocktail with the rims of the glasses dipped in a citrus mixture.

There is, however, a verbatim account of President Taft's remarks to the New Orleans convention of the Lakes-to-the-Gulf Deep Waterway Association. He said: "This trip has been illuminating to many of us, not so much in offering a solution of the problems presented in trying to develop the Mississippi and other rivers for that kind of transportation [that is, less costly conveyance of bulky merchandise] which will be most beneficial to the country, but rather in showing all the difficulties we have to meet and overcome in order that those rivers shall occupy their proper place in transportation. . . . The Mississippi River Commission says that in order to carry on . . . they ought to have two millions of dollars more a year and certainly Congress ought to be ashamed not to give it to them."[10]

Before speaking to the assemblage of businessmen and political leaders in New Orleans, Taft completed his down-river voyage, including his two stops in Mississippi riverfront communities as president. The first of these was in Vicksburg on the last Thursday in October; the second was the following day in Natchez.

October 28, 1909—Vicksburg

Delays vexed the president's trip downstream, and they became worse as the flotilla moved deeper into the South. Boats could not maintain a caravan in proximity to each other, and the dozen or so craft separated for many miles up and down the river. At one point, frustration overtook several in the party. A journalist reported: "The governors and congressmen debarked at Greenville today and came to Vicksburg by train. They will board their boats again tonight for the run to Natchez. The schedule of the river trip has gone all to pieces."[11]

Citizens in Vicksburg expected President Taft to arrive late afternoon or early evening, but his steamboat, the lighthouse tender *Oleander*, actually docked at 9:40 p.m. Newspapers reported a disappointed committee because there were extensive plans for a five-hour visit complete with an automobile tour of the community, the national cemetery, and the national military park.[12] While there were still several hundred people gathered to greet the president, they resigned themselves to a greatly reduced agenda with but one late event, namely, a buffet supper held at the Elks Club.[13] "The president made a speech in which he expressed his deep regrets and chagrin that the schedule of the river trip had gone so far awry as to cut his visit to Vicksburg so short."[14]

Journalists reported a verbatim record of Taft's comments in Vicksburg, though there is logically some variance from the president's actual text, given the historical context of the voyage. As with most materials assembled from shorthand symbols and longhand notes, the exact wording, punctuation, and other grammatical niceties of the remarks likely varied somewhat from the published version. It appears that the printed text may join the address after salutations were spoken; also, it is likely that what the president surely said in closing—for example, thanks to his hosts—was omitted from the newspaper account.

According to the published text, President Taft began with a jab at the congressmen who were also traveling in the flotilla. Apparently, some accused the president of going on a junket. He answered: "Well, that depends upon what you mean by a junket. If it is to be defined as the man defined his pleasure when he did not take his wife with him it is a junket. If a junket is a journey full of pleasure and with no work and no effort in it, then I deny that it is a junket."

Taft was on a roll and enjoying the exercise of his humor—sarcastic and self-deprecating: "If you had seen the efforts made at oratory on board the congressional steamer as it came down the river, you would understand they were still practicing their profession. If you had attended the meeting of the governors, heard their innocent investigation into what is meant by that phrase that rolls off our tongue with so much ease, the conservation of our natural resources, you could understand that the governors were pursuing their constitutional duty on board that vessel that comes with due slowness down the river, and if you had taken passage in those narrow bunks which can be compared only to that permanent resting place toward which we are moving with so much reluctance, you would understand that no one would have fought that means of passing the night unless it was in the earnest discharge of duty."

His conclusion to this matter? "Therefore, I deny that this is a junket. It never is a junket where the winners have gone home and the losers are getting even."

Of course, there was serious business for the president and his traveling companions—but his transition was still a bit tongue-in-cheek: "I would not have you think, those of you whose experience fits you to fully interpret the meaning of my remarks, that our eyes, in going down the river have not been properly directed to the waterway before us, under us, and back of us, and to the shores on each side in the study of the very difficult question that presents itself as to the improvement of this river."

At the heart of the presidential message were a position statement the residents of Vicksburg found encouraging and a caution that likely frustrated them: "There are those of us who are convinced beyond any change at all as to what ought to be done . . . as to the policy that ought to be undertaken in improving this waterway. That it ought to be improved, I think most of those on this trip sincerely believe." Still, the president acknowledged that "there is a long fight ahead and the enthusiasm of their rivalry, the enthusiasm of the people of the states in the valley, does not accomplish the improvement or bring it about in the way in which ultimately it will come. It has to be thrashed out in Congress and throughout the country and the country has to be satisfied that in expending the $200,000,000—it will probably take $200,000,000—it will be well spent."

The president's own commitment was couched in that language of caution: "Now I have no doubt that ultimately the country will be convinced as the details are worked out and the demonstration is made, but I would for the moment put a brake on the expectancy of immediate conviction of everybody. . . . I want to find the way to make this river accomplish all that my friends would wish it to accomplish."

Finally, there was a less definitive conclusion than the audience surely desired: "Now $200,000,000 seems on the one hand to a man who is administering the appropriation bills and framing them a very large amount. It is a large amount, but it is not a large amount for the United States to pay to develop a waterway that is as important as the Mississippi. And yet we are governed by all the people, and we must pursue the ordinary course of convincing them in order to bring this about."[15]

October 29, 1909—Natchez

Issues with the schedule continued to plague the flotilla. From the journalists' reports: "The president was nearly three hours behind time. . . . This was due to the fact that the Oleander [the steamship carrying Taft], which shook off all the other boats yesterday in the run to Vicksburg, got into difficulties herself last night and could not make her usual speed."[16] As this account implied, the boats were racing from one stop to another, and this pattern caused mishaps, confusion, and occasional congestion. Taft's own vessel was said to have taken on an inexperienced crew member to replace one who had a family emergency, and this individual accidently choked the coal fires heating the boiler and extended the tardiness.

Arrival at Natchez occurred just before 10:00 a.m. on October 29, 1909. Wire stories reported: "Not since the day the battleship Mississippi visited Natchez and won the river speed record from this city to New Orleans has there been another such crowd on the bluff as greeted President Taft. . . . [He was met] by Mayor Benbrook and a reception committee. The mayor made a brief address of welcome and the president and many of the visiting governors who arrived on the steamer St. Paul were taken for an automobile drive through the city. The ride ended at a court of honor on the bluff where the president made a brief address."[17] Excerpts from the Natchez address are reproduced below, as they ran in two different newspaper sources—one from Florida and the other from New York. Clearly, there was sufficient national interest in the president's trip and the issue of river development that journalistic coverage made his comments widely available.

In his address at Natchez, President Taft continued a theme McKinley and Roosevelt included in their speeches while in Mississippi: "I have one ambition; perhaps I have others, but one figures largely in my dreams. It is that when I lay down the staff of office, the people of the South may feel that by my administration the bonds between them and other parts of the country have been drawn closer."[18]

Yet the president moved quickly to the main purpose for his trip down the Mississippi: "After the beauty of this scene, I hate to come to commercial questions. But we cannot get along without clothes, and we cannot get along without bread and meat. While this trip, undertaken under the auspices of the Waterway Association, combines most of the beautiful, it also has a deeper purpose, and that is to draw to the attention of the country the need for some action in developing the utility of the great waterway that flows at the base of these bluffs. The problem is not solved, but I believe that it is in the process of solution. I believe it because we of the American nation admit no obstacles that we cannot overcome."

Taft's conclusion made his point, but he framed it in language that no twenty-first-century, politically correct officeholder would use: "The Mississippi River, in its willingness to make eddies and trouble, in its beauty, for it has great beauty, reminds one—dare I say it—of a beautiful and powerful woman. Properly directed, only by suggestion, she is the greatest aid to progress and happiness that we have in life. But treated without discretion, sought to be hemmed in where she will by the force of her character break out, she loses the opportunity for usefulness, and sometimes wrecks everything she strikes."[19]

November 1, 1909—Biloxi and Jackson

After Natchez and brief stops along the way in Louisiana, President Taft and his large party of dignitaries and journalists made their way down the Mississippi River to New Orleans, where he kept his appointment to address the convention of the Lakes-to-the-Gulf Deep Waterway Association. He and his traveling companions enjoyed scheduled events in the city, and then the president boarded a train for several days over the rails home to Washington, DC. Taft made a brief stop in Biloxi, where photographers snapped his picture in front of the White House Inn, and then he traveled north to his first major stop on this final leg of the extended trip home, Jackson, Mississippi.

Timeliness in arrival meant no alterations to the planned celebrations were necessary, as was the case both in Vicksburg and Natchez. Taft's train arrived in Jackson at 8:45 a.m., barely five minutes behind schedule. City leaders formed an escort committee to usher the president to the Edwards

Hotel, where the larger general reception committee met him. "At 10 o'clock a street parade formed and the president, with Governor [Edmond] Noel[20] in an automobile, led the procession.... The party proceeded to the state fair. An immense throng greeted the chief executive and he was given an ovation."[21]

Taft addressed the crowd at the fair, offering an interesting message: "In his speech at the fairgrounds the president congratulated Mississippi on its having been able to restrain the tendency of the young men to go into great cities."[22]

Jackson was the site of several competing events during the visit—the capital city had apparently ignored the *Aberdeen Weekly*'s advice to not "overdo the reception."[23] In addition to the state fair, Jackson's social calendar included a circus, a balloon ascension, and a parachute drop, and the city's population at the time was just over 21,000. Still, having the nation's president in town was a major attraction, and the reception committee kept him busy with activities for most of the nineteen hours he spent in the city. Notably the governor welcomed Taft to the executive mansion for a meal with state and community leaders.

There was, however, a controversy connected to this item on the agenda: "The dinner had caused considerable fuss between the wets and drys in the city. The drys were opposed to having wine served and they carried the matter into the pulpits of some of the churches. The wets, however, refused to give in and then the temperance people threatened to get out an injunction restraining the wets from using wine at a banquet."[24]

It was a dilemma for those wishing to serve alcohol to President Taft because Mississippi was by law a dry state. However, conviviality prevailed, and someone made a trip to New Orleans to secure a supply of wine.[25] In spite of the squabble, a journalist observed: "Jackson did her best to make the president's stay pleasant."[26]

Taft's address in Jackson offered a rationale for his theme of national unity: "I have gone from the Atlantic to the Pacific Ocean, down the Pacific coast to the southwest corner of the country, through the territories and that last great domain of Texas to St. Louis, down the Mississippi to New Orleans ... and I am able to say that we never in all our country's history were as homogeneous a people, as closely allied in all our hopes and ambitions, and in all our pride of country and patriotism as we are today."[27]

November 2, 1909—West Point and Columbus

Citizens in Columbus were excited about the prospect of a visit from the president of the United States, first announced on the front page of the *Columbus Commercial* on July 18, 1909. Organizers expected as many as 20,000 people to come out for Taft's visit,[28] a number more than twice the size of the city's population. A few days later the Columbus Commercial Club sent a letter to Secretary of War Jacob Dickinson, a Columbus native who was instrumental in securing Taft's visit, "convey[ing] our keenest love and patriotic devotion and loyalty." Community leaders assured Dickinson that the welcoming committee was willing to do as much—or as little—as the president desired to make his stay comfortable.[29]

Anticipation and attention to details in the town persisted throughout the summer and fall. The city even passed an ordinance requiring that residents sweep their sidewalks in time for Taft's visit.[30] On September 9 the *Columbus Commercial* reminded residents that they had "better buy those new clothes. Taft will be here."[31] About two weeks later, the newspaper stated that "we are as jubilant as a child waiting for Santa Claus."[32] Obviously, Columbus was eager for its moment hosting the president.

These preparations paid off in a grand celebration. Two days prior to the event, the *Commercial* stated: "In forty-eight hours Taft Day will be with us and Columbus for the first time will welcome a president. . . . The town is already dressed up for the occasion, and much more decoration will be done. Flags and streamers of national colors, framing portraits of the president, wave a welcome from homes and business houses, as well as from the hearts of the people."

Columbus also decided upon a theme. The article continued: "Simplicity is to be the keynote. It was this simplicity, allowing something character-istic, that led the president's advance guard, Mr. Wheeler, of the Secret Service . . . to say . . . that of all the towns the president had visited, none had so 'ideally, so considerately, and so characteristically arranged for his entertainment as Columbus.'"[33]

When the day arrived, again Taft's schedule lagged, but in Columbus by only about forty-five minutes. He and his party arrived at 11:43 a.m. on November 2, 1909. Earlier that morning, members of a welcome committee traveled to nearby West Point, Mississippi, to witness remarks made by the president from the rear platform of his train, and then to join him for the last few miles of the trip into the community. At the moment that Taft arrived and stepped down from his railcar, every whistle in Columbus sounded, and the crowd, estimated to be the largest ever assembled in the town, gathered around the Southern Depot. Two thousand children lined the sidewalks and sang to the motorcade as it passed.[34]

Visiting journalists noted a unique aspect of the enthusiasm: "The rebel yell was heard at Columbus as the president spoke as it has not been heard in years. . . . Nearly every sentence of Taft's address from the stand on Main Street was punctuated with cheers."[35]

Showing community pride in its local college, Columbus took the president to an event on the campus of the Mississippi Industrial Institute and College (now Mississippi University for Women). There were both a welcome by the college's president, Henry L. Whitfield, and an address by President Taft. Students, faculty, and staff treated their distinguished visitor to a meal on the lawn: "[They] gave him the first barbecue of the 13,000-mile tour—800 girls to wait on him while he ate, to sing to him on the college campus, and to shower him with roses."[36]

President Taft delivered remarks twice in Columbus, first from a speakers' platform at Main and Market Streets (Market is now Fifth Street), and later at the Mississippi Industrial Institute and College. Both of these addresses demonstrated Taft's oratorical talents, and they illustrated that time changes not only issues but also the language of popular discourse and cultural understandings.

Addressing the crowd from the speakers' platform in the heart of Columbus, Taft complimented his hosts with a nod in the direction of fondly recalled Confederate culture: "I have been spending a considerable part of the week in Mississippi, and I want to say that I like Mississippi. I am glad to be in the city of your great General Lee. I am indeed sorry it was not given to me to meet him in person and receive that kindly, gentle influence that he shed wherever he moved. I am especially sorry not to be able to come into his presence and to talk in regard to the relations in the South to the rest of the Union, because he represented that spirit which I would invoke on the part of every southerner with respect to the whole country."

There were respects to pay to the local resident who occupied an important post in the president's administration: "I am glad to be in Columbus because when I was looking for a man by whose selection for my cabinet, I could not only secure rare ability, but at the same time express an earnest of what I wished to do for the South, I selected Mac Dickinson to do that very thing. When I wanted, on the other hand, to have a man with the energy of a steam engine to build the Panama Canal, I selected J. M. Dickinson.[37] There has been no town in the 13,000 miles of my trip that has shown me more to convince me that you are glad to see me, as I am glad to see you."

Of course, the president had to make a transition to his themes of a unified country taking its place on the world stage: "[I] cannot come in the capacity in which I come, as your president, without thanking God that the past is over—not that we are attacking what the past is, but that we have passed through that awful trial on both sides that certified to the world the fiber of our natures and the strength of our American people, in order to show to the world that we are equal to any of them as a world power."

Then Taft spoke of shared values, differences in outlook between the South and the North, and the character required of all contemporary citizens: "You are not in favor of war, and I am not in favor of war.... Now, you southern people are an emotional people. We have some emotions in the north too, but if there is any difference, your hearts expand more easily and you are more sensitive possibly than we are.... [However,] one must know that your hearts and emotions are broad enough to entertain entire loyalty to the issues of the past, which you fought so nobly to sustain, and entire loyalty to our present government, for which you would be willing to lay down your life if the occasion required it."

Having enjoined the crowd with his homily on citizenship, Taft returned to his charming aspect: "I cherish your cordial reception, and I cherish it the more because you had so little to do with putting me where I am.[38] That is what gives flavor to your cheers, that is what gives an extra grip to your hand, and that is what makes me value the kindly look in your eyes."[39]

After his address from the speakers' platform, Taft and his escorts moved to the local college campus, where the president, once again, took to the podium to address those assembled. In this case, the audience comprised the students of the Mississippi Industrial Institute and College—a public institution serving female students—along with faculty, staff, and other guests of the campus celebration. President Taft's speech to this assemblage was certainly the most nuanced of his entire journey through Mississippi, aimed, as it was, directly at the young women gathered before him. One is tempted to surmise that it is nothing less than a US president offering fatherly advice. It is, in the opinion of the coauthors, a gem of early twentieth-century cultural attitudes toward gender roles and issues, and, for that reason, what follows is the available and uninterrupted verbatim record of the remarks:

"Young ladies, it is a great privilege to address you. Your being here and the character of the education that you are receiving and the results to be accomplished are all in line with the thought that I would like to emphasize.

I have a lot of maxims, a lot of principles that I would like to advance to young ladies in your situation. I wish that every woman in the world was so situated that she would not think it was necessary for her to marry if she did not want to.

"Now that is a proposition that I am prepared to defend against all comers. I am the last one to take a position against that old doctrine of the common law that there ought to be nothing to interfere with matrimony, but I would have matters so arranged that young women, in making their choice, should have a full and free choice. That can only be reached when they are put in a situation when that which they choose is not a livelihood that they select, but a life that is looked forward to of unmixed happiness.

"I think the most important education that we have is the education which now I am glad to say is being accomplished, which ought to be more widely diffused, that enables young men and young women to place themselves in a position from which they can by their own efforts work themselves to independence. And I am glad to know that principle obtains here, in its fullest sense, and I am glad to congratulate these young women on the opportunity which this great institution affords them to carve out their own future.

"I know that it is generally supposed that those who inherit wealth are in the best position for a future happy life, I mean in this world. But I venture to say that the best legacy that can be left to a young man is a good education, a good character, good traits in a family, and good moral standards, and nothing else. The necessity that he is under to get out and hustle is an advantage that he does not appreciate, when he is going through the process. But after he has won success and looks back and compares his own life with that of the man who when he entered life had money and means to support himself and enjoy himself, he will convince himself of the fact.

"And the same thing is true with regard to young women, who are given a fair chance in life of earning their own livelihood and carving out their own futures. The trouble has been that we have not given the young women a fair showing. We have not opened out all the avenues whereby she could win success.

"I am not a rabid suffragist, the truth is I am not in favor of suffrage for women, and I never will be until I have been convinced they are the ones who desire it. When they want it, they will get it. But I do believe that one of the advantages of giving them that kind of influence will be more certain means of opening the avenues of self-support to them than has heretofore been done.

"The great weight of popular opinion against it is that every community assumes that it still has enough men to look after its interests, and therefore while husbands respect the wishes of their wives, if they are good husbands, and know what is good for them, I do not know that they are always good men. What we are bound to do in the future, through influencing work, the effects of which we can see and the growth of which we know, anticipates that women are going to be given credit, independent of the matter of earning their livelihood.

"My boys, of whom I have two, I shall be glad that I shall not have any property to leave to them, only I hope a good character, and a pride in themselves, and a good education; but for my daughter, I am going to scrape together as much as I can, and give her as good an education as I can, so that she can take in the rest. I would so situate her that she not need to marry unless she choose.

"And now, my dear young ladies, I am delighted to have met you, and thank you for your appreciated attention to this speech."[40]

★ ★ ★

William McKinley, Theodore Roosevelt, and William Taft were the first three US presidents of the twentieth century—all Republicans—and they became the first chief executives of the United States to visit Mississippi while in office. What each encountered and noted in public remarks was a state steeped in both resentment and nostalgia regarding its Confederate past. Except for unvarnished hostility toward Roosevelt during and after his 1902 visit—owing primarily to his party affiliation and his appointments of African American citizens—all three presidents experienced hospitable receptions despite the Democratic sympathies of Mississippi's electorate at the time.

Brief editorializing in two Mississippi newspapers contemporary with the Taft visits may help twenty-first-century readers understand the balance citizens of the state in 1909 felt between the history of tension and the reawakening of national identity. From the *Macon Beacon*: "Mr. Taft's respectful mention of Jefferson Davis, his own predecessor in the chair of Secretary of War, while only just and proper, was yet done so graciously and genuinely as to give it extra force. Mr. Taft has not made Mississippi any more Republican than heretofore, but he has made us certainly have a greater respect and kindlier feeling for the Republican Party."[41]

And from the *Okolona Messenger*: "The *Indianapolis Star* says the reason that President Taft drew such large crowds in the South was because a Republican is naturally a great curiosity down here."[42]

CHAPTER FOUR

WOODROW WILSON

Twenty-Eighth President of the United States
Democrat
Elected 1912 and 1916
Served March 4, 1913, to March 4, 1921

Thanks in part to a split in the Republican Party's quest for the presidency in 1912—Theodore Roosevelt mounted a third-party challenge against incumbent Republican William Taft, dividing the party's votes—Woodrow Wilson became the first Democratic president of the United States since Grover Cleveland's term ended in 1897, and only the second Democrat elected president since the Civil War. A native southerner hailing from Virginia, he moved to New Jersey to become the thirteenth president of Princeton University, and then the state's voters elected him their thirty-fourth governor.

Wilson spent the longest visit in Mississippi of any sitting president, but it was also the least newsworthy. Traveling with his first wife, Ellen, and their three daughters, the president vacationed in Pass Christian over one Christmas and New Year holiday for nearly three weeks. The impetus for the visit in late 1913 came from the president's physician. Dr. Cary Grayson prescribed the break as a restorative for his patient whose exhausting schedule left him wrestling with "the grip" barely ten months into his first term.[1] To monitor the ailing president, Dr. Grayson also made the trip to Mississippi.

Aside from health troubles, the president also sought respite during an increasingly tumultuous period both in Washington and around the globe. On Wilson's mind were a number of brewing troubles, both across the

Atlantic and just across the southern border of the United States. Disputes between restive European powers were escalating toward an unprecedented conflict that soon came to be known as the Great War. Closer to home, tensions between Mexico and the United States appeared to be moving in the direction of armed conflict as well, as President Wilson publicly refused to recognize Mexico's counterrevolutionary government led by General Victoriano Huerta. During his sojourn in Pass Christian, the president had no choice but to devote some time to these issues, but it appeared from the published reports that he was able to relax and enjoy golfing and other recreational pursuits.

News that the president was coming occasioned hurried preparations. In recounting Wilson's arrival a century later, historian Edmond Boudreaux Jr. wrote that "all along the Mississippi Gulf Coast trees and bushes were trimmed. Beaches were cleared of debris, wooden fences were painted and streets were cleared. American flags were flying along the coast for the first time since the Civil War."[2]

Because the White House billed Wilson's southern trip as a holiday for the first family, accompanying journalists were generally reduced to human interest reports from the Gulf Coast. There was this story, for example: "President Woodrow Wilson . . . opened a mysterious letter handed to him by a pretty, dark-haired girl. . . . Willa Green had stepped forward as Wilson's car drove slowly through Gulfport. She handed him the letter, a box, and instructions not to open it until he reached Beauliau (also referred to as Herndon Cottage or the Dixie White House), the antebellum home where he stayed in the Pass."[3]

According to the report, Wilson read the letter as he sat on the front porch of Beauliau, untied the ribbon that held the box closed, and watched as a white dove fluttered out and perched on a nearby tree before flying off into the sunset. Media features across the globe said that Willa Green found an injured dove and nursed it back to health. Journalists portrayed her gift to the president as a symbol of longed-for peace in a world that was racing toward war.

December 25, 1913, to January 11, 1914—Pass Christian

When the White House made the decision that the president should travel to a warmer climate for recovery from both intensive work and his illnesses, several locations vied for the visit. After considering the available options, the White House made this announcement: "It has been practically decided

that President and Mrs. Wilson and family will spend a three-week vacation at Pass Christian, Miss., on the gulf coast. . . . The president's family
hopes to leave [Washington, DC] some time Tuesday [December 23, 1913]. . . .
Senator [James] Vardaman [D-MS] has been arranging some of the details
with the White House. A furnished cottage will be placed at the disposal of
the president, and the Mississippi people give him every guarantee of an
uninterrupted and beneficial vacation."[4]

Then as now, such a news item regarding the first family drew significant
attention, and the *New York Sun* offered readers more details on the day
following the initial announcement. The community where Wilson and his
entourage planned to stay was reportedly a Gulf Coast resort. Family members intended to stay in an 1851 mansion owned by Mrs. J. M. Ayers of New
Jersey and occupied by renters, Mrs. Thomas Herndon and her daughter,
Alice.[5] Mrs. Herndon expected to remain in the home throughout the visit
to assure appropriate hosting for the presidential party.[6]

Despite a White House request that there be no public demonstration
when Wilson arrived on Christmas morning, "a number of leading citizens
met and decided that it would be unworthy of southern hospitality to allow
the chief executive to come in unheralded." Thus, when a procession of
automobiles picked up the visitors at the train depot and drove them to the
Herndon residence, every available steam whistle blew, followed by a large
display of what were termed "Christmas fireworks."[7]

After the grand welcome, locals settled down to allow the president his
desired relaxation. On December 28 Wilson celebrated his fifty-seventh
birthday, and journalists reported that letters and telegrams of congratulations from all parts of the nation brought the chief executive much pleasure.
Late on the morning of his birthday, the president attended a worship service
at a nearby Presbyterian church that was set on the edge of a beach, and he
was said to be "taking life just as easy as possible." Though he occasionally
dictated a few letters, Wilson reportedly spent most of his time golfing, reading newspapers, and even napping.[8]

Limited attention to national concerns meant that journalists searched for
whatever stories they could find, even humorous moments. One wrote about
the observation of a youngster who caddied for Wilson and said afterward:
"I didn't think he played so good, considering he's the president." However,
the newspaper writer opined: "President Wilson really plays a good game in
view of the fact that he took up golf a little more than a year ago."[9]

World affairs intervened in the visit on January 2 when a US special envoy
to Mexico, John Lind, arrived by naval cruiser in Pass Christian to meet

with Wilson. Though rumors arose immediately that a war with the nation's southern neighbor was imminent, the United States undertook no military action with Mexico until later in the year, during the so-called Occupation of Veracruz that was related to the Mexican Revolution.[10]

On another day Wilson and his party were driving home from a golf course when the president noticed smoke pouring out of a large home they were passing in Gulfport. Taking immediate action, Wilson ordered his automobile to stop, and he sent two Secret Service men and two chauffeurs to assist with a bucket brigade, while he directed the overall effort. According to the report, the makeshift fire crew quickly extinguished the blaze.[11] This incident earned Wilson an honorary membership in the Gulfport Volunteer Hook and Ladder Company.[12]

Near the end of first family's Gulf Coast visit, a delegation from the Mississippi legislature visited the president at the Herndon residence to invite him for an address at the state capitol. Mississippi was, after all, part of the solidly Democratic South during Wilson's era, and nearly 89 percent of the state's voters had marked his name on their 1912 ballots. Legislators were eager to welcome the first Democratic president in sixteen years, and offered to receive him at the capitol formally and with great fanfare. However, Wilson informed the committee that he was working hard on the issue of antitrust reform, and he could not extend his stay in Mississippi for an address in Jackson. The visiting legislators apparently anticipated his response because they brought laudatory resolutions to share with the president, who said, in turn, that their praise was too generous. Wilson assured the delegation that the state had fulfilled his expectations and provided a wonderful retreat for him and his family.[13]

★　★　★

Evidently, Wilson enjoyed his stay on the Gulf Coast. Though official public appearances were few, the chief executive made his gratitude clear. On January 9 the president visited a school in Pass Christian, where several hundred students gathered to meet him and present flowers.[14] Also, Wilson and his wife hosted a reception at the Herndon residence on January 10, the day before their departure, to express formal thanks to the people of Pass Christian and surrounding communities; more than 2,000 persons populated the event.[15] Among those in attendance was a ninety-five-year-old African American woman, Lucy Marshall, who presented the Wilsons with a large photograph of herself. Another guest was a uniformed Civil War

general, A. C. Oxford, commander of the Fourth Alabama Brigade of the
United Confederate Veterans. He gave the president a card printed with the
Confederate veteran's pledge.[16]

Surely the festive nature of Mississippians in welcoming the president
resulted from more than just southern hospitality. For the first time since the
largely despised Andrew Johnson, the nation's president was a native-born
southerner, and Wilson had the added credibility for the state's citizenry that
he was a Democrat. Though this visiting president made a name for himself
in New Jersey, his southern roots and his party affiliation opened doors and
hearts in the Deep South.

★ ★

CHAPTER FIVE

FRANKLIN D. ROOSEVELT

Thirty-Second President of the United States
Democrat
Elected 1932, 1936, 1940, and 1944
Served March 4, 1933, to April 12, 1945

★ ★

Three times during his twelve years as president Franklin Delano Roosevelt traveled into Mississippi. Of these visits, the first was tremendously important in the context of national efforts at economic recovery and rural development; the second was more of a courtesy for the public as one element of a longer presidential vacation; and the third went largely unrecognized for years, as it was done under a cloak of secrecy during World War II.

The election of Roosevelt to the presidency in 1932 caused no small amount of both celebration and mixed feelings in Mississippi. On one hand, a Democrat was again residing in the White House, a welcome development after the state had suffered mightily in the first years of the Great Depression with the Republican Herbert Hoover at the helm. On the other hand, Roosevelt's insistence that extensive federal intervention was necessary to bring an end to the Great Depression troubled those who saw Washington as more of an intruder than a savior.

Also troubling for some in Mississippi was the fact that Franklin Roosevelt was the second straight Democratic nominee who hailed from New York, following Al Smith in 1928, a sign to southern voters that their centrality to the party was on shaky ground. Party faithful in Mississippi during the election of 1932 preferred Texan John Nance Garner, Speaker of the House and a hopeful in the race for the Democratic nomination. However, Garner dropped his candidacy after three convention ballots and agreed in a back-room deal to accept the vice-presidential spot on the ticket. This allowed Roosevelt to win more than two-thirds of the delegate votes on the fourth ballot, a plateau necessary at the time for a candidate to be nominated.

Still, Roosevelt's overwhelming victory in the 1932 election included a winning margin of more than 92 percent in Mississippi, his second largest margin among all states. Whatever reservations existed, Mississippians obviously gave the Democratic candidate an opportunity to right the ship.

As a savvy politician, the president knew that a resounding victory did not mean unconditional acceptance of all his proposals, and he understood that each new piece of New Deal legislation required salesmanship. It was with such a spirit that in 1934 he made his earliest visit to Mississippi. Franklin Roosevelt and his wife, Eleanor, traveled through the state by train and car to celebrate two early New Deal accomplishments: an experimental homesteading program championed by the First Lady, and the successful beginnings of the rural electrification juggernaut known as the Tennessee Valley Authority (TVA). Corinth and Tupelo shared the honors as first beneficiaries of the TVA, while Tupelo had the further distinction of being one of the initial sites for the construction of new affordable housing known as Subsistence Homesteads. In his remarks to enthusiastic crowds, Roosevelt recognized that a significant measure of resistance to the New Deal existed in the region, in no small part because of fear of federal incursion into farmlands and rural communities, areas that remained happily remote from Washington's reach since the founding of the nation. In response, the Roosevelts sought to portray the work programs as federal-local partnerships, spurred by regional leadership and realized through individual, independent effort.

The Roosevelts' goodwill tour of the region shined a light on an early New Deal program that had a significant and positive impact on Mississippi, and another, more utopian project that never reached its full potential. The latter and less successful of those two—a Subsistence Homestead project intended to provide inexpensive homes and small farming plots to struggling families—eventually collapsed under the weight of cost overruns and competing interests. The TVA, however, was a resounding success that survives to this day. In an essay for the Mississippi Historical Society, historian Sara E. Morris described the need for the TVA in the largely rural state: "By 1930 . . . 84.8 percent of all US homes in large urban areas and small towns had electrical service, but only 10.4 percent of rural homes had this luxury. In that same year, only 1.5 percent of Mississippi farm homes had electrical lights, the least of any state in the country. . . . Created by the US Congress on May 18,

1933, the Tennessee Valley Authority aimed to better the living and economic conditions of citizens in seven southeastern states, including Mississippi."[1]

November 17, 1934—Corinth

Near the end of their second year in the White House, President Franklin Roosevelt and his wife, Eleanor, made their way to Mississippi by rail, stopping for appearances related to the Subsistence Homesteads and the TVA in Corinth and Tupelo, and then paying a courtesy visit to the community of Amory, as they traveled toward Alabama. John E. Rankin, Mississippi's First District Democratic congressman, represented the citizens of Amory. He coauthored the bill that created the TVA and spent significant effort promoting the legislation.

Prior to building a power grid to serve many southern communities and individuals who lived in more rural settings, federal officials made the decision to test the model they were developing. What came to be known as "The Corinth Experiment" in Alcorn County, Mississippi, offered citizens the opportunity to join a cooperative funded by the members' monthly fees generated from base commitments and actual usage. In other words, those who chose membership agreed to pay each month not only for their actual, metered use of electricity, but also they subscribed at a base fee calculated upon a minimum number of kilowatt-hours.[2]

In honor of the role Corinth played as a test site for the newly created TVA system, the president made a stop to speak to an enthusiastic crowd from the rear platform of his train. "I want to congratulate you," Roosevelt said, "and tell you how happy I am in hearing about the fine public spirit that Corinth and Alcorn County are showing to the United States of America." The TVA, a "friend of the people," as Roosevelt saw it, brought about a more equitable society, thanks to the pioneering early adoption by Alcorn County's residents. In setting up the Alcorn County Electric Power Association, which served all residents regardless of proximity to towns, residents were "giving an opportunity to the people who live on the farm equal with the people who live in the city."[3]

November 18, 1934—Tupelo and Amory

After overnighting "in his special sleeper car on a siding near Corinth,"[4] the train carrying President and Mrs. Roosevelt traveled the fifty or so miles to Tupelo, where a large and enthusiastic crowd awaited. As Sara Morris recalled, "Tupelo, Mississippi, was near the TVA's Wilson Dam in Muscle Shoals, Alabama." Due to its advantageous location, "Tupelo officially became the first municipality to purchase TVA power."[5]

Prior to the speech, though, the First Lady insisted on visiting a newly created community, known locally as the Tupelo Homesteads. These newly constructed houses were part of a larger, nationwide program being over-seen by the powerful secretary of the interior, Harold Ickes. Set up within Ickes's Interior Department as part of the National Industrial Recovery Act, the Division of Subsistence Homesteads (DSH) sought to construct small communities of inexpensive housing all around the country on a few acres of land each. Potential residents applied to move in and lease the homes, with an eventual option to purchase. But the house itself was only one piece of the innovative properties residents inhabited; the homes were built on a plot of roughly three farmable acres, and were further stocked with, as historian Fred C. Smith recounted in his article on the Tupelo Homesteads site, "fruit trees, berry bushes, farming equipment, fertilizer, seed, a cow, two shoats, and twenty-five chickens," along with a garage, water pump house, and outbuildings for the livestock.[6] Residents were to produce most of their own food using the provided land, equipment, and livestock, and then they worked part-time to cover other expenses.

According to Smith, the Roosevelts' arrival came just two days after the first homesteaders moved into the two dozen homes, and Eleanor, who was an early advocate for the DSH, wanted to see how they were getting along. "The women of the [Tupelo] Garden Club carefully prepared and decorated two of the vacant homesteads for her inspection. Mrs. Roosevelt, however, insisted on visiting a homestead family. She stopped randomly at Number 20, the Barron residence, and she became so engrossed in conversation with Mrs. Barron in examining the house and the appliances that she strained the patience of the president. Franklin Roosevelt waited impatiently in his car, and he sent one of his staff members to 'fetch her.'"[7]

Though an innovative attempt at government-supported subsistence living, cost overruns and competing priorities doomed the DSH. The cost of the houses turned out to be exponentially higher than originally planned, especially at the Tupelo site, where the presence of the TVA led planners to electrify the homes—a feature included at only a few of the approximately 100 other DSH communities. These budgeting issues led Ickes and others in Washington to look for more cost-effective programs, and they shut-tered the DSH office soon thereafter. Still, many of the houses built north of Tupelo, including Number 20, stand yet today, a testament to New Deal–era

Washington's willingness to reimagine its role in American lives.[8] But while the DSH as a utopian dream fell short, the TVA demonstrated that government intervention in local issues could bring success. Tupelo was ground zero for this vital new program.

Proud of this cornerstone role in a successful national project and eager to see and hear the Democratic president, the citizens of Tupelo and surrounding communities overflowed city streets and Robins Field, an athletic facility, that November 18, 1934, afternoon. Estimates ranged to a crowd of 75,000 people, and the throngs impressed Roosevelt: "they have not come by the thousands—they have come literally by the acres."[9] The crowd was there to celebrate their contract with the TVA that offered power at rates well below those charged by the private utility previously serving the city. A parade featured the president and First Lady waving from an open touring car.[10]

Roosevelt's speech that day is a particularly significant one, and deserves to be read in full; the complete text can be found in Appendix A. The president's remarks at Tupelo clearly demonstrated that Roosevelt was deeply invested in the TVA project, not only politically but also emotionally. "Two years ago, in 1932, during the campaign, and again in January, 1933, I came through Kentucky—through the Tennessee Valley—and what I saw on those trips, what I saw of human beings, made tears come to my eyes." Campaigning in the midst of the Great Depression, Roosevelt laid eyes on some of the most devastated rural areas in the nation. "There was not much hope in those days," the president said. "People were wondering what was going to come to this country."

But time and the hard work of those building the power network of the TVA effected great change. "Today I see not only hope, but I see determination and a knowledge that all is well with the country, and that we are coming back." Roosevelt professed the belief that the electrification of the region would make life better for many families, and he saw his vision fulfilled beginning in northeast Mississippi. Clearly, the people of the region were also excited, as the number in attendance on this Sunday morning in the park exceeded even the most generous expectations.

As the text of his speech demonstrates, Roosevelt eagerly touted the great successes of the TVA, both in the form of statistics and in anecdotal evidence. "The number of new refrigerators that have been put in, for example, means something besides just plain dollars and cents. It means greater human happiness. The introduction of electric cookstoves and all the other dozens of things which, when I was in the Navy, we used to call 'gadgets,' is improving human life."

Life in northeastern Mississippi changed drastically in a few short years, thanks both to the president's vision and the diligent work of citizens throughout the Tennessee Valley. Roosevelt assured the crowd that he recognized and saluted their centrality to this effort. The TVA's positive showing, he said, was "not coming from Washington. It is coming from you. You are not being federalized. We still believe in the community; and things are going to advance in this country exactly in proportion to the community effort. This is not regimentation; it is community rugged individualism."[11]

As an interesting aside to the Tupelo visit, in the 1936 session of the Mississippi legislature, lawmakers adopted House Bill No. 77 with this title: "An act to appropriate the sum of sixteen hundred dollars ($1600) to reimburse the city of Tupelo, Mississippi, for funds used to pay the expenses of certain units of the National Guard, which were used in said city on the occasion of the visit of the President of the United States, Franklin Delano Roosevelt, on November 15 [sic], 1934."[12] From a twenty-first-century perspective, costs at this minimal level to provide security for a visiting president of the United States are nearly unimaginable. It is clear, as well, that the crowd exhibited positive feelings for this visiting chief executive.

After the stop in Tupelo, the Roosevelt train traveled to Amory for the second Mississippi stop of the day. The November 22, 1934, *Amory News* reported that the welcome for the Roosevelts was upbeat. "Thousands and thousands of people from Mississippi and Alabama greeted President and Mrs. Roosevelt here Sunday, when their special train passed through Amory. Congressman John Rankin, who was aboard the train, presented Mrs. Roosevelt and then the president. Mrs. Roosevelt expressed her gratitude being able to visit north Mississippi."[13] The unnamed author of the story called attention to the president's recognizable smile and remarked on the attentiveness and enthusiasm of the large crowd.

So memorable was this presidential visit in the history of Amory, in fact, that the Frisco Railroad eventually donated Engine 1529 to the community, and it sits in an Amory city park to this day. This is the very engine that pulled Franklin and Eleanor Roosevelt's special train during the 1934 whistle-stop.[14]

Franklin Roosevelt made two other stops in Mississippi during his long presidency; however, as mentioned previously, neither carried the significance of this early tour. He stopped briefly in 1937 on his way to the Texas coast for tarpon fishing on the Gulf of Mexico. Also, he included Mississippi's Camp Shelby as one stop on a 1942 secret tour of industrial and military sites that were strategic to the nation's efforts in World War II.

April 29, 1937—Biloxi and Gulfport

At 11:37 p.m. on April 27, 1937, Franklin Roosevelt left the White House, according to the *White House Usher's Diary*, for travel by railcar to New Orleans, where he boarded a naval destroyer, the USS *Moffett*, as the first leg of a fishing cruise.[15] Roosevelt needed a break in the middle of a rough patch during this fifth year of his presidency; the US Supreme Court and the president engaged in conflicts for months over several elements of his recovery agenda, including minimum wage laws, Social Security, and various other New Deal programs. The ultimate destination for the weeklong fishing trip was Port Aransas, Texas, where on May 1 Roosevelt met his son, Elliott, a resident of Fort Worth. The presidential yacht, the USS *Potomac*, traveled to the Aransas Pass channel to serve Roosevelt and his party.[16]

Though there is some confusion among published sources regarding the precise date that Franklin Roosevelt visited the Mississippi Gulf Coast on this trip, this account accepts the transcript of White House records as the most accurate. It contains this note for April 29, 1937: "Arrived Biloxi, MS, 9:00 a.m., inspected US Veteran's Facility nearby, accompanied by governor and mayor, and then proceeded to Gulfport, Mississippi, by auto, where that mayor joined the party."[17] According to the same source and for this same day, the president arrived in New Orleans at 2:30 p.m., and thus a length of stay in Mississippi approximating four hours can be established.

Apparently the presidential train proceeded from Biloxi to Gulfport, even as its passenger in chief motored in an automobile the few miles between the communities. This is apparent because the collections of the National Archives of the United States contain the single typewritten sheet on which are Roosevelt's brief remarks from "the rear platform of the presidential special train" in Gulfport. Mississippi's senator Pat Harrison introduced Roosevelt, and the president recalled a meeting the two of them had "nearly a quarter century ago" when Harrison was a congressman and Roosevelt was assistant secretary of the navy. The president teased, "I do not know about Senator Harrison's fishing promises but if Texas does not work out I am coming back here to make him prove them."[18]

Looking back from a perspective sixty-five years after the event, the Biloxi *Sun Herald* reported that Roosevelt's brief stop in the city was nevertheless a welcome and celebrated one. "[FDR] was on his way . . . to fish for tarpon, but kindly consented to be feted on the coast, where most of the mayors had declared official holidays because of the prized visit. . . . Roosevelt was celebrated with a motorcade through Biloxi, while local citizens cheered and waved flags. He visited the Veteran's Administration and other locations in the community." Biloxians presented the president with tokens of their esteem: "He left with such goodies as a gavel made of Beauvoir cypress and a magnolia wreath."[19]

Though the Civil War was more than seventy years in the nation's rearview mirror, the remnants of that conflict in Mississippi must have been clear to Roosevelt during his visit. One of the "other locations" he visited in Biloxi was the Jefferson Davis Home for Confederate Veterans,[20] and his gavel of "Beauvior cypress" came from the grounds of the retirement estate occupied by the president of the Confederacy.

September 29, 1942—Camp Shelby

Of the visits to Mississippi made by President Roosevelt, this one was kept confidential—at least, initially. In the fall of 1942 the commander in chief traveled to inspect selected strategic industrial and military sites related to the war effort; these installations occupied locations across several states in the eastern half of the country. Public information regarding the trip went unpublicized, presumably for purposes of security and to avoid giving any information to the nation's enemies. One of the places on the president's schedule was Camp Shelby near Hattiesburg.[21] Local citizens were not made aware of the president's visit for more than a decade; in the *Jackson Daily News* for March 22, 1953, was this revelation: "President Franklin D. Roosevelt ... made a secret visit to this state during World War II and inspected Camp Shelby."[22]

The FDR Presidential Library provided a bit more detail about the secretive visit: "FDR arrived in New Orleans, inspected the City Park Plant of Higgins Shipbuilding Corp., joined there by Governor Sam Jones of LA. He left at 9:55 a.m. for Camp Shelby, MS, which was inspected in the afternoon with Governor Paul Johnson of MS."[23]

Much more entertaining was this account from a soldier at Camp Shelby who witnessed the president's visit: "Early one morning in September 1942, orders were passed down to the eighty-fifth division to begin an immediate police-up and check the neatness of the entire camp. A review of the troops was scheduled in the afternoon. Something big was about to happen. Obviously someone of importance was coming. . . .

"[After lunch] a long, black limousine arrived. . . . President FD Roosevelt stepped out, as the general saluted his commander in chief. Then General Haslip [*sic*, General Wade H. Haislip] accompanied the president as they reviewed the troops in the limo. The president had stopped by during one of his 'secret' tours of the nation and the industrial plants."[24]

★   ★   ★

While Franklin Roosevelt's visits to the state were few relative to his number of years in office, his presidency impacted Mississippi in ways that remain observable. The TVA's relationship with Mississippians continued through to the present moment. The impact of its benefits throughout the rural Tennessee River valley is difficult to overstate, having brought electricity and modern conveniences that hastened both economic development and cultural progress in the state and across the broader region. Roosevelt's presence in Tupelo to celebrate the advent of the TVA made clear its significance.

Rapid change became the norm nationally over the next few decades, as Americans returned from the war and began to fight battles at home over the nature of citizenship and civil rights. Roosevelt's secretive 1942 tour of military installations included the last visit to Mississippi by a sitting president for more than a quarter century; when he departed after his visit to Camp Shelby, the state he left behind was home to an overwhelmingly Democratic electorate. But between his departure in 1942 and the Republican Richard Nixon's arrival in 1967, social upheaval across the country brought about seismic shifts within the national parties, shifts that realigned the political affiliations of the Deep South.

CHAPTER SIX

RICHARD NIXON

Thirty-Seventh President of the United States
Republican
Elected 1968 and 1972
Served January 20, 1969, to August 9, 1974

The national Democratic Party and the voters in Mississippi were in the midst of an ideological split by the middle of the twentieth century. As the Supreme Court struck down legalized segregation in its 1954 *Brown v. Board of Education* decision and Democrats within the offices and agencies of the federal government moved slowly toward support for integration, the party was already splintering into incompatible ideological factions. Beginning formally with the segregationist Governor Strom Thurmond's (D-SC) third-party run in the 1948 election against sitting Democratic president Harry Truman, it was clear that a historic realignment was under way, and that conservatism—most notably practitioners whose philosophy was tinged with racial prejudice—was growing increasingly alienated from its traditional party base. Thurmond and his supporters bolted at the 1948 Democratic convention and formed an alternative party known as the States' Rights Democrats, or the Dixiecrats.

In the South, Democratic voters attempted to keep the diminishing conservative wing of the party alive into the 1960s. Mississippi voters—an almost entirely white bloc built largely on discriminatory voter registration laws—led that increasingly quixotic effort, even casting the state party's entire lot of electoral votes in 1960 for a noncandidate, Democratic governor Harry F. Byrd of Virginia, who had been a prominent face of resistance to ongoing attempts at school integration. As the party moved into the turbulent 1960s with the progressive John F. Kennedy at its head, the Democrats found that they could no longer count on the formerly solid South to help win federal elections.

By the following contest four years later, when Republican Barry Goldwater took on Democrat Lyndon Johnson, party platforms—and the electoral map— reflected a drastically changed political landscape. Johnson, a driving force behind the 1964 Civil Rights Act that sought to eliminate legal discrimination from schools to voting booths, bested primary challenger and strict segregationist George Wallace, governor of Alabama, in the primaries. The incumbent Johnson's triumph over Wallace affirmed the party's move away from the explicitly white supremacist ideology that guided much of its platform before, during, and after the Civil War. In Mississippi and across the Deep South, the selection of a civil rights advocate emphatically brought about the end of regional conservative support for the national Democratic Party.

Looking back at that 1964 election, Republican Richard Nixon saw a chance to wrestle the South away from the Democrats in 1968. Goldwater fared terribly everywhere in the country except for the South, and Nixon perceived in those former Democratic strongholds a potential voter base to build upon. Mississippi delivered Goldwater's largest statewide margin of victory, giving the Republican 87.14 percent of the Magnolia State's votes, versus 12.86 percent for Johnson. The next closest was the 69.45 percent Goldwater won in Alabama, the only state where Johnson wasn't even on the ballot. Continued disfranchisement of black voters assured that the Deep South would overwhelmingly favor the candidate who best represented the concerns of conservative white electors.

With a region full of voters who felt left behind by the Democrats, Nixon knew that a more conservative turn in his party, coupled with regular nods to white separatist ideology, could solidify the southern conversion to the Republicans for the foreseeable future. Well chronicled in history books today, this "Southern Strategy" delivered the Republican nomination to Nixon in 1968.

The candidate walked a fine line on racial issues throughout the nominating contest, tailoring his take on civil rights issues to each audience he addressed. To appeal to northerners, he voiced his support for an open housing bill then in Congress that aimed to end housing discrimination. However, a secretly made recording of Nixon speaking to southern Republican delegates from Mississippi and elsewhere prior to the convention made clear that political calculations were far more important than civil rights in his support for the legislation. His goal, he confided, was to force Congress to "vote for it and get it out of the way. . . to get civil rights and open housing issues out of sight so we didn't have a split party over the platform" at the convention. Moving the legislation through to President Johnson's desk also meant quickly taking it out of the news cycle, and out of consideration for voters. Nixon's Machiavellian maneuvering assured that he appeared both supportive of basic civil rights in public, and at best indifferent to the same issues to the conservative southern delegations. Further tipping his cap to the South's long-held antifederalist position, the nominee concluded that he "would have preferred that it be handled at the state and local level."[1] In 1968 candidate Nixon demonstrated that he knew how to work a crowd.

While Nixon's double-speak on many such issues carried him to victory in the fall, Wallace outflanked Nixon in the Deep South, running as an outspoken white supremacist third-party candidate that summer (American Independent Party). With few exceptions, in fact, Nixon's carefully moderated conservative message won votes virtually everywhere in the general election. His setbacks came in the progressive Northeast, where he lost territory to the liberal Democrat Hubert Humphrey, and in the very conservative Deep South, where Wallace's right-wing message bested the Republican candidate. Still Nixon's Southern Strategy paid off in the long run. His tailored, conservative positions, such as opposition to federally mandated school desegregation, won him the entire Deep South—along with every other state in the Union but Massachusetts—four years later. Though Nixon did not single-handedly convert the South to his party, his two successful presidential elections added measurably to the result that Mississippi and the rest of the Deep South became Republican territory for decades to come.

Clearly, Nixon knew how to play politics to his advantage, even in the midst of a summer of upheaval brought about by vital issues from civil rights to the war in Vietnam. While such gamesmanship is a necessary skill for all electorally successful politicians, Nixon performed the role of calculating politician with a remarkable—and frequently unscrupulous—talent. He knew how to win an audience, and at times would create one when the political advantage was clear. As an example, Nixon spent nine hours in Alaska during the return from his historic 1972 trip to China to assure that a triumphal homecoming played live on prime time television.[2] Accordingly, Nixon's three trips as president to Mississippi had multiple purposes, but in each case the reasons included: to enhance his image, to repay faithful voters in the state with presidential attention, to woo past or potential donors, and/ or to acknowledge influential Mississippians in the US Congress.

In their book *Mississippi Politics: The Struggle for Power, 1976–2006*, Jere Nash and Andy Taggart pointed to the phenomenon of trips with more than one intention, as they recalled Nixon's first presidential visit: "In 1969, Nixon endeared himself to Mississippians when he toured the ruins of the Gulf Coast in the aftermath of Hurricane Camille, in the process becoming the first sitting president since 1937 [*sic*, 1942] to set foot on Mississippi soil."[3] Furthermore, Nash and Taggart set the Nixon political relationship with Mississippi deeper in history, recalling that as early as the 1960 Republican National Convention, Nixon made a commitment to bring his candidacy to the state in exchange for the support of the delegation despite controversy over the civil rights plank in the party's platform. "Nixon kept his promise and campaigned in Mississippi on September 24, 1960, the first time a presidential candidate had appeared in the state in more than a century."[4]

September 8, 1969—Gulfport

Though the 2005 paired hurricanes Katrina and Rita were more destructive across the states of the Gulf Coast in terms of both property and lives lost, Hurricane Camille in August 1969 was a more powerful storm, with wind speeds greater than 200 miles per hour—estimated following the destruction of the instruments recording the measurements. Camille made landfall on the Mississippi Gulf Coast early on Monday, August 18, and brought widespread devastation with its sustained winds and tidal surge.[5]

President and Mrs. Nixon made an aerial inspection of the region on September 8, 1969. What they saw shocked them, though by then residents had cleared some of the debris. On the day following landfall, the *New York Times* ran a page-one story that asked, "Just what will a hurricane wind of 190 miles an hour do?" The answer? Terrifying things. The report gave a glimpse at the storm's terrible power: "[The hurricane] will snatch three large oceangoing ships from their moorings and set them down on the beach. . . . It will make a concrete-block service station disappear."[6] Mississippi fared worst of all. "The wreckage extends all along the Mississippi coast and beyond. Mobile on the east and New Orleans on the west were also in the hurricane's path, although neither was damaged as heavily as the little Mississippi towns in between."[7]

Late in the twentieth century and early in the twenty-first, rapid presidential response grew as a critical factor in the politics related to natural disasters, and chief executives learned—sometimes by misstep, as in the case of George W. Bush (see chapter 12)—that there was great significance attached to being on-site as soon as reasonably possible. Expectations differed, however, half a century ago. Nixon's visit to Mississippi's Gulf Coast followed Camille by nearly three weeks. The White House tagged the disaster visit on to the end of a longer day trip that began in Del Rio, Texas, for an event with President Gustavo Diaz Ordaz of Mexico. Nixon participated in the dedication of the newly constructed Amistad Dam on the Lone Star State's southern border. This ceremony occasioned a page-one story in the *New York Times* on September 9, 1969, that extended on page thirty-five and was followed by a brief note that the president returned to Washington, DC, at 11:45 p.m. The only storm story in the news on the day of Nixon's stop in Mississippi was about a hurricane watch for New York City and New Jersey. Hurricane Camille was apparently a faded memory for much of the nation.[8]

However, Mississippians certainly had not forgotten the destruction that still surrounded them every day, and Nixon used an opportunity of convenience to fly over the damage. He made an 8:25 p.m. stop at the Gulfport Municipal Airport, and showed with his presence and his words that he and the federal government cared about those living with Camille's aftermath. It was a significant political stop, and the cadre of state and local officials that welcomed the Republican president made clear the strength of Nixon's continuing appeal to southern conservative Democrats. Governor John Bell Williams and both of Mississippi's powerful US senators, James O. Eastland and John C. Stennis, were in attendance, as were Mississippi's US representatives William M. Colmer, Charles H. Griffin, and Gillespie V. "Sonny" Montgomery; all six were popularly elected conservative Democrats. The lone Republican official of note, Clarke Reed, was the sitting chairman of Mississippi's Republican Party.[9] Nixon's visit was also tremendously important to the people of the coastal communities, and estimates for the size of the crowd at the airfield ranged from 25,000 to 75,000.[10] Though he hailed from a different party than the state's elected representatives to the federal government—and he finished a distant third in the election the year before—southern conservatives believed Nixon's view of the world aligned closely with theirs.

Speaking to what was surely the largest group to descend to that point on the Gulfport airfield, Nixon offered the hurricane-ravaged region both his own sympathy and the support of Washington:

"On the part of your federal government, I can certainly pledge to you a continuation of the interest that we have already shown, an interest that is not partisan—it represents all the people of this country; an interest in terms of all the departments of government, all the agencies in government; an interest which is shared by the members of the house and the senate, led by your own house and senate delegation."

The president sought, as well, to align himself with the assembled Mississippi politicians, heaping praise on Governor Williams and others. For at least a century prior, responses to massively destructive events relied on the guidance of local—rather than federal—leaders, while Washington offered sympathy and limited support from afar. Mississippi's recovery in 1969 was little different, but Nixon took pains to paint the state's own response as "unprecedented."

"Under the leadership of your governor and working with the members of the house and the senate, and also the state legislature . . . you have set up an unprecedented group of private citizens and government officials to work together for a new kind of cooperation, a plan in which you will not just rebuild as it was, what was old, but in which you will build a new area, not only new buildings, but new ideas and new opportunities for all of the people of this great state."

It was the can-do spirit of common Mississippians, Nixon asserted, that would carry the state through such a difficult time. "No matter how many millions of dollars we get from Washington, no matter how much you are able to get from the state government or from your county government, no matter how much comes from the various volunteer organizations from all over America . . . what really counts are the people.

"Because, if the heart of the people and the spirit of the people and the strength of the people are not sound, then all of the money in the world will not help. As I come to Mississippi today, I say that the heart and the spirit and the strength of the people of Mississippi has never been stronger. And that means you are going forward to a greater future than ever before."[11]

His visit that day surely bolstered his position as a favorite among the voters of the state. Three years later, Nixon won more than 78 percent of Mississippi's votes on his way to reelection. Despite that strong showing, Nixon was under a cloud by the time he returned to the state in 1973. During his first visit in 1969, Nixon was accompanied by a cast of aides who were, by 1973, linked in the minds of the public to the events that would eventually end Nixon's political career. At his side in Gulfport were not only his wife but also Attorney General John Mitchell and other administration insiders, including John Ehrlichman, H. R. Haldeman, Henry Kissinger, Ronald Ziegler, Dwight Chapin, and Alexander Butterfield, all of whom would play roles years later in the Watergate scandal.[12]

April 27, 1973—Meridian

Nixon and his administration's troubles began on June 17, 1972, when security caught five men breaking into the Democratic National Committee headquarters at the Watergate Hotel in Washington, DC. The discovery of financial connections between the burglars and members of Nixon's reelection committee soon ballooned into a full-blown political conspiracy and cover-up that eventually implicated the president himself as a willing participant. By the time Nixon arrived in Meridian to dedicate a new Naval Technical Training Center, the US Senate was within three weeks of convening nationally telecast hearings on the scandal.

While the president's attention was surely focused elsewhere, he was in Meridian to christen the new training center in the name of Democratic senator John Stennis, a man who provided leadership of national significance as the chairman of the Senate Committee on Armed Services. Like Nixon, Mississippians had more than Watergate on their minds; the president's visit, just as in 1969, came in the wake of a destructive natural disaster. Nixon and Stennis together flew over areas of the state devastated by historic flooding on the Yazoo and Mississippi Rivers, and when the president's aircraft reached Meridian, his staff issued a statement regarding the federal response to the devastation. Apparently, the president and his advisers determined that they could set a better tone for the dedication event by segregating the nuts and bolts of the disaster message from the ceremonial address, leaving for Nixon's public remarks the compliments about the heroism and tenacity of Mississippians.

Though they were in opposing political parties, Nixon praised Stennis extensively at the dedication ceremony, recognizing both the senator's assistance to the president and his standing in the South. First, Stennis offered unwavering support of Nixon's approach to the Vietnam War. Second, Stennis was a popular conservative Democrat in a state of critical importance to Republicans' continuing expansion south of the Mason-Dixon Line. To build and maintain inroads in the Deep South, Nixon and his party needed to stand in conspicuous friendship with Stennis and other conservative stalwarts. These were contentious times for the president—aside from the still-developing scandal, opposition to the war in Vietnam was growing more virulent by the day—and Nixon had strong incentives to court the powerful senator. Thus, not only did the president fly over the flooded counties with a revered state figure, he also used some of his time at the microphone in Meridian to remind everyone of his attention to the Camille disaster in 1969 and to praise the strength of character evident in the citizenry. With all the vexation surrounding him, a positive and receptive crowd was cathartic to the beleaguered Nixon.

"This morning I have made a low-level airplane flight over the swollen headwaters of the Yazoo River in Mississippi and from there west to the Mississippi River and downstream to Vicksburg," read the White House statement. More than a sympathetic observer, Nixon sought to cast himself as a driver of federal aid in a time when the role of a president in such situations was evolving. "To deal with this emergency, federal agencies have been mobilized to assist state and local governments in the most massive flood-fighting effort of this century. . . . So far the [US Army] Corps [of Engineers] has provided materials and assistance for flood mitigation and prevention amounting to $24 million. . . . I can assure all of the people who live in the stricken areas that full federal assistance will be provided as long as needed."[13]

When Nixon later stood atop the dais and began his speech in honor of Stennis, he shared an anecdote from his earlier plane ride intended to set the tone for his assessments of both Mississippi's then junior senator and Mississippians themselves. Nixon told of his initial wonder at how anyone could rise from such devastation. "Senator Stennis looked me in the eye and he said, 'Look, the folks in Mississippi always come back. They don't desert the land.' I recalled then the spirit that I saw in the eyes and faces of those on that night in Gulfport, people there who had been driven out of their homes. The winds had come and destroyed them, and they were living in trailers, or even worse, but I recall that what impressed me about it is that while others may have given up on them, they haven't given up on themselves. And that is why the spirit of the people of this state has always impressed me and impresses me today."[14] Stennis, the steely-eyed public servant, reminded the president of the great resilience of the people of Mississippi.

Seeking an opportunity to burnish both Stennis's image and, by extension, his own, Nixon used the occasion to remind the crowd that the man of the hour was also a fan of the president's aggressive pursuit of the war in Vietnam. "Senator Stennis has made some very kind remarks about the leadership of the President of the United States over these past four years and particularly the year 1972. . . . [A] president can make a hard decision, but a president is not able to carry out that decision unless, in the final analysis, he has the support of the people. And in this case, whether it was the decision which I thought was essential on May 8 to mine Haiphong and bomb North Vietnam, which triggered the first negotiation, or whether it was the decision, the much more

difficult one, at Christmastime to renew the bombing of North Vietnam with
B-52s, another very difficult decision, whatever the case was, I understood why
many disagreed."[15] The senator, though, was not among those many. "What has
really meant something, a great deal to me, has been the personal association
as well as the personal support that I have had from and with John Stennis
in that period. . . . John Stennis, night after night, went down through long
[debates in Congress] and stood there holding the fort, fighting for that kind
of strong defense because of the conversations we had had, knowing what
was on the line, and winning those votes."[16]

   Before a supportive crowd, the embattled Nixon sought to hitch his star
to the night's honoree. "That is John Stennis—not thinking of himself, but
thinking of the president." Stennis, in the president's view, was the ultimate
patriot. "He is a man who does not think of himself first, who does not think
of his party first, but who thinks always of America, his country. . . . John
Stennis will be remembered not as a man of war, but as a man who was strong
enough to help America lead the way to peace."

   With that, Nixon left the comfortable confines of a ceremony far from
Washington in celebration of the legacy of a political ally, and he headed back
to the nation's capital, where his own legacy was emerging as a decidedly less
patriotic tale. By the time Nixon returned to the state for his final visit as a
sitting president one year later, he was serving on borrowed time.

April 25, 1974—Jackson

President Nixon's last trip to Mississippi came at the invitation of the
Mississippi Economic Council (MEC) on the occasion of the organization's
twenty-fifth anniversary. An audience comprising the powerful business
interests of the state gave a tailor-made opportunity for the president to
make a strong public statement about his perspectives in the face of the
difficult political environment surrounding him. America's participation
in the Vietnam War had, by then, ended badly. The economy was spiral-
ing downward. Worst of all for Nixon personally, the Watergate scandal
had matured into a legal and political crisis that was sucking the life from
his administration. His lengthy and unfocused remarks to a large crowd
attending the MEC meeting at the Mississippi Coliseum revealed much
regarding the president's state of mind and his desperation to win support
(see Appendix A for a verbatim rendering of this significant address).

Nixon's attempts to win over the crowd included everything from appeals to football fans—"to all of those in this great state, whether it be from Ole Miss or Mississippi State or one of the other universities or colleges, let me say, if you ever find a good quarterback who can throw and who can run and who is young, call me"—to a rebuke of unnamed naysayers who claimed throughout the previous five years that the country was on a downturn due to social unrest and an unpopular war: "Those were the pessimists, but they were wrong. They were wrong then, and they are wrong today. America's greatest days are ahead of us, because it is not the easy times that test either an individual or a nation, it is the hard times. And America has withstood the hard times and has come through even stronger each time."[17]

The president's scattered remarks demonstrated that his days as a composed, wily politician were behind him, reflecting the continued unraveling of his administration; the speech itself went on for nearly an hour. Nixon's talk to the members of the MEC and others in the large audience stretched to nearly 6,000 words, roughly three times the length of either of his inaugural addresses, each of which lasted about seventeen minutes. The politician who was by then largely despised seemed to be struggling to acknowledge the public's distaste, and to paint a picture of the nation's future that required his unshakable, informed, and experienced leadership. His approval rating cratered at 24 percent by July, a low that no chief executive matched for decades following Nixon's presidency.[18]

At times Nixon's tone ranged from pleading to sarcastic to defensive, often in the space of a few sentences. "Let me look at the economy a minute with you. And I am sure out here in this audience we have lots of experts who may have differing views about it. I can only give you the best judgment that I have from the economic advisers, not only from the administration but from outside, who look at the American economy today, analyze it, and wonder where we are going."[19]

Throughout the early portion of his remarks, Nixon tried to present a plan for revitalizing the economy that included lower energy prices, higher production of staple agricultural and fuel products, and economic and environmental deregulation, which he argued would increase coal mining and spur the development of nuclear power. Nixon then pivoted to a rosy assessment of the disastrous end of the Vietnam War, followed by an explanation of the philosophy of long-term peace guiding his talks with leaders in China and the Soviet Union. More than anything, the rambling speech sounded unprepared and entirely off-the-cuff; by the time his remarks concluded, he had, for example, circled back to the topic of solving inflation three distinct times, largely repeating himself at each phase.

★ ★ ★

A reading of President Nixon's last Mississippi speech is remarkable in the sense that it reveals a doomed politician struggling to maintain his grasp on a presidency that was sliding toward an inevitable, premature, and ignoble end. Less than four months after his 1974 trip to Jackson, Nixon became the only individual in the nation's history to resign from the presidency. His earlier visits, though, were as emblematic of the deftness of his political skills as his last visit was of the dangers of his vanity.

Still, and despite his failings, Nixon's impact on southern politics was seismic. Though he did not originate the move of states in the Deep South toward the Republican Party, his 1968 candidacy affirmed for white southern conservatives that there was not only a place for them in the GOP, but that the party could produce politicians with the skill to win national elections upon a solidly conservative platform. While southern Democrats saw their winning appeal return one more time in the election of Georgian Jimmy Carter in 1976, the region has remained unfailingly Republican for more than a half century.

CHAPTER SEVEN

GERALD FORD

Thirty-Eighth President of the United States
Republican
Never Elected to the Presidency
Appointed to the Vice-Presidency under the Twenty-Fifth Amendment
Assumed the Presidency upon the Resignation of Richard Nixon
Served August 9, 1974, to January 20, 1977

★ ★

Near the bottom of the front page in the *New York Times* on Tuesday, August 6, 1974, was this headline, "President Considered Resigning but Rejected Idea, Aides Assert." According to the report, when President Nixon received information on the previous day that newly disclosed materials from White House tape recordings contradicted public statements he had made regarding the Watergate scandal, he considered several options, one of which was submitting his resignation. However, he "discarded it at least for the time being." On page nineteen of the same edition was the headline, "Ford Seeks to Stand Aloof in Impeachment Debate." Accompanying this story is a photograph with the caption, "Vice President Ford returning from New Orleans to Andrews Air Force Base, MD."[1]

Standing aloof from the Watergate fray apparently meant that Gerald Ford found it more comfortable to lend in-person support to the campaigns of various Republicans across the nation. He became an avid traveler, thereby having regular excuses to get away from Washington. On Saturday, August 3, "he stumped all day in the Mississippi heat for Republican congressional candidates," the *Times* reported on August 5. Stops for the vice president, as mentioned by the reporter, included Columbus, Jackson, and Hattiesburg.[2]

This interesting anecdote led the story: "One small sign appeared among the banners and placards of all sizes sprinkled through the enthusiastic crowd of 1,500 that greeted Vice President Ford at the Pine Belt Regional Airport near Hattiesburg, MS, yesterday. 'Ford Support the President for Us,' the sign read. That was unusual because the growing crowds turning out for Mr. Ford in his seemingly endless travels . . . have shown little evidence that they were there to demonstrate loyalty to President Nixon in his struggles against impeachment. Mostly, they seemed to want to look at the man who may be the next president."[3]

Just a few days earlier, according to the same article, 13,000 turned out to watch Ford and House Majority Leader Tip O'Neill partner in a pro-am golf tournament in Massachusetts. The previous year there were barely half that many spectators at the event.

Clearly, citizens across the United States sensed that a change was coming and that Gerald R. Ford would ascend to the presidency sooner or later. However, few who cheered him on August 3 in Mississippi guessed that his elevation would occur before another week passed. Friday, August 9, 1974, became resignation day for Richard Nixon. Gerald Ford took the oath of office as the thirty-eighth president on that same day.

President Ford had an unexpired term of less than two-and-a-half years ahead of him, and as he grew comfortable in the office, he made the decision that he would seek election in 1976 to a succeeding four-year term. Looming on the Republican horizon, however, was Ronald Reagan, formerly the governor of California and a formidable candidate with presidential ambitions of his own. Ford's two visits to Mississippi while serving as president were both related to his 1976 campaign.

July 30, 1976—Jackson

In their book *Mississippi Politics*, Jere Nash and Andy Taggart write that, during the 1976 campaign for the Republican nomination, Reagan led in the contest for the support of the Mississippi delegation. However, on Monday, July 26, Reagan announced his unexpected choice for a running mate. It was Pennsylvania's liberal Republican senator, Richard Schweiker, ostensibly to balance the ticket. Party leaders in Mississippi were shocked and disappointed; the announcement was considered not only a mistake but also a betrayal of conservative principles.

Thus the support of the Mississippi delegation became both vulnerable to Ford's candidacy because of Reagan's decision and available because the members had decided to arrive at the Republican National Convention uncommitted and determined to vote as a thirty-delegate bloc, a strategy known as the unit rule. Journalist Jules Witcover wrote: "Though the national party prohibited imposition of the unit rule, there was no way it could stop a state party from using it, and the rule had a long and solid tradition in Mississippi."[4] When Mississippi Republicans adopted the unit rule at the 1976 state party convention in April, leadership assumed that because of primary contests in other states, a nominee would be a foregone conclusion. Furthermore, there was an expectation it would be Reagan, and delegates preferring his candidacy were in the majority on the Mississippi delegation. Mississippi expected to vote with the winner but had little inkling it would be pivotal in choosing the nominee.[5]

In this transitional moment, Ford's campaign saw an opportunity to turn Mississippi to his side. On July 30, 1976, President Ford flew to Mississippi accompanied by members of the state's congressional delegation. When Congressman Thad Cochran heard the news of Reagan's announcement, he said, "[Schweiker] is the most liberal kook on Capitol Hill, and it scares me to death to think that he could be a heartbeat away from being president." This influential opinion soon became known to the Mississippi delegates.

According to Nash and Taggart, "President Ford traveled to Jackson on Friday to court the delegation.... The Ford visit boosted the work of his team in Mississippi and netted public endorsements from Congressmen Thad Cochran and Trent Lott."[6] Even a subsequent visit to the state by Reagan and Schweiker to meet the delegation could not lock down the commitment they sought. At the Republican National Convention at Kansas City in August, maneuvering made the Mississippi delegation's votes pivotal in a fight over a proposed new rule that presidential candidates would be forced to name their favored running mates prior to the balloting on the floor. Eventually, there was a conclusion referred to by some as the "Great Mississippi Compromise" owing to the significant role the state's leadership and delegates played from one stage of the skirmishing to the next.[7] President Ford won the Republican nomination in 1976, and Ronald Reagan had to await the election of 1980 for his appointment with history.

On the front page of the *Jackson Daily News* for July 30, 1976, was a photograph of President Gerald Ford and First Lady Betty Ford waving to the crowd as they emerged from Air Force One. Details reported in the story included a crowd of several hundred at the airport, together with a vanload of elephants arranged to provide a visual symbol of the Republican Party. Adapting a familiar slogan from Herbert Hoover's successful 1928 run for the presidency,[8] one campaign sign proclaimed: "A Ford in the White House and a Chicken in Every Pot." President Ford headed for a closed-door meeting with the delegation that was likely to tip the balance of votes in his direction.[9]

Speaking at the Ramada Inn in Jackson early that evening, Ford affirmed that he had just finished "a very good give-and-take with the delegation that is going to Kansas City," and was optimistic of earning their support. His public speech at the hotel was a boilerplate address; the incumbent candidate reviewed his accomplishments since taking over from his disgraced predecessor two years prior, then he followed with a promise to lead a strenuous campaign throughout the summer and fall. Nevertheless, close examination of his points opened a window into the pitch he gave Mississippi's electors and voters. From the president's perspective, the previous two years resulted in a triumphant renewal of the people's faith in the institution of the presidency. "We have done a good job in restoring the confidence of the American people in the White House, itself," Ford proclaimed, a statement he would repeat nearly verbatim a few moments later. In doing so, he said, "we have turned this economy around." Ford also touted the end of the Vietnam War and a return to peace as proof that his leadership steadied the nation.

In looking forward, Ford's pronouncements were equally rosy, if also equally vague. He promised to continue vetoing costly bills from the Democrats in Congress as he had in his first partial term. "I vetoed fifty-three bills, forty-two of them have been sustained," Ford recounted, "and the net result is we have saved the taxpayers of this country thirteen-billion dollars. And I might add parenthetically, if they send any more of those bills down with those wild spending programs, they will be vetoed again and again and again." Allowing Georgia governor Jimmy Carter to take his place in the White House, Ford said, would eliminate that vital check to Congress's power.[10]

In an interview at the Jackson airport prior to his departure later that evening, a journalist challenged Ford on those same vetoes. "There has been some criticism of you, Mr. Ford," the interviewer stated, "concerning your veto of certain programs dealing with social programs, school lunch measures, what have you. Do you think that is warranted criticism, that you are not attuned to the poor in this country?" President Ford defended his actions, as he did from the dais at the Ramada. "If you look at the budget I recommended, in almost every category I recommended more money for education, more money for health, more money for many of the social programs than had been previously recommended or approved. It is just that you can do just so much. And it was a sound recommendation, and I fully stand by it."[11]

September 26, 1976—Bay St. Louis, Gulfport, Biloxi, and Pascagoula

Ford's second presidential visit to Mississippi had the singular purpose of campaigning for a victory in the November election, and his time on the coast followed hard on the heels of a visit by the Democratic candidate, Jimmy Carter. The incumbent's popularity on the Gulf Coast showed during this late September visit. Eight thousand attended his rally at Bay St. Louis, and 13,000 cheered him in Pascagoula. His numbers in Biloxi were twice those of Jimmy Carter's stop a few days earlier. While on the coast, the president picked up the endorsement of Democrat John Bell Williams, formerly the governor of Mississippi, who said he admired Ford's support for the state's recovery from Hurricane Camille. For a portion of the campaign motorcade across Mississippi's Gulf Coast, the legendary Paul "Bear" Bryant, head football coach of the University of Alabama, joined President Ford.[12]

Speaking at the Hancock County Public Library in Bay St. Louis, Ford echoed his argument made the previous July, framing his brief time in the White House as a restorative period for the presidency and the nation. "As you will all recall, in August of 1974, just a little over two years ago, this country was in trouble. The American people had lost faith in their government. We were in serious economic circumstances. Inflation was high, over 12 percent. We were on the brink of a recession, the worst in forty years. We were still involved in Vietnam, and this country had to turn it around." Ford sought to make the case that the nation was better off. "We are over our troubles of the last two years.... The Ford administration is going to win the battle against inflation. We're going to hold down the cost of government."[13]

The president delivered a similar speech at the Main Post Office in Gulfport a short while later. Ford again pushed for limited government as a solution to inflation, and he recounted his record of presidential vetoes (which, by this time, had climbed to fifty-eight). Recognizing the presence of the Naval Construction Battalion Center in the city, Ford drew contrasts with his opponent on defense spending. "In the two years that I have been president, I have submitted to the Congress the two largest defense budgets in the history of the United States.... My opponent wants to cut the Defense Department budget by $5 to $7 billion. That would be disastrous. We need to keep America number one, and under a Ford administration we will.

You don't stand up to the pressures around the world by having less power; you need more power, and we are going to keep it that way." Ford knew that full-funding promises for the Seabees helped his cause in Gulfport.[14]

In Biloxi at Mavar's Cannery, Ford again fine-tuned his message for the local audience. "I'm mighty proud of the people out at Keesler Air Force Base," Ford said, referring to Biloxi's own military installation. "You're a very vital part of this great national defense team that we have. I believe that the United States—in the Army, the Navy, the Air Force, the Marine Corps—we're unsurpassed. And under a Ford administration we're going to stay number one."[15]

A final stop in Pascagoula's Beach Park that evening rounded out his swing through the Magnolia State, and again the president recognized a local defense-related contractor in his otherwise thematically identical remarks. "This is my third visit to Pascagoula," Ford said. "I came down here in 1962 with my wife, Betty. She commissioned a new submarine over here in the Ingalls shipbuilding yards.

"But let me talk about the Navy and what the Ingalls shipbuilding yard means to the kind of a Navy that we have to have. We are being challenged by the Soviet Union on the sea. We have had our Navy gradually go down in ship numbers, although we've done very well in tonnage. But you have a big shipbuilding contract out here in Ingalls shipbuilding. I understand 27,000 people work here building those fine ships. I compliment you. But let me say this: we need a first-class Air Force; we've got one. We need a superb, first-class Army; we have one; we need an outstanding Marine Corps; we've got one. And we've got a swell, first-class Navy, and you are a big part of it."[16]

★ ★ ★

Ford departed the state with thirty-seven days of campaigning left and, as it turned out, just a few months remaining in the White House. He lost his bid for election on November 2 to Carter. Both men made missteps during the campaign that hurt their chances in one region of the country or another, and Mississippi turned out to be one of the ten closest races among all the states. Jimmy Carter won Mississippi's delegation to the Electoral College by fewer than 15,000 votes statewide and a plurality under 50 percent.[17] Surely helped by his status as a southerner, Carter was the last Democratic candidate to the present day to carry Mississippi. Gerald Ford, a northern Republican who had represented Michigan in the US House of Representatives for twenty-four years before his appointment as vice president, lost the presidential vote in Mississippi by less than 2 percentage points.

★ ★

CHAPTER EIGHT

JIMMY CARTER

Thirty-Ninth President of the United States
Democrat
Elected 1976
Served January 20, 1977, to January 20, 1981

★ ★

Mississippi experienced a heady year of electoral politics in 1976. First, the state's delegation to the Republican National Convention became uniquely pivotal in the decision to nominate Gerald Ford despite the surging popularity of Ronald Reagan (see previous chapter). Second, following a hard-fought, months-long campaign, a slim majority of Mississippi votes went to Jimmy Carter, with the final tally coming during a tense election night in November. Victory belonged to the Democratic challenger. According to Jere Nash and Andy Taggart, at the 2:30 a.m. announcement, Carter phoned Democratic governor Charles Clifton Finch to say: "Cliff, Mississippi just put me over the top. I love every one of you."[1] Finch was the sitting governor and was the latest in an unbroken string of Democratic chief executives elected in Mississippi since the days of Reconstruction.[2] However, Carter was and remains the only Democrat to win the state's presidential delegation to the Electoral College since Adlai Stevenson in 1956 captured over 58 percent of Mississippi's popular vote.

Jimmy Carter was, in many ways, an improbable candidate in 1976. He was a farmer by profession who had a relatively short political history, serving four years in the Georgia senate and later one term as the state's governor. He chose the right moment—the national election following the Watergate scandal that led to Richard Nixon's resignation from the presidency—and the right campaign strategies to capture not only the Democratic nomination for the presidency but also to win the office. In 1976 he defeated Republican Gerald Ford, Nixon's successor, and he lost in 1980 to Ronald Reagan, who became the most revered Republican of the modern era to hold the job.

In addition to an uneasy political mood in the nation, several other factors helped Carter achieve his 1976 win in Mississippi. Running as a third-party candidate, George Wallace captured the state's electoral votes in 1968, and he remained popular among many conservatives. Speaking in Jackson during the 1976 campaign, Wallace said, "If Jimmy Carter loses this election, it will be the last opportunity for someone in the South to win the White House."[3] Campaign advertising for Carter used a recording of this statement as an endorsement throughout the fall on southern country radio stations. In the background was a stirring rendition of "Dixie."

There was also an unusual development. "To stop the growth of Republicans a coalition of Democrats formed in 1975 and 1976 that most thought was unbeatable. For those two campaigns, black voters joined with rural white voters first to elect Cliff Finch governor and then to carry Mississippi for Jimmy Carter."[4] This coalition as negotiated by Democratic leaders was short-lived, but decisive for the 1976 election.

Finally, James Eastland, the politically powerful Mississippian who was president pro tempore of the US Senate, added his endorsement. During a September 1976 visit to the state by candidate Carter, Eastland said to the press: "I'm for him all the way."[5] Regardless of whether the senator or other Mississippi Democrats had misgivings, the party leaders faithfully promoted their presidential candidate.

Jimmy Carter never forgot the loyal support he received, as he showed during his visits to the state while in office. He traveled to Mississippi three times—first to hold a town meeting, second to declare federal support in a disaster situation, and finally as he tried in vain for reelection. Though the statewide margin of victory was quite thin, Republican Ronald Reagan won the state's 1980 popular and electoral votes.

July 21–22, 1977—Jackson and Yazoo City

Barely six months into his presidency, Jimmy Carter decided to take a flying trip through the South to discuss foreign policy—particularly his perspectives on the Soviet Union—and other issues that were occupying his administration and members of Congress.[6] He scheduled his first stop in Charleston, South Carolina, where he addressed the Conference of Southern Legislators. From there he traveled on Air Force One to Jackson, Mississippi, made brief remarks at the airport, and then flew by helicopter to Yazoo City for a town meeting with about 1,500 Mississippians. A nationwide network scheduled his question-and-answer session for a ninety-minute telecast. He stayed overnight with a local family and motored back to Jackson the next morning.

This strategy of using a town meeting in a small community and bunking in a household suited Carter's understanding of symbolism. James Wooten, a journalist who knew Carter both during his days as governor of Georgia and in the White House, wrote that the president "had increased his capital considerably by investing skillfully in symbols." Wooten reported that Carter understood the need to establish himself in the public mind, and that the image he preferred was that of "a common man, just another American hired to do a particular job."[7]

Yazoo City may have seemed a strange choice to many in the nation, but those who knew the recent history of the 1976 presidential election recognized it as the home of a prominent businessman who helped Carter out of a difficult situation. Owen Cooper had not only business success, but he also served as the lay president of the Southern Baptist Convention. He and Jimmy Carter were well acquainted from the president's own affiliation with the same church denomination. When Carter chose to grant an in-depth interview to *Playboy* magazine during the campaign, certain of his supporters were shocked and outraged. The piece was wide-ranging, touching topics such as adultery, homosexuality, and even a statement about Lyndon Johnson that seemed to accuse the former Democratic president of lying and cheating.[8]

Members of the public, and particularly Carter's fellow Southern Baptists, decried the candidate's appearance in a publication that regularly ran photographs of naked women, and the assessment of many conservative Christians was that his perspectives did not match their stricter morality. Staffers enlisted Owen Cooper to provide public support through the crisis, and his endorsement helped smooth ruffled feathers.[9] Thus it was Cooper and his family that hosted the president of the United States not only in their community but also at their home.

Journalist Laura Foreman wrote a piece for the *New York Times* introducing readers to Yazoo City. It ran in the morning edition on the day of the town meeting. Her perspective ran well past a simple eyewitness account of the community and revealed how she thought her readers would view the venue President Carter had chosen for his event. She wrote: "Confederate monuments are as inevitable as magnolias or mosquitoes in Mississippi Delta towns." She went on to describe the twenty-foot-high pedestal in Yazoo City with a "proud-faced . . . Confederate soldier holding a rifle and a woman cradling a flag."

Foreman saw the community through the lens she polished: "Not that any monument is needed to perpetuate memory here where memory is as palpable as heat. . . . Of the 600 persons listed as heads of families in the 1840 census in Yazoo County, nearly 500 have descendants still living here, and to them the local tales and legends are as real as the Union bullet holes in their porch posts." The journalist's observation of folks living in Yazoo City included that they were civil, even mannerly, but that they were slow in giving up "a rigid caste system."[10]

Illustrating Foreman's article were a map of Mississippi with Yazoo City located in the state's eighteen-county Delta region and a photograph of two young girls playing leapfrog in the shadow of the town's Confederate monument. There was also a charming photograph of Owen Cooper with his wife and grandchildren preparing food for the president's overnight stay.

Flying into Jackson on Air Force One for an event in Yazoo City was certainly a study in contrasts, that is, international attention focused on an unapologetically rural setting. This was surely not lost on President Carter, who said on another occasion, "The aura of Air Force One is an overwhelming factor of power and prestige."[11] Indeed, the president's message both in his remarks at the airport in Jackson and during the town meeting in Yazoo City assured his hearers that the opinions and support of individual citizens were critical to those taking action on a world stage.

During his brief comments delivered about 5:30 p.m. at Allen C. Thompson Airport in Jackson, Carter recalled election night 1976 and Mississippi's pivotal role as the state that put him over the top in electoral votes. He said, "Over a period of time, the people of your state and the people of the country came to realize that I felt the same way that you do, that I tried to search in my own heart for those things that are conservative."

Though a Democrat, Carter seemingly understood the power of the Republicans' Southern Strategy, as he spoke of the "kinds of principles [that] have bound us together," among which he listed "deep religious conviction." However, he pushed beyond the boundaries normally observed by politicians of the Republican Party to more progressive ideas, when he mentioned to Mississippians "a willingness to change when we saw that the future could be better than the past," as well as referring to the reaching of "our hands out to our black neighbors." Recognizing that "this was not an easy thing for us to do," he maintained that "we have done it, and we are better off for it."

Finally, Carter said to the airport crowd that he was "proud to be an American" and "proud to be a southerner." He concluded by asking for everyone's help, encouragement, advice, sound judgment, and prayers.[12] Following his remarks and some hand-shaking, Carter boarded a helicopter for his short flight to Yazoo City, located about forty miles to the north, where he was transported by automobile to the site of his 8:00 p.m. town meeting that was carried live across the nation by the Public Broadcasting Service (PBS). In conjunction with the presidential event, the community's leaders used the occasion to dedicate the new Yazoo City High School building, and they scheduled Carter's forum in the gymnasium.

Below is a sampling of the evening's interaction between President Jimmy Carter and citizens attending this unique town hall event in Yazoo City. The coauthors include this abbreviated verbatim material from a considerably longer transcript to illustrate Carter's personality, his attempts to mix southern conservative values with his oftentimes more progressive outlook on social issues, themes aimed at a broader audience on PBS, and the remarkably varied interests of the attendees. Through the ninety-minute course of the program, questions from Yazoo City residents for their president ranged from regional to national and international issues.

PRESIDENT: It's a great pleasure for me to come to the dedication ceremony of the Yazoo City new high school. . . . I want to say just a word about the school itself, because I think it typifies the South, Mississippi, [and] Yazoo City attitudes. In a lot of places in our country you couldn't get a school bond issue passed, particularly if the school classrooms were going to be filled with roughly two-thirds black students and one-third white students, but the people of Yazoo City, believing in your young people, having confidence in one another, and looking forward to the future with great anticipation and courage and confidence, overwhelmingly voted to build this new school. . . .

I've enjoyed this first, almost exactly six months of being your president. I've tried to open up the decision making process of our country to you and the people like you all over the nation. I think presidents, members of Congress, cabinet officers, [and] federal administrators can make better decisions to the extent that we receive the judgment, common sense, and the benefit of the experience of people around the country. . . . Tonight I want to take about an hour and a half to listen to your questions and try to give you the best answers I can. . . .

Q: My name is Herman B. DeCell of Yazoo City. My question, Mr. President, relates to your proposal to balance the budget by 1981. I think most of us agree with that proposition, but many of us are concerned about possible impairment of ongoing programs that are vital to our local people—revenue sharing, the youth work programs, our educational programs, and related programs that provide job opportunities. My question is, how will you go about establishing priorities to determine which of these programs may be modified or altered, and in what way?

PRESIDENT: Fine. That's an excellent question. Our projections of the future economic growth of our country, based on normal circumstances, show that we can continue the programs that are doing a good job . . . and with proper management, reorganization of the government itself, with the elimination of overlapping and duplicating federal programs and bureaucracies, we can have enough growth in federal revenues to give us both expanded programs and/or tax reductions which are very important to you, or a balanced budget.

Q: Hello, Mr. President, I'm Ted Webb, a student at Ole Miss. You have been in office for about six months now. At this point in time, are you personally satisfied with the progress made by the programs you sponsored, and if not, which program has been your biggest disappointment and why?

PRESIDENT: I've been very pleased so far with the progress that the Congress has made in the programs that I've put forward in the campaign. . . . I asked them to give me the authority to reorganize the executive branch of government, and the Congress gave me almost exactly what I wanted.

I asked the Congress, in addition, to help me create a new Department of Energy, to bring all the forty or forty-five or fifty different agencies that have been responsible for energy together in a coordinated, well-organized, bureaucratic entity so we could have a carrying out of an energy policy. . . . I asked the Congress to help me stimulate the American economy, and they did so to the tune of about twenty-one-billion dollars to put our people back to work. . . . So far we've had good progress. . . . I would say that the major programs that we put forward already are well on the way to being passed. . . .

The things that have disappointed me, of course, are the things that disappoint you. We've still got too many people unemployed. Last month, we had 270,000 new jobs, but the workforce has increased to such an extent that we still have about 7 percent of our people without work. . . . I think we've done a lot of new things that had been avoided or ignored for a long time, and I have been, overall, pleased.

Q: Hello, Mr. President. My name is Sue Tatum, and I come to you tonight with a question on behalf of my friends who are low-income people and fixed-income people. As you can imagine, they are having increasing difficulty paying utility bills. . . . Is there anything on the horizon to help these people?

PRESIDENT: I wish I could give you good news, Miss Tatum. But I think no matter who's in the White House, no matter who's in the Congress, that the price of energy is going to go up. We are simply running out of oil and natural gas, and the production of coal, atomic energy, solar energy is going to be more costly in the future. . . . The only solution, it seems to me, is a much fairer distribution of energy and also a great reduction in how much energy a family uses to meet its own needs. . . . I would say that private homeowners, business leaders, industrial producers, and government, all have to work together to hold down inflation, hold down the consumption of energy; but we can't depend on cheaper energy in the future. I'm sorry.

[Note: Questions and answers continued for an hour and twenty minutes. Among the other topics raised by members of President Carter's audience were: oil companies and the competitive position of independent refiners; the Small Business Administration; human rights; abortion; federal housing subsidies; the Panama Canal Zone; health care and national health insurance; local projects of the US Army Corps of Engineers; tax reform; federal regulatory agencies; the neutron bomb; labor laws; and aid to Vietnam for rebuilding after the war.]

PRESIDENT: Before I leave you, I would like to say this: I've enjoyed being here. The quality of your questions has been no surprise to me and, as you can see, they've covered a wide range of subjects—from the history of the South to the future of Vietnam. And this is typical of the intense interest in public affairs that exists among the American people.

As I said to begin with, I don't claim to know all the answers. I'm learning every day. I have a lot of people who believe in me. I have a lot of people who have doubts about me. I have a lot of people who voted for me; a lot who didn't. But I think it's accurate to say that almost every American wants to see me succeed in being a good president. Because to the extent that I do succeed, your own lives and those of your families will be better, freer, and fuller lives.

We are partners in shaping what our country will be. You are partners with me. And I hope that I can serve in such a way that would increase your own confidence in our government, increase your own confidence in the federal government, which in the South sometimes has not been a pleasant phrase, and that I can convince the American people that the government in Washington is your government.

These hopes that I have are dependent on you for realization. If you withdraw and lash out and condemn and criticize your own government as a general proposition because you don't like one or two things that happen, our whole country is weakened.

But to the extent that you participate in the debates and try to correct mistakes and let us know what you want done in Washington, and participate with us, to that extent we'll be a success.[13]

As if to prove the point that, even in a small town high school gymnasium, words from the president of the United States were significant, there was a media report two days later about one of the president's brief comments: "State Department officials expressed concern today that an off-the-cuff response yesterday by President Carter in Yazoo, Miss., to a question about the Panama Canal would seriously complicate the delicate negotiations for a new canal treaty. Diplomats said they believed the president's reference to the United States exercising 'partial sovereignty' over the Canal Zone until the year 2000 would be particularly offensive to Panamanians."[14]

Of a different character entirely was an interaction between Carter and a nine-year-old girl that caught media attention and was widely reported. There were even follow-up stories months later. A Yazoo City youngster, Mary "Digger" Tucker, stepped to the microphone and asked what it was like to be a president. Obviously charmed, Carter encouraged Mary to learn for herself by running for the presidency in about thirty years. He also invited her to the White House for a visit and a play session with his own young daughter, Amy.

President Carter went on to say: "In general, it's been a very pleasant job. The working conditions are good. My office is near my home and the people have been very nice to me so far."[15]

Follow-up press stories one month later reported that Mary Tucker from Yazoo City didn't make it to the White House, and that despite the national limelight, her school friends didn't pay much attention to her interaction with the president. There was even a report that she missed the rerun of her television appearance because she was in Bible school when it played on the local network affiliate.[16] A second follow-up by media one year later reported that Mary Tucker had decided the presidency was not as interesting a career choice for her as becoming a gymnast because "they get to do a lot of things."[17]

September 14, 1979—Pascagoula

President Carter's second visit to Mississippi followed the 1979 landfall of Hurricane Frederic, an event that was cataloged at the time as one of the three most destructive storms in the nation's history.[18] The *New York Times* based its report of the storm's fury on early information from the site and set the scene for the president's trip: "Hurricane Frederic ... moved far inland today after punishing the central gulf coast last night with battering-ram winds of up to 130 miles an hour.... The storm caused widespread destruction along a 100-mile front."[19] Half-a-million people evacuated the region, and, as a result, only eight deaths resulted from this devastating storm, though there could have been many more. Mississippi and the two other states ravaged by Frederic received presidential disaster area declarations within twenty-four hours.

"Mobile, Ala., and Pascagoula and the surrounding areas bore the brunt of the hurricane, and both cities showed it.... Pascagoula had no electricity, no drinking water and a lot less intact glass than it had twelve hours before. The Ingalls Shipyard in Pascagoula, Mississippi's biggest industry, suffered extensive damage and was not expected to reopen for several days."[20]

When Frederic reached its peak in the Gulf of Mexico, the winds were in excess of 130 miles per hour, making it a Category Four hurricane on the Saffir-Simpson Hurricane Scale. Landfall came on September 12, 1979, as the storm struck the border between Mississippi and Alabama. Forty-eight hours later—on September 14—President Carter visited the Gulf Coast, inspecting the storm damage by helicopter. Around midday, he addressed residents at Ingalls Shipyard in Pascagoula.

Carter began his remarks by expressing the concern of the entire nation; he also shared the widespread admiration for Mississippians' preparedness in a situation that could have killed hundreds of people. The president said his positive comments extended also to Governor Cliff Finch, local officials, and Mississippi's members of Congress, many of whom were on the coast to meet with the president that day.

At the heart of his rather brief message were the sorts of assurances presidents offered throughout history as they arrived to examine disaster sites: "The other thing that I'd like to say is that we will be here on a long-term basis, because the repair that's got to be done to the community structure is not going to be quickly resolved. I hope that the people who are farmers will know that we've got assistance available for them; businesses, large and small, that have been shut down, we've got unemployment compensation, and we'll have extra people that have been here from the Labor Department to process those claims. If anything should arise in the future that's a problem for you, or is delayed in being delivered, in delivery of services, if you'll let ... me [know] directly in the White House, we'll take care of it without delay."[21]

October 31, 1980—Jackson

Though historians understandably disagree whether the problems vexing the later years of Jimmy Carter's presidency were of his own making or would have victimized anyone holding the office, all agree that reelection in 1980 was a serious challenge, if not a near impossibility. Inflation was higher for US citizens than at any other time in recent memory. Gasoline prices peaked. American industries reported financial losses. Crime statistics rose in response to the difficult economy. European nations expressed unhappiness with American leadership in the world. The Soviet Union invaded Afghanistan, despite warnings from the United States to discontinue the attack. Perhaps worst of all for American pride, militants in Iran overran the US embassy and took American hostages. This hostage crisis headlined the nightly news month after month, and neither diplomatic nor military responses proved effective.[22]

Carter faced reelection problems also in Mississippi, as the fragile coalition between black and white factions of the Democratic Party dissolved and weak attempts to repair the rifts were ineffective. When Republican presidential candidate Ronald Reagan appeared at the Neshoba County Fair in August 1980, he struck a resounding chord for many with his jab at the president: "People have been telling me Jimmy Carter is doing his best. That's our problem."[23]

Candidate-to-candidate sniping became commonplace for both Carter and Reagan, and each man declared himself offended by the insults. Five days before the election, Ronald Reagan campaigned in Texas, Arkansas, and Louisiana. "In response to a question about whether he and President Carter disliked each other, Mr. Reagan appeared to vent a long-simmering sense of outrage.... [He said,] 'I can hardly have a warm feeling in my heart for someone who's been attacking me on a personal basis for many months now in the campaign.'"[24] Of course, Reagan also engaged in the back-and-forth. For example, he said in several speeches: "A recession is when your neighbor loses his job. A depression is when you lose yours. And recovery is when Jimmy Carter loses his."[25]

One day later, on October 31, 1980, President Carter made campaign appearances in Memphis, Tennessee; Jackson, Mississippi; and Houston, Texas. The *New York Times* termed the trip a "final, sometimes sentimental swing through his native South" and reported that he "denounced Ronald Reagan and his supporters . . . for what he said was an attempt by them to portray Mr. Carter's views as contrary to the teachings of the Bible." The specific Reagan inferences to which Carter referred were apparently his positions on the federal Equal Rights Amendment and rights for gays and lesbians.[26] For example, in his *Playboy* interview the president had said, "For us to engage in homosexual activities . . . these are sins. But Jesus teaches us not to judge other people."[27]

President Carter's late-afternoon campaign rally in Jackson took place on the lawn at the governor's mansion, occupied at the time by Democrat William Winter. Media sources placed the crowd size at about 5,000. Despite widespread predictions to the contrary, Carter professed confidence in his reelection, even as he remained feisty about perceived slights.

From the outset of this speech just four days ahead of the election, President Carter emphasized his most obvious connection to the crowd standing before him: "I want to talk to you for a few minutes about the southland, about what it means to be a southerner and about what Mississippi has meant in my own campaign to become president of the United States, the first president from the Deep South since James Polk was elected in 1844." He reminded his audience that Mississippi was pivotal in his 1976 election as the state that put his electoral total over the top, and he said, "Mississippi came through then. You've set a good tradition. I'm counting on you Tuesday night."

There were lengthy reminders in the speech about rural electrification, minimum wage laws, Social Security, and Medicare—Democratic initiatives that meant much to people across the South. Carter reminisced about his early life experiences as a southerner, pointing out Republicans opposition to federal programs that made life better for average Americans.

Using humor to transition to the 1980 campaign, the president said: "You've been listening lately to the Republican candidate, Governor Reagan, who's running against me, and you know he's been trying to wrap himself in the mantle of Democratic presidents. . . . Every time a Republican starts running for president, you always notice they quote Democratic presidents. Have you ever heard a Republican candidate quote a Republican president? No." This charge against Ronald Reagan may have arisen from his early history as a Democrat, or it may have originated when he gave a speech in 1964 in support of Barry Goldwater's presidential candidacy. In it he used the phrase "rendezvous with destiny," words that came from an address by Franklin Roosevelt in 1936.[28] (In a 1984 campaign speech in Gulfport, Mississippi, Reagan mentioned and quoted Harry Truman, Franklin Roosevelt, and John Kennedy—see the next chapter.)

Each issue in Carter's address came out of a regional context; for example, on national defense he said: "Southerners know what it means to protect our nation. We've always been in the forefront of volunteering to go to war, to give our lives, if necessary, to defend our nation. . . . We know what it means to have a strong defense."

As he got to comments on his opponent in the election of 1980, Jimmy Carter also critiqued him and his outsider's perspectives from a regional point of view: "When Ronald Reagan was asked about subsidies, he said he wasn't familiar with the subject. And only recently he's heard about the Tennessee-Tombigbee, which is going to take those farm products to market. Recently he said, 'You subsidize the inefficient, when you put a floor under the price for farmers.' He said, at a later time, that farmers should start planning for an end to government assistance in production and in the marketplace.

"Well, people of Mississippi, I know what it means to have a stabilized price for farmers, because you can have a devastating drought that wipes you out one year. You can have the highest production in the world the next year. Farmers don't want a handout. Farmers want to stand on their own feet, but they want to have markets that are stable and predictable, because they can't control the weather. And almost all of our programs that we have don't cost America anything. They help the farmer, yes, but they help our consumers as well. It's the best investment I know in the economy of this country."

Characterizing the election as "a contest between two men who disagree on every major issue," Carter upped the stakes for his supporters and for undecided voters by telling the crowd that the campaign would "decide the future of this nation, the rest of this century and perhaps beyond." On that basis, he made a plea: "I need your help." He offered his four years of experience as the reason to support his reelection: "I've made thousands of decisions. In each one of those decisions in the oval office, I have been learning about this country. Every decision I make leaves me better qualified to make the next decision." He recognized the decision facing each individual "next Tuesday in the voting booth." To all voters he said: "Your decision will make a difference."

Then the president returned to the theme of regional identity politics: "Let's win a victory for the South, for the ideals and beliefs that we have, the vision that we share for a greater nation even than we've had before. You join me. We'll have a partnership. We'll whip the Republicans and have a great nation. Thank you very much. God bless you."[29]

★ ★ ★

Just as historical events—the Watergate scandal and the pardon of a Republican president implicated in dirty politics—doomed Gerald Ford in his 1976 bid for reelection, so the events between 1977 and 1980—especially a steep recession and the hostage crisis in Iran—made it nearly impossible for Jimmy Carter to win a second term. In his 1976 campaign for the presidency, Jimmy Carter became the single exception to Mississippi's otherwise unbroken string of election victories for Republicans beginning in 1960.

One obvious conclusion is that Carter simply fell prey to the normal and expected trend in Mississippi in the election of 1980. However, Ronald Reagan barely captured the state with a margin slightly over 1 percent. Carter actually came much closer to winning in Mississippi than he did in most states. Reagan swept into the White House in 1981 with 489 of the nation's 538 total electoral votes, a winning ratio of nearly 10 to 1. Thus it is possible to argue that in Mississippi the slim victory for Reagan meant Jimmy Carter's southern roots won votes that would otherwise have gone to the Republican candidate in 1980 as well as in 1976.

CHAPTER NINE

RONALD REAGAN

Fortieth President of the United States
Republican
Elected 1980 and 1984
Served January 20, 1981, to January 20, 1989

★ ★

Ronald Reagan's journey through the history of presidential electoral politics in Mississippi was both progressive and epic. In 1976 he lost the support of the state's delegation to the Republican National Convention when he prematurely named one of the few liberal members of the party as his preference for a running mate. In 1980 he eked out an 11,000-vote general election victory over the Democratic incumbent president, Jimmy Carter, who won the state four years earlier by a margin nearly as thin. By 1984 Reagan's popularity throughout Mississippi was so strong that he garnered the state's support for his reelection by a plurality approaching a quarter-million votes.

Writing for the 2001 publication *Campaigns: A Century of Presidential Races*, Ted Widmer, historian and director of the Center for the Study of the American Experience at Washington College, characterized Reagan's second presidential victory succinctly: "The 1984 campaign proved that Reagan was not relinquishing power anytime soon.... [He] repeated the ideas that had brought him to the presidency, advocating supply-side economics, a strong military, smaller government, and old-fashioned idealism.... Even his gaffes were forgiven.... November brought a landslide. Reagan won 59 percent of the vote and Mondale won 41 percent. The electoral discrepancy of 525 to 13 was even more overwhelming."[1]

Barely two months into Reagan's presidency, an assassination attempt nearly took his life, and security-conscious members of the White House staff were reluctant to send the president on the road. However, the overly protective approach became incompatible with developing national issues and Reagan's preferred style. "As the economy slid into recession in the spring of 1982, administration officials worried that the president was being perceived as 'remote from the problems of average Americans' and recommended the president travel more to counteract growing impressions that his was a regal presidency."[2]

Reagan won support with his humor, his likability, and his ability to choose and address a limited set of issues that aroused popular interest. He was far too great an asset to keep closeted in the White House. Party leaders in the early 1980s were reshaping political images, attempting to build greater popular support, and Ronald Reagan quickly became the pivotal figure of the Republican efforts. Jere Nash and Andy Taggart summarized this period thusly: "Working in both parties, activists sought to sharpen and narrow the public policy positions of each party and purge those who disagreed. This process of definition, which began in 1960 and reached its apex in 1984 with the reelection of Ronald Reagan, is the key to the transformation of what used to be the one-party Democratic South. By 1984, Republicans would proudly proclaim themselves conservative while Democrats were stuck with the liberal label. While those words would take on different meanings with different people, they gradually began to signify where the two parties stood on a broad range of cultural issues. And for better or for worse, the overwhelming majority of white Mississippians are 'conservative' on all of them."[3]

Ronald Reagan regularly made his positions clear on issues that came to be labeled "conservative"—for example, smaller government, less federal regulation, a massive military, returning prayer to public schools, opposition to affirmative action, opposition to abortion rights, and states' rights over federal management when it came to election laws, education, and a range of other policy areas.[4] The impacts of this political strategy both nationally and in Mississippi have held sway since Reagan's presidency: "Mississippi Democrats have been in a quandary [since those years]: how to reconcile their national party's 'liberal' platform with a majority of Mississippi voters who are not only culturally conservative, but whose votes are motivated more by their cultural perspective than their economic status."[5]

Writing during the Reagan presidency, history professor and prolific author Garry Wills of Northwestern University, observed: "Reagan is that most disarming of political apparitions, the kindly fanatic . . . the demagogue as rabble-soother, at a time when people do not need to be stirred up but assuaged, to have anxieties dispelled, complexities resolved. They need to believe that the simpler past not only perdures but prevails. . . . Reagan not only represents the past, but resurrects it as a promise of the future."[6] This dynamic was observable through Reagan's words during his presidential visits to Mississippi.

As he served his eight years in office, Ronald Reagan traveled to Mississippi only twice, and he made each visit for the purpose of a political campaign. In June 1983 the president spoke at a Republican fund-raising dinner in Jackson, furthering state party efforts to elect or reelect several key candidates. In October 1984 Reagan headlined a huge rally in a city park on the Gulf Coast, as he campaigned for his own reelection.

June 20, 1983—Jackson

President Reagan honored the Mississippi Republican Party for its faithful support in 1980 by his presence at a fund-raising dinner in June 1983 at the Mississippi Coliseum in Jackson. He spoke to the dinner crowd at 5:30 p.m., but earlier in the afternoon he attended a smaller reception for major donors, as well as Republican Party leaders, officeholders, and candidates, at Dennery's Restaurant across the street from the scheduled site for the larger event. Reagan began wooing Mississippi's voters during his August 3, 1980, campaign visit to the Neshoba County Fair where he won the crowd with homespun, often self-deprecating humor; took verbal swipes at President Jimmy Carter and other Democrats; told stories about such icons as John Wayne and Ole Miss football; and offered that if elected, he would "reorder priorities and restore to the states and local communities those functions which properly belong there."[7]

When Reagan arrived at Jackson in the summer of 1983, he was among friends. He shared the dinner platform with state and federal Republican officeholders and office seekers, including, US senator Thad Cochran, US representative and House Majority Whip Trent Lott, Republican candidate for the House of Representatives Webb Franklin, and Republican gubernatorial candidate Leon Bramlett. The president was careful to include praise and support for each in his remarks. Of Trent Lott, for example, Reagan said, "I only wish we had another 434 just like him in the House of Representatives." Why? Because Lott opposed "the taxing and spending irresponsibility that shoved our country into the economic turmoil and decline from which we're now just emerging."[8]

At the very outset of his speech, Reagan recognized the success of the Republican Party's so-called Southern Strategy: "Isn't it wonderful to see so many Republicans in Mississippi? Times have changed and for the better." Yet he evidenced hunger for greater numbers: "We have to understand the importance of reaching out to Democrats with whom we have fundamental agreement. [Most Mississippi] Democrats have little in common with the national and state Democratic platforms. And I'm quite sure there are many here who were and some who still are Democrats but who have found it more and more difficult to follow their party's leadership. . . . I think it is time to point out that there are many fine, patriotic Democrats in this country who are beginning to recognize that the present leadership of their party and the leadership in recent years has strayed far from the principles that once characterized the Democratic Party in the days of Jefferson and Jackson. They would no longer be at home, I think, with the present leadership of that party and what it advocates."

Recalling his promise in the 1980 election to "Make America Strong Again," Reagan spoke of his struggles with recalcitrant Democrats and their "attempts to get our program before it had a chance." However, he was proud to report success in the difficult battles he fought. Indeed, he assured everyone that "those who think they can pull the wool over the eyes of the voters and return to the tax-and-spend and spend-and-inflate policies of the past are badly mistaken." And he—Reagan—would continue to lead: "If confronted with budget-busting spending bills or any attempt to take away the people's tax cuts or indexing, I will not hesitate to veto—indeed, I look forward to it." Righteousness was his banner, as he recited recent achievements, including gains in retail sales, productivity, and real wages.

According to Reagan, not only was the economy suffering when he took office, but the nation's "military strength was permitted to erode dangerously." Here the president took an opportunity—in the classic phrase of nineteenth-century politics—to "wave the bloody shirt."[9] He set the context: "At a time when the Soviets were dramatically increasing their military effort, real spending for our defense needs was reduced by almost 20 percent." As he had with the previous issue, Reagan reminded his audience that in 1980 he promised to "turn this threatening situation around." With the help of congressional Republicans, the president claimed to have "set in place a program to rebuild our defensive capabilities." He was sorry to report that "providing this country with an adequate defense is an expensive undertaking, especially when you're forced to make up for the irresponsibility of so many past years." But whatever the cost, the president and the Republican faithful would "not send our brave young men and women in the military out to defend us with second-rate weapons and bargain-basement equipment. If they can put their lives on the line for us, we can afford to give them what they need to do the job right."

Patriotism was never far from President Reagan's imagery, and he often coupled it with talk of the divine: "What we have in this country is the most precious gift God has given to mankind. Our country, more than any other, has been blessed with liberty and abundance. A few years ago some people were counting America out, claiming that our best days were behind us, that our country was in decline. Well, not anymore. That pessimism is something else we've turned around."

Likewise, for Ronald Reagan, heroism and kindness were at the heart of American character, and during the disastrous floods of the Mississippi River in 1983, "your citizens, young and old, white and black, proved that the American spirit is alive. . . . During the floods, there were numerous accounts of neighbor helping neighbor, of heroism and kindness crossing all racial and economic lines. The people of Mississippi showed the country that when the chips are down, we are all Americans."

At that point in his speech, the president returned to a plank in the Republican platform. He recalled the promise "to make government smaller," and he pointed to a goal that within three years of his ascension to office, the number of federal employees on the domestic side would shrink by 75,000. After only eighteen months of his term, he reported: "We're ahead of schedule, because we've already reduced it by 65,000." He also stated that his administration had eliminated 2,200 federal publications. In that same vein, he shared this news: "There's going to be another surprise pretty soon, come budget time, when they find out how much we are able to cut, how many billions of dollars simply in the improvement of management."

As savvy as any politician in the history of the nation, Reagan demonstrated in this address not only his attentiveness to the interests of his audiences but also his readiness to support fellow Republicans. Perhaps most obvious of all was his ability to turn every political situation into a rally banking credit toward his own reelection and legacy.

October 1, 1984—Gulfport

Preserved video from WLOX-TV's live coverage—available online—shows Ronald Reagan's second visit to Mississippi as president. It is an engaging visual of a well-run campaign rally that occurred more than three decades ago.

A crowd numbering in the tens of thousands flooded into Jones Park in Gulfport. Excited and curious people held campaign signs by the dozens. The president arrived at the nearby airfield on Air Force One, met with Republican leaders, and then motored to the site of the rally. Along the way he made a reportedly unscheduled stop to banter with an elementary school group. After proceeding to the park, Reagan mounted the red-white-and-blue speakers' platform, and US representative Trent Lott introduced him. Cheers of "Four more years" rang out, and he quieted everyone so as to address the assembly. Spontaneous cheering interrupted throughout his remarks. The video left no reasonable conclusion other than the crowd at the rally presaged a resounding Reagan victory.[10]

Equally as interesting is a piece that ran in the *New York Times* on October 3, 1984, under the title "Two-week Countdown to a Reagan Rally." What made the story engaging is that it provided an insider's look at how major campaign events occur, and, further, it answered the question why the president visited Mississippi during the fall of 1984 when polling predicted a certain win for him in the state. Below are excerpts from the story:

"A crowd, estimated at 40,000 people by local police jammed a vast, sandy park on the shores of the Gulf of Mexico to hear Mr. Reagan appeal to their pride and patriotism. Mrs. [Gia] Catchot, a thirty-five-year-old hairdresser in a green velvet warm-up suit said: 'When Reagan won, I felt really safe. I feel like he's doing the best that he could do.'" Such impressions did not happen by accident, as the article went on to explain by following the efforts of the campaign organization: two weeks of planning, efficient use of resources by bundling additional stops into scheduled trips, and a persistent awareness that no locale can be taken for granted.

As campaign staff searched for an appropriate event location, "the Gulf Coast was picked because it contains the highest concentration of Republican votes in the state, and its news media reach into both Louisiana and Alabama. With several large military bases and contractors here, people in the region seem to like Mr. Reagan's pro-military message and the military spending that pours into the local economy." More than one week prior to the event, there were advance people from Reagan's campaign on-site, and they recruited Republican faithful to help with the preparation. More than 500 volunteers staffed eighteen committees assigned to deal with the details.

"The White House advance team met every morning with the local organizers. . . . No expense was spared in drumming up a crowd . . . commercials on nine radio stations and in four newspapers . . . direct mail . . . schools called to release students early. . . . In the publicity efforts the organizers stressed two things: ample parking and free admission. . . . The campaign spent upwards of thirty-thousand dollars" on the Gulfport event.

Even the placement of individuals within the expected throng of people came under scrutiny: "The only spectators allowed between the press stand and the speakers' platform were special guests holding tickets issued by the local Republican Party. Thus it was virtually impossible for any dissenter to hold up a sign within range of a camera."[11] In this regard, one photograph of the rally available from the Reagan Library shows the large crowd seen from speakers' platform. There is a sea of smiling faces with several excited individuals holding poster-size signs supporting Reagan's candidacy. As far back in the gathering as the eye can see by straining—that is, at a spot that a casual look at the image would not notice—there is one banner that reads "Keep Nuclear Waste Out."

Given the degree of preparation and the minute-by-minute control exercised by professionals at planning campaign messages and campaign events, it was nearly impossible to believe that between the airport and the site of the rally, Reagan's motorcade happened upon a group of Gulfport's students from an elementary school in exactly the right location that the president could stop for an interchange and media could record the chance encounter. Furthermore, some of the questions asked by the young children were sophisticated enough to appear planted at a preplanned event. See below for the extant verbatim record. (Note that bracketed words in the transcript replace "inaudible" in the original, but they represent what was said by individual children. Also, the material below omits children's questions as repeated by the president in favor of showing the give-and-take.)

PRESIDENT: I am very proud that you'd come out this way, and, see, I think you even kind of came back early, didn't you, to be here? Well, and all those signs. Thank you very much. Tell me, I know I've only got a few seconds here, but sometimes some of the others, some of you must have said to yourself, 'Boy, if I could ask him, I'd sure ask him.' Would you like to throw a question at me, somebody?

Q: [Do you support federal aid for foreign countries?]
PRESIDENT: Yes, I think this is traditional with America. We've always tried to help our friends out and help developing countries. But I tell you, from the old days of just throwing money out there and not knowing where it went, we're trying to do it in a way now that will enable them to become self-sustaining and build their economy. And the biggest help we're being is buying from them the things that they have to sell that they make there.

Q: [Are you going to put nuclear waste in Mississippi?]
PRESIDENT: Well, our director of energy has said that we just were not going to do anything against the state's will, and having been a governor myself of a state, I'm a great believer in state's rights.

Q: Do you think you're better than Mondale?
PRESIDENT: No, I don't think in this country anyone thinks that you're better than anyone else. I just think that I should keep on being president for four more years.

Q: Can you beat Mondale?
PRESIDENT: Wait a minute until I turn to where the people of voting age are. [Applause] I think so. They just told me I can.

Q: [Are you going to raise taxes?]
PRESIDENT: Oh, here's a question I have to answer. And I know the people behind me, after the signal they just gave, will be very happy. The young lady wants to know, am I going to raise taxes? No.

All right, thank you all very much. God bless you all. They tell me I have to get in the car and go.[12]

Below are excerpts—with occasional commentary on the structure of his outline—from Reagan's remarks at the Gulfport rally. It is instructive for any who might wish to persuade an audience. Many referred to him as "the Great Communicator," because he demonstrated time and again during his presidency that he was able to tailor his image and his message to the crowd he was addressing as well or better than most public figures. That dynamic was on full display in Gulfport.

After thanking the people of the coastal communities for hosting him and complimenting Mississippians serving in the US Congress, Reagan began with a sentence and a paragraph sure to bring cheers, hauling out and dusting off regional notions of valor and values and even marching out the Stars and Bars with the mention of "Dixie." This was his opener for the red meat of the speech:

"It's great to be back in the South. You know, I'm always happy when I visit this part of the country, maybe because you make me feel so much at home. You in the South have always given our country more than its share of greatness and courage. Here are the traditions and values that shaped our land. Here is steadiness of purpose, fidelity to ideals, [and] love of country. Our opponents may be ready to ignore this region, but Vice President Bush and I happen to consider that the South is worth respecting, worth listening to, and, yes, worth fighting for. We've come here for one reason, and one reason only: to win! And we ain't just whistlin' *Dixie*."

At this point, Reagan had the crowd firmly on his side. He reminded them that when he took office, the nation was suffering from economic woes and frustrating military weakness. He proclaimed: "The choice between us and our opponents is the clearest our country has faced in more than fifty years. . . . Our opponents' rhetoric of gloom and doom is nothing but a nightmare. It's time for them to wake up and look at the facts.

"Four years ago, the economy of the South and of all America was in a shambles. . . . Our defenses had grown so weak that many of our planes were too old to fly. . . . Many of our ships couldn't leave port.

"Today, just four years later, the United States of America is a very different place. It's stronger, more prosperous, and bursting with patriotism. . . . This isn't a Reagan recovery, this is an American recovery."

Then he offered his list of achievements:

"This great nation is moving forward again, and we're not going back to that unhappy past. We've knocked inflation down . . . productivity is up, consumer spending is up, and take-home pay is up. . . . During the past twenty months, we've created six-million new jobs. We've been creating more jobs every month than our allies in Europe have created over the last ten years."

Reagan knew that everyone wanted the good times to continue, therefore he presented his prescription—the important reasons he must be reelected:

"My friends, I believe our great nation has turned the corner. . . . But I wouldn't want to take that for granted, so let me just ask you: Do you feel better off than you did four years ago? [Audience: 'Yes!'] Is America better off than it was four years ago? [Audience: 'Yes!']¹³

"Well, now, despite this strength of this expansion, there's one sure way to ruin it. . . . [Our opponents] want to give the American people a massive new tax increase. They call it bitter medicine, but that's just because they think they can get us to swallow anything. I think the word shrimp means something different to our opponents than it does to Gulfport. To you, it's a livelihood; to them, it's your paycheck after they get their hands on it. . . .

"Our pledge is for tax simplification. . . . We'll fight for enterprise zones, to help Americans in disadvantaged areas get off unemployment and welfare and start climbing the economic ladder. And we'll keep government under control by working for a line-item veto. I had it as a governor. . . . And then a constitutional amendment mandating that government stop spending more than government takes in.

"A southerner named Thomas Jefferson, back shortly after the Constitution was ratified and put into place, said it had one lack. It needed a clause to prevent the federal government from borrowing. Jefferson was right, and it's time we recognized it.

"Now, you might have noticed that our opponents are trying to appeal to traditional Democrats by comparing themselves to Harry Truman. Well,

President Truman kept a sign on his desk that said, 'The buck stops here.' But if our opponents are elected, their sign will say, 'Your bucks stop here.'

"Forgive me, but Harry Truman believed, with F.D.R. before him and John Kennedy after him, in strength abroad and self-reliance at home. Now, to all those Democrats here today . . . come walk with us down the new path of hope and opportunity. Add your strength to ours, and all of us can build something new for America, something far better than before. And it will be a true bipartisan achievement between millions of patriotic Democrats who know they can no longer follow the leadership of that party.

"As our economy grows, we'll need to go forward with bedrock values that have always sustained the people of the South—the values of faith, family, neighborhood, and good, hard work. And together, we're already making an impressive start.

"We've helped lead a grassroots revolution for excellence in education that will reach every child in this land. Recently, we learned that scholastic aptitude test scores have gone up a full four points. Now, that's the second improvement in the past three years and the biggest increase in those scores in twenty-one years.

"We must continue to crack down on crime. We say with no hesitation, yes, there are such things as right and wrong, and, yes, for hardened criminals preying on our society, punishment must be swift and sure. In 1980 the crime rate was rising. Well, last year, reported crime dropped 7 percent, and that's the steepest decline since 1960.

"In foreign affairs, America is at peace. Since 1980 not one nation has fallen to communist aggression, while the people of one country, Grenada, have been set free. . . . I pledge to you that we will give firm support to the forces of liberty, democracy, and economic progress and that we'll do so as long as I hold this office. [Audience: 'Four more years! Four more years! Four more years!']

"Now, I know that many of you have a special interest in the great effort to defend our freedom. . . . We're determined to give America defenses that are second to none."

Of course, the Great Communicator never forgot to wave the bloody shirt:

"Well, now, I'm supposed to end my speech. . . . But I can't help but remark about something that I've seen more and more at rallies of this kind all over the country: so many bright, young faces here today, so many young people. . . .

"You know, by any measure, those young people I've mentioned are just the best, [as] General Marshall said [in World War II], 'The best damned kids in the world.' Well, the young men and women serving today are the grandsons and granddaughters of those heroes. And I'll tell you, he was right; they are still the best damned kids in the world.

"Now and then on the news a commentator will be talking to one of our young people in uniform. And it's kind of struck me that so often when the young man in uniform or woman in uniform answers, you hear the proud and lilting cadence of Charleston or Memphis or Jackson or Gulfport, or Biloxi. The South was the home of patriots in 1776, when a southerner wrote our Declaration of Independence. And today, more than two centuries later, the South is the home of patriots still.

"So, maybe when you see one of our young people in uniform walking along the street here in Gulfport or Biloxi or wherever, maybe, if you think of it, just nod and smile and say hello, and maybe let them know how all of us feel about them. It'll make you feel real good, and I know how good it'll make them feel."

Finally, he left the crowd with a fond farewell:

"Well, now I do have to go. . . . God bless you, and God bless America. Thank you very much."[14]

Statewide and national media representatives attended the Gulfport rally because the story of the likely Reagan landslide was building. The publisher of the local *Ocean Springs Record*, Wayne Weidie, provided coverage of the event. His piece on the Opinion Page mirrored the sentiments of his readers, a solidly Republican citizenry:

"President Ronald Reagan and his supporters stormed into the Mississippi Gulf Coast earlier this week and took no prisoners. . . . The fifth district has strong Republican voting habits. In 1980 the district gave Reagan 59 percent of its vote, the highest of any congressional district in the state." Weidie noted that symbolism was as much or more in evidence as national policy—"flag waving and religion being ingredients of the 1984 campaign."

Optimism was high: "The crowd roared its approval when Reagan asked if they felt better off than they were four years ago. They roared approval again when he asked if America was better off than it was four years ago." Weidie's observations led him to predict an outcome: "If the mood of the nation doesn't change before November, Walter Mondale and Geraldine Ferraro [Reagan's Democratic opponents] won't be eating general election steak."[15]

★   ★   ★

Good practitioners of the art of homiletics—that is, well-schooled and well-prepared preachers—know that every good sermon addresses three points, summed half a century ago by Richard R. Caemmerer in three simple terms: goal, malady, and means.[16] Those who listen to a sermon must be able to identify what belief or behavior the preacher is aiming them toward (goal), the barriers in the way of reaching the goal (malady), and the enablers that will overcome the malady and lead the hearer to the goal (means).

Read Ronald Reagan's speeches and his intuitive understanding of that simple structure is obvious. As he campaigned during his two trips to Mississippi, for example, the message could not have been clearer. Reagan's goal was that voters would support him and other Republican candidates. The malady, by his reckoning, was a Democratic, big government platform of tax increases, liberal social programs, and dangerous mismanagement of the nation's military. The means was a Republican platform that he assured his hearers matched their cherished values: reduced federal budgets, tax cuts, a strong national defense, and conservative social policies.

Goal, malady, and means is a simple formula for persuasive sermons that preachers have employed for centuries to win hearts. It is little wonder that by using the same time-tested approach Ronald Reagan won votes.

CHAPTER TEN

GEORGE H. W. BUSH

Forty-First President of the United States
Republican
Elected 1988
Served January 20, 1989, to January 20, 1993

Two men from the same family made more than half of all visits to Mississippi by sitting US presidents through the second term of the forty-fourth chief executive, Barack Obama. On twenty-four occasions, one or another president with the surname Bush traveled to the state. During his one elected term in office, George H. W. Bush visited Mississippi five times. His son, George W. Bush, had eight years as president, during which he traveled to the state a remarkable nineteen times. Hurricane Katrina's destruction brought the latter Bush regularly to Mississippi, as he spotlighted recovery efforts and offered support and encouragement to a devastated region.

George H. W. Bush, on the other hand, visited for a variety of reasons during his presidency, but most trips occurred within the context of Mississippi's acceptance of the man and his message. In 1976 the state voted for the southern Democrat Jimmy Carter by a thin margin. Other than Adlai Stevenson twice in the 1950s, Carter was the only Democratic candidate to win Mississippi since Franklin Roosevelt in 1944. By 1980, even though Carter was again on the ballot, the state was back in the Republican column. Twelve years later and following eight years of the Reagan presidency, Mississippi gave George H. W. Bush nearly 60 percent of its votes, as he swept into the White House.

Though a tough economy spelled problems for Bush by the 1992 election and the popular Democratic governor of Arkansas, Bill Clinton, won nationally by a margin of 5.5 percent, the incumbent president carried Mississippi by 9 percentage points. Unsurprisingly, whenever George H. W. Bush visited the state of Mississippi, he received an enthusiastic reception for both him and his political positions.

According to historian Richard J. Ellis, it wasn't a given that the public would welcome Bush so generously: "John Quincy Adams, Martin Van Buren, [and] George Herbert Walker Bush [were] all presidents who were seen as lacking a common touch. In a democratic age, the most damaging charge against a president is not that he has acted in a vulgar or undignified manner but that he is aloof or distant, out of touch with the people's interests and wants."[1] Ross Perot, who garnered nearly twenty million votes as an independent candidate in the 1992 election, went a step further, claiming that Bush was actually afraid of the American people and that he could only move among the public "in a motorcade two blocks long."[2]

Such criticism stung Bush, and he worked to blunt issues that his travel raised. For instance, when the manufacturer delivered a new version of Air Force One in the late summer of 1990, there were editorials about the eighty telephones, seven bathrooms, and an elegant, on-board presidential suite. "Some reporters were given a tour of the plane and Bush twice asked whether they were aware that Congress approved the purchase, and he made sure they wrote down that it was [ordered] under the previous administration."[3] Also, when opponents raised the question of international trips during the 1992 election—Bush was one of the most enthusiastic overseas visitors to occupy the White House—the presidential travel schedule was severely curtailed. He left the country for only nine days in the nine months prior to Election Day.[4]

Thus it was comfortable and encouraging for Bush to travel to Mississippi, where citizens warmly welcomed him and enthusiastically assured him of their continuing support. His message in 1988 was that his Democratic opponent, Governor Michael Dukakis of Massachusetts, held perspectives unlike the traditional values of many Americans, particularly voters in the South, where politics, racial attitudes, and opinions on social issues were generally conservative. The so-called Southern Strategy of the Republican Party played to the region's politics, particularly during and after the Nixon years. (See the discussion of the Southern Strategy in chapter 6.) It flowered fully during George H. W. Bush's time on the presidential stage.

Jere Nash and Andy Taggart, in their history of Mississippi politics, recalled: "In his acceptance speech at the Republican National Convention,

Bush went through the list: Dukakis supported abortion and gun control, opposed the death penalty and school prayer, and had even vetoed a bill requiring teachers to lead their students in the pledge of allegiance."⁵ Thus, whenever he visited Mississippi even after his election, President Bush made sure to reinforce the voters' appreciation of his positions on those issues where Republicans thought Democrats were vulnerable.

In an interview years after the Bush presidency, his southern campaign coordinator, Lanny Griffith, explained the importance of the values strategy: "I think [the 1988 election was] the first time we ever fully realized how potent [the cultural issues] were." Griffith defined these issues as "hunting, fishing, and your lifestyle," as opposed to "the ACLU, the liberals, sort of arrogant, we're smarter than you, look down on you, [and] East Coast type thing."⁶

May 13, 1989—Lorman and Starkville

Many presidents accept invitations to speak at college and university com-mencements—usually at the larger ceremonies that occur in the spring—and George H. W. Bush obviously found that practice inviting. During his first year of office, he addressed graduating classes at five institutions. His speaking schedule included the commencement ceremonies at Texas A&M University, Alcorn State University (Mississippi), Mississippi State University, Boston University, and the United States Coast Guard Academy (Connecticut).⁷

Bush's two stops on one day in Mississippi for this purpose underscored his relationship with the state's voters. He was conveniently able to address large commencement crowds at both Alcorn State University—one of the state's three historically black schools—and Mississippi State University—the state's primary land grant institution.⁸ Many of the state's leading Republican politicians made both stops of the trip with him on May 13, 1989, a spring day just four months after Bush took office.

In the *Los Angeles Times* on May 9, 1989, journalists reported that an invi-tation for President Bush to give the commencement address at a Mississippi postsecondary institution came first from the president of Alcorn State University in Lorman. Bush accepted, and White House planners added a second stop on the same day for a commencement address at Mississippi State University in Starkville, as it offered broader visibility at a larger institu-tion. Thus this particular Saturday became a significant day of hosting for two universities and for the state's system of higher education. Also there was this obvious dynamic: the first stop gave a Republican president positive exposure within the African American community—a group that by the late twentieth century rarely supported Republican candidates—while the second stop more than balanced the ledger for white southerners who had been faithful Republican voters.

National media attention that generally attends presidential trips and addresses focused on Mississippi, and major urban newspapers covered the events. That same *Los Angeles Times* article drew a contrast between Bush's tightly scheduled time in Lorman and Starkville: "The president of Alcorn State University finally got the kind of RSVP that he wanted. Walter Washington has asked every U.S. president since Lyndon B. Johnson to speak at commencement. . . . President Bush is the first to accept. He will speak on Saturday. Alcorn State, which with 2,757 students is one of the smallest of Mississippi's eight public universities, is located in the rural hills of southwestern Mississippi, seven miles west of Lorman—an unincorporated hamlet consisting of a post office, two service stations, a general store, and a few houses. 'Roots' author Alex Haley attended Alcorn. Bush also will travel Saturday to Mississippi State University in Starkville to give another graduation speech. The predominantly white school has about 12,000 students."[9]

An interesting juxtaposition of the regional and the international occurred in a story from the *Philadelphia Inquirer* where the speeches at Alcorn State University and Mississippi State University included information on an announcement by Mikhail Gorbachev that the Soviet Union would remove 500 nuclear warheads from Europe. These were interesting times for the United States, as stresses grew within the Soviet Union. There were evolving struggles with internal politics, even as unrest boiled over among the subnational republics within the union. About two-and-one-half years after this visit by President Bush to Mississippi, the Soviet Union dissolved.

As he made his trip to Mississippi, across the state, and home to Washington, DC, President Bush answered questions from journalists traveling with him about the likely reaction of the United States to the Soviet leader's decision regarding nuclear warheads in Europe, and he even took time for public comments related to the situation in both of his commencement addresses in Mississippi.[10] Though the president tailored his speeches in Lorman and Starkville to each university community, still he commented on this critical international issue, and he used exactly the same carefully crafted sentence regarding the Soviet Union in both instances: "As the Soviet Union moves towards greater openness and democratization and as they meet the challenge of responsible international behavior, we will match their steps with steps of our own."[11]

Contrasting the two commencement addresses from May 13, 1989, offers an unusually sharp opportunity to see how Bush handled the varying sensitivities of two related, yet different communities. The first was the community of a small, historically black university, and the second the community of a larger research university historically serving a majority of white students—different in many ways, yet both located in the same southern state, Mississippi. While the president's topics were generally the same in both speeches, his speech writers chose different approaches to those topics. We offer paired quotations on specific topics to illustrate the sometimes obvious and sometimes subtle differences.

TOPIC: Change and Transformation in American Life

[*Alcorn State University*] For some American families—those fortunate families where children are raised assuming that they'll have the opportunity to go to college—the drama of today's ceremony is difficult to appreciate. Many of you are the first, though, in your families ever to attend college, let alone stay the course through graduation. The economic transformation wrought by the historically black colleges such as Alcorn is nothing less than astounding. While 85 percent of the United Negro College Fund alumni come from blue-collar families, almost all go on to professional or managerial positions, and in many cases, they're the first blacks to hold these particular positions.

[*Mississippi State University*] Some things haven't changed. . . . Our values haven't. We see these values everywhere: a church-based child-care center, choir practice, or the PTA. And they uplift American society, for they reflect the tenets of "do unto others," tenets I respect and which I will try hard to serve as President of the United States. And they are the values of America's good, quiet, decent people. Americans who know that we are not the sum or our possessions but of how we conduct ourselves. And these people form the heart of our society, and they enrich its central unit, the family. Here these values play a special role, for they teach that life is not a celebration of self and our fate is not divisible.

TOPIC: Recognizing Congressman Sonny Montgomery (D-MS)

[*Alcorn State University*] I'm very pleased that my good friend, Sonny Montgomery, a congressman whose home is in Meridian, is here.

[*Mississippi State University*] Congressman Montgomery and I were elected to Congress on the same day. I'm delighted he's here. His great-grandfather, Colonel W. B. Montgomery, was instrumental in rebuilding Mississippi after the [Civil] War, and he played a major role in founding this university. And so, this afternoon I want to recognize those pioneering efforts and to salute my dear friend, the colonel's great-grandson, your own congressman, Sonny Montgomery.[12]

TOPIC: Character of the University and the Definition of Values

[*Alcorn State University*] The threads woven through the fabric at Alcorn, and any place where excellence is sought, are what used to be called simple family values. We're not talking about two sets of values, family values are the same regardless of race, color, or creed. Family values—they're not complicated: honesty, faith, frugality, acceptance of responsibility, the importance of work, a tradition of helping one's neighbor. Martin Luther King argued that "intelligence is not enough." He said, "Intelligence plus character—that is the goal of the true education."

[*Mississippi State University*] Today, my friends, the eyes of America are upon Starkville, Mississippi. For we meet, to begin with, at a special school, special because for 109 years MSU has made education a lasting legacy and opportunity its bequest. We gather, also, in a very special state, special for its people. You realize that who we are matters more than what we have. And you value home and family and tradition and service to country.

TOPIC: America's Recent History

[*Alcorn State University*] The past 40 years embrace an era of tremendous change for Alcorn and for the United States of America, a time of upheaval and, finally, a time of growth, and maybe something like wisdom.

[*Mississippi State University*] Today I look back upon those times, the past 40 years, and I am struck by the wonder of how much this country has achieved. What newly married vet in his early twenties could have envisioned just how wide the golden door of opportunity would swing in four short decades.... We believed in the simple, the basic truths like kindness and civility, self-sacrifice and courage, compassion and concern for others, timeless values which span the generations, values which show that America is great because America is good.

TOPIC: Opportunities for World War II Veterans

[*Alcorn State University*] Like my classmates in Connecticut, many of the men at Alcorn in 1948 were veterans, soldiers who had fought for democracy, many of them serving in segregated units. And like many of you today, the Alcornites of 1948 were graduating with skills that would enable them to feed the hungry, nurse the sick, and reach out to help the young through education.

[*Mississippi State University*] With the end of World War II, America was unified as few could have imagined. I'm sure many of you have seen that famous Life magazine photo that captured the spirit of those times: the sailor in Times Square embracing a woman in the mass exultation of V-J Day, a victory for freedom that came after so much sacrifice. Like the woman swept off her feet, the spirit of rejoicing, and more importantly the limitless possibilities of America, swept us all. And I, too, felt that sense of idealism and opportunity and headed on out with Barbara—headed out to Texas to make the most of the American Dream.

TOPIC: Achieving Worthy Goals for Self and Others

[*Alcorn State University*] For some of you, I hope there comes a day when you ride winds into the political arena to fight for what you believe in, to grapple not only with your own dreams but also those of your countrymen.

[*Mississippi State University*] Community service works because it's real, not abstract. It makes achievements feasible. Compassion helps one child escape heroin addiction. Generosity allows another to eat a decent meal. And through faith in God, still another overcomes the curse of bigotry and hatred.

TOPIC: A Concluding Benediction

[*Alcorn State University*] America is proud of you and of your families that you represent. God bless you in the challenge to come.

[*Mississippi State University*] Good luck to each one of you. My heart-felt congratulations! May your future be worthy of your dreams.

October 12, 1989—Gulfport

George H. W. Bush's second trip to Mississippi during his time as president was as the headliner at a campaign event for a Republican candidate for the US House of Representatives. Tom Anderson worked for several years as an aide to Trent Lott, who represented the Fifth Congressional District until his election to the US Senate. Lott's elected Republican successor, Larkin Smith, served only eight months before he lost his life in a plane crash near Gulfport. The district's characteristics included "native conservatism," and it was a place where "popular [Republican] presidential candidates have built a political force that has won offices down to the county level."[13] However, Anderson's victory in a special election was not certain because he was running against Gene Taylor, a popular Democratic state senator who likewise held conservative political views. Thus Republican leaders enlisted President Bush to make a campaign appearance on behalf of Tom Anderson.

Taylor held clearly conservative views, but he also advocated strongly on behalf of the defense industry, an important issue for voters in the area. As the *New York Times* coverage of Bush's trip pointed out: "Much of the district's economy is built on military spending generated by the huge Ingalls shipyards in Pascagoula, four military installations, and the large number of retired military personnel who live in the district."[14]

That same story observed: "Indications of just how high the stakes are in the race could be seen earlier this week in the campaign visit here by President Bush, who touted Mr. Anderson for his Washington experience and for the conservative philosophy he would bring to the office. The Democrats countered with a letter signed by the house speaker, Thomas S. Foley, and other Democratic leaders promising to install Mr. Taylor on the Armed Services Committee."[15]

Things didn't go as smoothly as the Republicans hoped in this district that was one of their strongholds. Both the *New York Times* and the *Washington Post* called attention to a politically pointed cartoon from Jackson's *Clarion-Ledger* that "greeted Bush." Captioned "Lapdogs," it showed Bush and Lott greeting each other at the airport, "each holding a leash tightly. Millie, the president's dog, was at the end of Bush's leash. At the end of Lott's was Anderson, crouched on all fours." The *Post* also quoted a local voter who said, "Everybody loves Trent, but I don't like Anderson. It seems like he was shoved down our throats."[16] These were the negative perceptions confronting President Bush as he arrived in Mississippi.

Speaking just prior to the lunch hour on the second Thursday of October in Gulfport's Jones Park—a favorite location for political rallies—the president took off his coat in the midday sun and said that he was ready to "go to work here." Politics is people, he told the crowd, and "good people is what southern Mississippi is all about." Also, he reminded everyone of the devastation of Hurricane Hugo on the South Carolina coast just a few weeks prior to this Gulfport visit, and he thanked the Mississippians who responded to the emergency that killed twenty-seven and left nearly 100,000 people homeless.

Then he launched into support for Tom Anderson, whom he termed "the right man," who "won't be your average freshman in Congress because he's already ahead of his class." Bush referred to Anderson's many years of experience working on a congressional staff.

The president knew that Anderson's opponent, Democrat Gene Taylor, promoted his candidacy on the basis of his local service and connections. Even though Anderson was born in Gulfport and graduated from the University of Mississippi, he spent many years living and working in Washington, DC, as well as serving as an ambassador to several Caribbean nations during Ronald Reagan's presidency. Thus it was important for Bush to establish Anderson's local bona fides for the crowd: "Tom knows the back roads of the fifth district, from Jones County right down to Jones Park, just as well as he knows those corridors of Capitol Hill, and that's a winning combination in the U.S. Congress."

Not only did Anderson know the lay of the land, according to the president, he also knew "what the fifth district needs: continued economic expansion. . . . Growth and jobs, real work, not make work. Let me tell you, we can't tax our way to richer growth." Though federal taxes grew during the Bush years, his hallmark pronouncement at the Republican National Convention in 1988 was "Read my lips: no new taxes."

Bush set the ambassadorial service of Tom Anderson into the context of a troubling issue he said was "on the minds of every American." It was "illegal drug use," and during service in the Caribbean, Bush reported that Anderson was "point man in drug interdiction efforts" and that he knew "what it is to stop those drug runners from reaching our shores."

But Anderson was not a one-issue congressman, according to the president: "There's the environment. . . . Living here on this beautiful Gulf Coast teaches a lesson every day on what it means to preserve our natural heritage. . . . I want to see action on the environment, and I know that Tom Anderson would support a strong advocacy."

Bush spoke confidently of Anderson's commitment to education as well, not the least because his wife, Katherine Anderson, was a teacher. "We need

Prior to the twentieth century, no sitting president of the United States visited Mississippi. However, President-elect Zachary Taylor stopped in Vicksburg during the 1849 journey to his inauguration in Washington, DC. *Private collection. Pat Hilpert, photographer.*

President William McKinley was the first chief executive to visit Mississippi while in office. His initial stop was in Corinth on April 30, 1901; on the following day he made stops in seven other communities throughout the state. *Private collection. Pat Hilpert, photographer.*

President Theodore Roosevelt visited the Mississippi Delta twice, first in 1902 near Smedes for a hunting expedition, and second in 1907 for stops in Vicksburg and Mound Bayou. *Private collection. Pat Hilpert, photographer.*

Clifford Berryman was a successful cartoonist in Washington, DC. His 1902 image "Drawing the Line in Mississippi" depicted the origin of the teddy bear legend. *Image courtesy of the Theodore Roosevelt Center at Dickinson State University and the Library of Congress.*

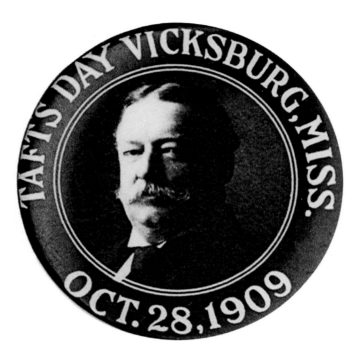

President William Taft visited several Mississippi communities during late October and early November 1909. This image is of a celluloid button made for his stop in Vicksburg. *Private collection. Pat Hilpert, photographer.*

President Franklin Roosevelt and his wife, Eleanor, visited Mississippi in 1934, stopping in Tupelo to celebrate the early success of the Tennessee Valley Authority (TVA). *Private collection. Pat Hilpert, photographer.*

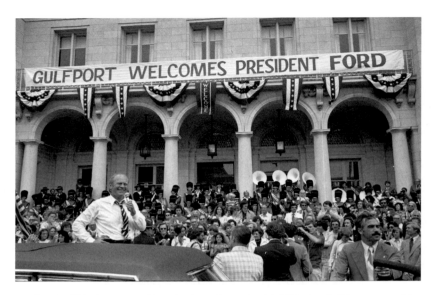

President Gerald Ford campaigned for reelection on September 26, 1976, in four Gulf Coast communities. His narrow loss to Jimmy Carter in Mississippi marked the only presidential election Democrats won in the state between 1960 and 2016. *Courtesy Gerald R. Ford Presidential Library.*

President Jimmy Carter overnighted at the home of a lay leader of the Southern Baptist Convention during a 1977 visit to Yazoo City. Owen Cooper, a Mississippi businessman, had supported Carter when a campaign interview with *Playboy* magazine riled conservative Christians. *Private collection. Pat Hilpert, photographer.*

This large and enthusiastic crowd greeted President Ronald Reagan at a rally in Jones Park during a 1984 stop in Gulfport for his reelection campaign. *White House photo, courtesy of the Ronald Reagan Presidential Library.*

On a single day in 1989 President George H. W. Bush addressed spring commencement ceremonies at both Alcorn State University and Mississippi State University (MSU). This image shows him speaking from the MSU podium. *Courtesy of Special Collections, Mississippi State University Libraries.*

President Bill Clinton enjoyed meeting and shaking hands with Clarksdale residents during a 1999 tour across the nation to promote his New Markets Initiative. *Reuters photo, Alamy Ltd.*

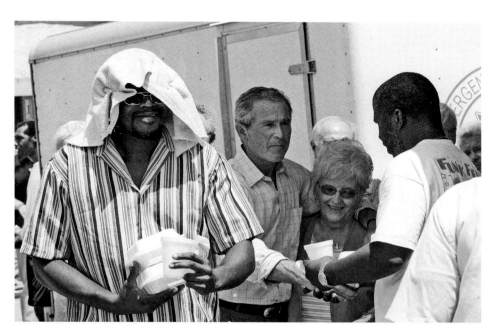

President George W. Bush made more trips to Mississippi than any other chief executive. Fourteen of his nineteen visits related to recovery after Hurricane Katrina. This photograph shows Bush comforting Biloxi residents at a food relief station. *Reuters photo, Alamy Ltd.*

On June 14, 2010, President Barack Obama met with Governor Haley Barbour and local leaders in Gulfport to discuss recovery following the Deepwater Horizon disaster. *White House photo, Pete Souza, photographer.*

people that understand this profession," Bush said. "I know I can count on Tom to speak out on Capitol Hill for a higher standard of excellence in our schools."

Each of the issues was "a matter of urgent concern," the president said, "and every one of them is one more good reason to send this good man to the Congress to help me get the job done." Lest the local voters forget, as the president was wrapping up his remarks, he reminded them that "the best reason to send Tom to Congress may just be this one: whatever the issue, you know where he's coming from philosophically. You know where his heart is: right here in Gulfport."

Finally, there was the Republican values closer: "You know, I know what makes this state click: Mississippi values, traditional values, Tommy Anderson's values. You need a man in Washington who makes sure the voice of southern Mississippi is heard in the halls of Congress. You need Tom Anderson."[17]

During the final weeks of the campaign, Anderson tried to distance himself from the criticism that he was an outsider to the district, but Taylor's hometown appeal was strong. Also, a revelation damaging to Anderson—that he accepted eighteen free trips on a Mississippi businessman's private plane and failed to make required federal reports on sixteen of them—added fuel to Taylor's momentum. In the end, President Bush's visit did not make the difference in this election. Taylor received 65 percent of the vote to Anderson's 35 percent. The victory meant that Democrats held all five of the state's US House seats for the first time in seventeen years.[18]

December 3, 1991—Meridian

President Bush sought venues in late 1991 to deliver a message about his proposed reforms to the economy, congressional hesitancy to work with him, and the need for the public to support his ideas. One of the places his staff identified to highlight these themes was Peavey Electronics in Meridian, Mississippi, a widely known manufacturer of high-quality audio equipment. Effects from a worldwide recession struck in late 1990. Both the president and his political advisers realized that reverses in the economy damaged his reelection prospects in 1992, and they knew it was critical to be seen as actively and aggressively responding to the looming problems.

This area of the state, near the border with Alabama, comprised Mississippi's Third Congressional District; its elected US representative was Sonny Montgomery, a Democrat who served in the US House starting in 1967. Montgomery was the long-serving chairman of the Veterans Affairs Committee, and he wielded considerable influence among the Democratic leaders within the House of Representatives. Indeed, in the third quarter of the twentieth century, Mississippi's congressional delegation comprised conservative Democrats who built seniority and stature beginning in the 1940s, but when Montgomery retired in 1997, he was the last of that powerful group. Republicans replaced nearly all the Democrats—except generally the representatives from the Delta—as the Republican Party's Southern Strategy succeeded. Bush was in Meridian to help himself politically but also to further Republican aims in a southern state.[19]

Peavey Electronics was quite active in international commerce. Company founder Hartley Peavey began constructing one-off amplifiers in 1965 above his father's store, and his was the classic American success story: start small, build an innovative and respected product, and grow to become a national or international success. At the time Bush came to town, Peavey Electronics was moving toward the manufacture of digitally controlled sound systems, units that CEO Peavey said in a subsequent interview were in use "in airports and stadiums all over the world."[20] In other words, Peavey Electronics was a firm with a solid track record of product development, manufacturing, and sales that was poised to become even more successful both domestically and internationally. That it was located in the heart of a region Republicans were determined to control politically was a plus.

The plan was for the president to tour the Peavey manufacturing facility and then to address a gathering of the employees. By the early December date of this visit to Mississippi, the US Congress adjourned for the calendar year, and the president hit the road to generate popular support for his proposed economic reforms.

The *Commercial Dispatch* of Columbus, Mississippi, ran its coverage on the day following the event, providing local details and color. Noting that the preparation was lengthy—as is typical for a presidential visit—the report stated that Meridian was "a city held a friendly hostage [for days] by the national media and a swarm of advance team officials from the White House."[21] When President Bush arrived on Air Force One at 1:40 p.m., landing at the local airport, more than 6,000 ticketed spectators from the general public greeted him. As invited guests arrived for the event at Peavey's main manufacturing plant, each individual passed through strict security.

One Columbus resident, Margie Joiner, recognized that Mississippi was in political transition. Her light-hearted comment to the journalist from the *Commercial Dispatch* captured the state's rapid political evolution: "Years ago, the Republican Party was not welcome in Mississippi. They said the name Republican to scare the children."[22] Bush's reception that day—and in his other visits to the state—proved that the Mississippi climate had changed for Republicans.

When the president took the podium he noted that Peavey's exports reached countries around the world, and that global sales made up 40 percent of the company's business. Bush advocated on behalf of his economic priorities, arguing against protectionism and drawing a direct line from globalization to more American jobs.

Throughout the 1990s and the first two decades of the twenty-first century, the issue of globalization grew in importance. Many Republicans and Democrats alike advocated the North American Free Trade Agreement (NAFTA) of 1994 and other international trade agreements with the strong support of the US business community. Popular support varied, however, as some political campaigns alarmed the electorate with warnings regarding the potential sacrifice of American jobs when manufacturing companies transferred operations abroad.

Thus Bush's address at Peavey Electronics came at an interesting juncture in this ongoing discussion about globalization. In the following excerpt the president made his argument for support in strong terms, calling opposition to globalization "a false division between foreign policy and domestic priorities." It was an address that illustrated issues still lively in the national political conversation of the twenty-first century. Bush began his remarks with thanks for the "great day," and he complimented "the people behind the power of Peavey" as well as "the pride in what you have accomplished." He termed it "a true American story."

An illustration of Bush's commitment to globalization was close at hand: "Hartley [Peavey] once remarked that 'Fat cats don't hunt.' Well, Peavey's been prowling the global marketplace with a hunger that won't quit. You export, I'm told, to 103 countries, accounting for more than 40 percent of your sales. Two amplifiers are top sellers in Japan. Peavey proves that more foreign exports means more American jobs. Ask the man, ask Hartley: he's playing a critical role in our Secretary of Commerce's Japan Corporate Program, he knows what I'm talking about. Cracking foreign markets that means creating more economic growth and more American jobs."

The president got right to the reasons for his trip and for choosing this setting for his televised speech: "Some in the Congress have tried to set up a false division between foreign policy and domestic priorities. But I think they're wrong. Anyone who's on the front lines of foreign competition knows that fighting the battles against foreign protectionism means a winning war on the home front. These things are related."

He also had a patriotic reason for hope and for dismissing the misgivings about potential job losses in this nation: "With a level playing field, I am absolutely convinced that American workers can out-innovate, out-perform, and out-produce any competition on earth. . . . Right here in this great state, more than 43,000 jobs are export-driven, and overall, every billion dollars in manufacturers' exports means 20,000 jobs."

President Bush had accomplishments to put on the table: "Over the years we have built a foundation in this new, revitalized world. . . . Inflation is down. Interest rates have fallen to the lowest level in years. Our exports have skyrocketed, as I said, 80 percent in the last five years. And, again, that does mean good jobs across the country for men and women."

Of course there was still much to do, and the president's plan charted a course: "But this is no time—I'm not here to sing some Pollyanna-ish view— this is no time to sit back and hope for the best. . . . I've traveled to forty- eight states since I've been president, talking and meeting with people, and listening and learning. . . . I've asked Congress to pass an important series of initiatives that would help put Americans back to work and set us on a long-term economic growth track: tax incentives, for example, to unleash investment; reforms to reform the banking system. . . . I believe that these measures would help the American economy."

Just after making a pitch for his policy proposals, the president assured the crowd, "I didn't come down here to talk politics," though he recognized "that both parties will spend a lot of time shooting at each other. That's already started [for the election of 1992]."

Despite the political rhetoric on all sides, the president recognized that it was time "to set this aside and to get the job done." He called on Congress to "act on an effective plan of action that I'm going to send out there to the American people in the state of the union message."

Finally, what was the Bush plan? "So, what I want to do as we work for peace and work to handle the changes that are happening in the Soviet Union and bring parties together for peace in the Middle East . . . is to take that newfound credibility, use it to hammer our way into these markets of Europe, these markets of Asia, so we will have more access. We will have more ready access to those markets, and that means more products like the ones you make, other products being made for export across this country, going into these foreign markets." In other words, globalization equaled success in the American economy.

As it was with Peavey Electronics, so it was with the Bush plan: "This is the American dream in action."[23]

March 6, 1992—Jackson

Surprising opposition arose for President Bush from the far-right wing of the Republican Party when Patrick Buchanan, a political commentator and syndicated columnist, declared his intention to seek the 1992 presidential nomination. Buchanan served as an adviser to three Republican presidents, including Bush's predecessor, Ronald Reagan. When Bush wavered on his pledge not to raise taxes and the economy went into recession, Buchanan saw an opportunity developing and threw his hat into the ring. Though Bush remained the presumptive nominee in the minds of most analysts, Buchanan made a stronger-than-expected showing in the New Hampshire Republican primary on February 18, 1992, and the battle lines hardened. For the president to establish his position as front-runner in the race for the party's nomination, he needed an overwhelming win on the day of primaries known as Super Tuesday, March 10, 1992. Eight states were in play; most of them were located in the South. Mississippi was one of the Super Tuesday states.

Thus the stakes were high when President Bush came to Jackson on March 6, just four days prior to Super Tuesday. Ahead of the event, the *Clarion-Ledger* announced that there would be a rally in Jackson with the president speaking for twenty minutes. Bush was the middle of three candidates to visit Jackson in anticipation of Super Tuesday. Arkansas governor Bill Clinton, the leading Democratic contender in Mississippi's polls, was planning a brief stop on Thursday, and Buchanan scheduled an event at Jackson International Airport for Sunday evening. Bush's campaign assured voters that his schedule included Mississippi even before Buchanan's surprisingly strong showing in New Hampshire.[24]

A flyer posted around Jackson promoting the president's event called it a "Mississippi Bush/Quayle '92 Rally" planned to occur on the "south steps of the new state capitol." Though Bush was not to appear until 4:30 p.m., the gates to the rally opened at 2:30 and entertainment began at 3:30. In other words, the campaign invited supporters and the curious to make an afternoon of it.

Following the rally, the *Clarion-Ledger* story provided details: "President Bush, courting Mississippi voters on Friday, hailed welfare reform and appeared to question his Republican challenger's racial sensitivity. A throng of 8,000 gathered on the capitol grounds to greet Bush and his wife, Barbara, whose visit comes just four days before the Super Tuesday presidential primary. Bush, who was often interrupted by applause, called for sweeping changes in government assistance programs."[25] The president advocated stricter policies regarding the necessity of work for those seeking public aid, and he repeated a common theme of the anti-Buchanan forces, namely, that the challenger was racist in his proposed policies and his rhetoric. There were, indeed, oft-reported instances of white supremacist groups advocating on behalf of Buchanan, though he forcefully denied any racial prejudices.[26]

Jackson's *Clarion-Ledger* opined after the event that "Bush offered few new initiatives to guide the country out of the recession." The newspaper reported Mississippi's growth in unemployment, including a full percentage point during January 1992, meaning that "an additional 12,000 are out of work."[27]

As to issues current in the campaign, Bush said the following while in Jackson: "We must allow common sense to prevail in our welfare system—we must restore the connection between welfare and work. . . . Let's stand up and reject the ugly politics of hatred that is rearing its ugly head again. . . . Racism, anti-Semitism, and bigotry have no place in the United States."

No Republican candidate could or would avoid talking about values; it was an important element of the Southern Strategy: "We're in a battle for our future. We're fighting to protect our most basic institution—the American family. That's why this year's decision is so important to America. This country was built on faith and family and freedom and we must renew those sources of strength."

According to Bush, problems with the economy were not so much of his making, as they were the result of inaction or misguided action by his Democratic opponents in Congress: "Instead of passing my plan [that is, the economic growth package], the big spenders who control the United States Congress had ideas of their own. Here's what it means to you: a tiny, temporary tax cut of a quarter per day. Tell Congress to keep the change and to keep their hands out of the taxpayers' budgets."

Then there was this pitch for a favorite Bush and Republican theme, globalization: "My opponents are peddling protectionism—a retreat from economic reality. That is not the American flag they're waving. It is the white flag of surrender."[28]

September 22, 1992—Greenville

Located in the heart of the eighteen-county Mississippi Delta region in the state's northwest quadrant, Greenville seemed an unlikely campaign stop for George H. W. Bush in 1992. Sparse population, heavy with African American voters who generally leaned Democratic, characterized this region of the state, but Washington County supported Bush in 1988, and the community of Greenville produced some of the state's most prominent Republican leaders.[29] Campaign staff chose this venue for a stop-by at the Mid-Delta Regional Airport. Two days before the event, the *Clarion-Ledger* mistakenly reported: "It will be the first time a sitting president has visited the Delta since 1902, when Republican President Theodore Roosevelt made a stop in the Delta."[30] In fact, there were four other presidential visits to communities in the Mississippi Delta between 1902 and 1992.[31]

Greenville residents also heard on that Sunday, September 20, 1992, that the president would be paying a visit to their community. The local newspaper, the *Delta Democrat Times*, ran this rather prosaic headline on its front page: "Bush Will Stop Here." Within the brief story was news of the announcement by the state chair of the Bush-Quayle Campaign in Mississippi, Clarke Reed, a Greenville businessman and statewide Republican leader. Reed had few details other than the date—Tuesday, September 22—and an encouragement to the citizenry to "show him a real good welcome."[32] The article also reminded readers that Bush made a previous Greenville stop in 1984 as he campaigned for the reelection of the Reagan-Bush team.

By the following day, questions remained about some arrangements, but local planners announced that festivities would take place at the American General Aircraft Corporation's hangar at the municipal airport. There was also information that the president would arrive between 4:00 and 5:00 p.m., and that bands and choral groups would begin a program of entertainment at 3:00 p.m. The political reporter with Greenville's *Delta Democrat Times* wrote: "Although Bush won the vote in Mississippi four years ago, he has recently continued to lag behind Democratic opponent Bill Clinton in the polls."[33] By the next day's edition, there were a specific time for Bush's address—5:15 p.m.—and news that in-state leaders of both parties were sniping about each other's candidates.[34]

Evidently, the president's visit was a hit with the audience. Following the event, the *Delta Democrat Times* led with the headline, "Bush Shoots and Scores; Mid-Delta Crowd Goes Wild." According to the report, the president attacked Clinton, a next-door neighbor as governor of Arkansas, saying in effect that he was a free-spending politician who thought nothing of raising taxes on the state's citizens. In addition, Bush promoted his record as president and maintained that the economy was moving in a positive direction.[35]

Of his Democratic opponent, Bush said that the Arkansas governor had more than doubled the state's spending since 1988 and "paid for it by raising taxes that hurt working families the most." Furthermore, the president reported that Clinton "raised and extended his state's sales tax repeatedly and doubled his state's gas tax. He even tried to tax food stamps until the federal government forced him to stop." Expanding the story, Bush said that Clinton "started taxing mobile homes and then he raised taxes on beer and then he tried to tax child care." Though the reference was a little foggy, the president's gist was clear: "I guess it doesn't matter whether the burp is from the beer or the baby bottle, he's going to slap a tax on it; and I don't think we need that for the United States of America."

After Bush accused Clinton of distorting the record of his presidency and reporting that there were new figures showing an eighteen-month high in housing starts, the president concluded, "Inflation is down, interest rates are low, and our economy is poised for a take-off—if we make the right choice in November." He concluded with this direct exhortation: "Elect me as president!"[36]

Less than one hour after his arrival, President Bush waved farewell to the crowd of 6,000 who attended the rally, and he departed aboard Air Force One. With him were sixty or so national media representatives traveling everywhere with the Bush campaign.[37] The president and his entourage headed to another of the five campaign stops scheduled for the day.[38]

★   ★   ★

George H. W. Bush's early life history predicted anything but popularity for him in the Deep South, including Mississippi. He was a Yankee through and through: born in Massachusetts, he grew up in Connecticut, attended Phillips Academy and Yale University, and vacationed at the family's seaside estate in Kennebunkport, Maine. In other words, he was from a moneyed family with the sorts of New England connections and political power usually gained only by the privileged and wealthy.

However, his history also included decorated service in World War II and an early career move to Texas to earn his own way in the oil business. He became a success, founding more than one profitable firm. He took on challenges to provide party leadership in Texas Republican circles, and his visibility gave him opportunities to run for the US Congress. Right place, right time, and right connections meant national Republican leadership, presidential appointments to key federal posts, and important ambassadorships. Then the Republicans chose him to share the national ticket with presidential candidate Ronald Reagan after coming up short in 1980 primary contests against Reagan.

Bush had the history to understand the Southern Strategy of the Republican Party and to use it to his advantage. His presidential visits to Mississippi during his four years in office showed that his Texas seasoning overcame his New England heritage as he talked the talk that those seeking so-called traditional, conservative values in their candidates found appealing. Mississippians rewarded George H. W. Bush in the 1988 presidential election for his party affiliation, his philosophy, and his political positions with a 20-percentage-point victory over Michael Dukakis, the Democratic governor of Bush's birth-state, Massachusetts.

Four years later, and despite regularly positive receptions in the South, Bush's efforts were insufficient to keep his job. The incumbent president's pitch captured the most votes in the election of 1992 cast for any candidate in Mississippi, but the same was not true in the nationwide tally. Bush lost to Clinton in the three-way race, finishing with 37.4 percent nationally to Clinton's 43 percent. Perot, in the most successful third-party bid for the presidency since Theodore Roosevelt's attempt to regain the White House at the head of the Progressive "Bull Moose" Party in 1912, garnered 18.9 percent of the final vote. While a plurality of Mississippi voters found Bush's family values platform appealing, the incumbent president's campaign failed on the basis of an economic downturn, a youthful challenger promising change in Washington, and another candidate who hammered the administration's economic policies incessantly. Bush's loss opened the White House's door to another southern governor—this one from Arkansas—twelve years after Georgian Jimmy Carter left the Oval Office.

CHAPTER ELEVEN

BILL CLINTON

Forty-Second President of the United States
Democrat
Elected 1992 and 1996
Served January 20, 1993, to January 20, 2001

★ ★

In terms of life experiences and proximity prior to his service as the nation's chief executive, Bill Clinton was surely the twentieth-century president most closely related to the state of Mississippi. Born and raised in neighboring Arkansas, his entire record of public service prior to running for the presidency was in the state next door. He was both attorney general and governor of Arkansas, the former for two years and the latter for twelve years. Both he and his wife made speaking appearances in Mississippi during his gubernatorial years, and he often crossed the border between the states to work with Mississippi officials on programs benefiting the region. Despite those connections and his national victory in the 1992 presidential election, Clinton lost the balloting for Mississippi's electoral votes in that contest to the incumbent Republican president, George H. W. Bush, by nearly 9 percent.

Economic measures suggested that Clinton succeeded in his first presidential term. Rates of unemployment and inflation fell to their lowest points in many decades. Homeownership climbed, and crime rates declined. Federal budgets balanced, and there was even a budget surplus.[1] Clinton's vice president was Albert Gore, who hailed from Tennessee, another state bordering Mississippi. In other words, no other modern president logically had a better chance—for geographical and cultural reasons—to win Mississippi's support for reelection. Surely it was Bill Clinton in 1996. However, Mississippians again disappointed their neighbor by giving their electoral votes to the Republican challenger, Bob Dole, who won with a margin slightly larger than 5 percent.

Viewing the history from Carter's slim win in Mississippi in 1976 through Clinton's two losses, Jere Nash and Andy Taggart reached an unavoidable conclusion: "For federal elections, at least, the shift in rural white voters had matured; even a southern governor could not overcome the ideological positions of his national party."[2]

Is it any wonder, then, that Republican George H. W. Bush visited Mississippi five times during his four years in office, while Democrat Bill Clinton visited the state just once while serving for eight years? Presidential trips require great expenditures of time and financial resources, and thus must be purposeful. For the most part, venues other than Mississippi offered the Clinton administration greater gains in terms of policy or politics.

Bill Clinton was never shy about traveling. He logged more time abroad during his years in office than any other president—230 days—and his time on the road for domestic travel was even more extensive—roughly 700 days.[3] During his trips, he made 2,500 appearances in various foreign or domestic cities, and these were in addition to his 450 appearances in Washington, DC.[4]

When Clinton did visit Mississippi, it was the middle of 1999, the third year of his second four-year term. Earlier that same year, the US House of Representatives impeached him on charges of perjury and obstruction of justice in a case related to his relationship with White House intern Monica Lewinsky, but the US Senate acquitted him at trial. Remarkably, he emerged from the process with strong public support, and his administration continued to address national and international issues in an aggressive fashion.

One of the targets Clinton chose as a focus was poverty, particularly those areas of the nation where chronic poverty and its effects persisted decade after decade. As an initial step in the political effort required for his economic development proposals to succeed—Republicans controlled both houses of Congress—President Clinton met on May 11, 1999, at the White House with "seventeen chief executive officers from major American corporations and investment firms to discuss ways to mobilize new private investment in America's most economically underserved communities." Clinton led discussions on several proposed programs flying under the banner the New Markets Initiative.[5]

His campaign to persuade passage of these proposals also took him on a nationwide tour of several economically challenged locations over four days.

In this effort, the president made visits to these sites: the Appalachian region of Kentucky; the Mississippi Delta, specifically Clarksdale; a blighted urban neighborhood in East St. Louis, Illinois; the Pine Ridge Indian Reservation in South Dakota; and a Hispanic community in Phoenix, Arizona.[6] Though Clinton made no trips to Republican Mississippi during the first six-and-one-half years of his presidency, a policy reason arose for him to visit a community vexed by poverty in a region labeled by one scholar "the most southern place on earth."[7]

July 6, 1999—Clarksdale

On Monday, July 5, 1999, President Clinton flew on Air Force One to Tennessee, and overnighted at the Peabody Hotel in downtown Memphis. At 7:00 a.m. the following morning, he left the hotel by motorcade for a quick trip to Memphis International Airport, where Marine One, the presidential helicopter, was awaiting him for a brief, seventy-mile flight to Fletcher Field, the airport serving Clarksdale, Mississippi. Upon arrival, several local and statewide officeholders met the president and his entourage. The welcoming committee included Mississippi's Democratic lieutenant governor, Ronnie Musgrove.[8] Traveling with Clinton were three cabinet secretaries—transportation (Rodney Slater), labor (Alexis Herman), and agriculture (Dan Glickman)—a senior administrator from the small business administration, and the Rev. Jessie Jackson, a prominent leader from the nation's African American community and an outspoken advocate for solutions to poverty and racism. This was the second stop for the travelers on their trip promoting the president's New Markets Initiative; on the previous day, the group visited Hazard, Kentucky, in that state's Appalachian Mountains.

According to the announcement that went out from the White House prior to the president's tour, the policies and programs upon which the administration built the New Markets Initiative were intended "to bring private enterprise and capital to distressed areas." Among the accomplishments claimed by President Clinton in this area were a "strengthened and simplified Community Reinvestment Act," a "Community Development Financial Institutions Fund," and the "designation of 135 new urban and rural Empowerment Zones and Enterprise Communities across the country." These programs were part of an agenda to bring "jobs and opportunity back to distressed areas." As congressional consideration of the president's new Fiscal Year 2000 budget approached, the administration offered provisions for a New Markets Tax Credit program, as well as other financial incentives that would encourage large corporations and small businesses to invest in "underserved rural and urban communities."[9]

Clinton's schedule for the Clarksdale stop included several elements. There was a motorcade from the airport to the downtown area—US representative Bennie Thompson (D-MS) and Clarksdale's mayor Richard Webster escorted—to meet local business owners and visit a retail shop. Following those stops, the president toured the Waterfield Cabinet Company's manufacturing facility led by CEO Bob Koerber. The principal program for the visit to Clarksdale also took place at the Waterfield plant, where Clinton made introductory remarks and then facilitated a roundtable discussion with eight employees in front of an audience of 700. Local and national media covered all events.

During his introductory comments, the president said, "I just want to tell you exactly why we're here. First of all, the people in the Delta know better than anybody else that, while this country has had an unbelievable run—we've had the longest peacetime expansion in our history—nearly nineteen-million jobs since the day I took the oath of office . . . in the Delta the poverty rate is much higher than the country as a whole. In this county, it's over twice as high. The unemployment rate is higher than the national average, and the investment rate is lower. . . . I want everybody in America to know that while our country has been blessed with this economic recovery, not all Americans have been blessed by it, that it hasn't reached every place."

Clinton went on to enumerate some of the economic gains experienced by most in the nation—for example, low unemployment rates, high homeownership rates, and record numbers of children lifted out of poverty. He claimed his share of the credit for these developments: "Ever since I became president, I have done what I could to increase investment in undeveloped areas through the empowerment zones, which give tax credits and put tax money into distressed areas, through the enterprise communities, [and] through getting banks to more vigorously approach the Community Reinvestment Act." Indeed, he reported that in the Mississippi Delta alone, the measures helped "to generate more than 5,000 jobs and 200 million dollars in annual sales."

The president continued: "Now, let me say, we've got a lot of other challenges in the Delta. . . . But fundamentally, what I want America to know is that every place in the country, and today this place, is full of good people, capable of doing good work, who can be trained to do any kind of work, and we are going to do everything we can in the government to give the financial incentives necessary for people to invest here."

Then there was this interesting argument from the president: "Everybody in America has a selfish interest now in developing the Delta. Why? Because most economists believe that, if we're going to keep our economic recovery going without inflation, the only way we can possibly do it is to find more customers for our products and then add more workers at home. If you come here, you get both in the same place. You get more workers and more consumers. So it's good for the rest of America as well."

His pitch for assistance with the New Markets Initiative concluded his introductory remarks: "I want all of you to think about, when we leave here, what we can do to show people the opportunity that's here now and what you could do to help me pass, on a bipartisan basis, the necessary tax incentives and loan guarantees to say to any investor, anywhere in America, if you come to the Mississippi Delta, you can get at least as good a deal as you could investing anywhere else in the world. And we're right here at home, and we need you."[10] At this point, Clinton led a lengthy discussion with eight panelists from the audience. In the course of the discussion, the president asked and answered questions about national and regional issues as they related to his New Markets Initiative.

As the program closed, Clinton, once again, made a pitch for support: "The story needs to go out across America. This is a good investment. This is a good deal. We will help you. We have institutions to help you. We have tax relief to help you. And more and more, our financial institutions are coming up with the money. But America needs to wake up and recognize that the best new market for American products and for new American investment is right here in the U.S.A."[11]

Following his tour and the program inside the plant, Clinton proceeded to the company's loading dock for an interview with CNBC journalist Ron Insana. Portions of the interaction between the president and Insana help to clarify perspectives and motivations that brought the president to Mississippi. These are presented in verbatim format below:

INSANA: Mr. President, this trip and your new markets initiative in some ways have already been compared to Lyndon Johnson's War on Poverty [and] Bobby Kennedy's swing through Appalachia. How will this program work where some of the other government programs on poverty have failed in the past?
PRESIDENT: Well, first of all, I think it's important to recognize that this is different because we don't say the government can solve all these problems, but we do say the government can no longer ignore them. And, in fact, we've been working on them for six-and-a-half years, ever since I took office.

This is a classic example, this approach to new markets, of the New Democratic or Third Way philosophy that I articulated back in 1991 and

1992. That is, the government's role is to create the conditions for success, give people the tools they need to succeed, and then in effect, empower people to make the most of it.

But we recognize, if you look at—go back to the War on Poverty, it did a lot of good in terms of giving children preschool and feeding hungry children and giving them access to health care. But in the end, if you want these communities to be self-sustaining, they have to get private-sector capital with private-sector jobs, and they have to prove that they can compete for it, they can win it, and that people can actually make a profit investing in these places and that it will be profitable to put people to work. . . .

INSANA: What specific items will be included in the legislation to advance those goals? What kind of tax credits?
PRESIDENT: Well, the big ideas in the legislation are a tax credit of up to 25 percent for people who invest in vehicles that will be creating businesses or expanding businesses in high unemployment, underdeveloped areas. In addition to that, once you get into those vehicles, then you would be eligible to borrow two dollars for every one dollar invested and have the money borrowed be subject to a government loan guarantee, which would mean the interest rates would be much, much lower. So by those two things, you lower the relative risk of investing in these new markets.

But we've seen—you heard the person from Bank of America say today, we heard the gentleman from a local bank in Kentucky yesterday or the people from Aetna or these other companies say, "These are good investments; we can make money here." So if you lower the relative risk of getting in, in the first place, and in effect, try to provide for the whole nation what now you can find in the empowerment zones that the vice president has worked so hard to manage over the last six years, I think we can get a lot more growth here. . . .

You know, sooner or later, results should account for something. Sooner or later, we [Democrats and Republicans] should stop having this debate as if there is no history, no evidence, no facts, and no results. Now, we've produced an economy with nineteen million new jobs, the longest peacetime expansion in history, and if we get out of debt, the average person will get much more than they would from an extra tax cut.

Second, I am for a sizable tax cut. I have proposed a sizable tax cut. I also supported the previous tax cuts, the $500 child credit, and the college credit which is $1,500 a year. I supported all these tax cuts. But first things first. If we take this country out of debt for the first time since 1835, then average people are going to have more money in their pockets than if we keep the country in debt and give them a tax cut now because we've got an election in a year and a half.[12]

After his interview, President Clinton lunched with those in his party at Hick's Superette, a local barbecue restaurant. The travelers returned to the Clarksdale airport following the meal, and just before 2:00 p.m. he boarded Marine One to return to Air Force One at the airport in Memphis. In the late afternoon, the president and his traveling companions made yet another stop on behalf of the New Markets Initiative, this one in East St. Louis, Illinois.

The next day's *Clarksdale Press Register* carried the front-page headline, "Clinton Visit Leaves City Optimistic." The article reported the details of the presidential visit, including a welcome announcement that new resources could become available: "President William Jefferson Clinton's brief but historic trip through Clarksdale has city officials and local residents believing that something good may come from the visit."

There were quite a few reasons for optimism, according to the story of the *Press Register*. At the head of the list was the president's proposed New Market Initiatives program that sought federal and private sector partnerships "in pursuit of both corporate profit and the creation of good jobs." As for good news of a more immediate character, "Clinton announced fifteen-million dollars in community development grants for the Mississippi Delta. The money is part of a forty-six-point-five-million-dollar funding package." Then came the dramatic icing on the cake: "Clinton later announced a $500 million capital investment fund entered into with the Bank of America."[13]

Three pages later in the same day's *Press Register*, the editor chose to deal honestly with the enthusiasm generated by the presidential visit. While acknowledging the good news in an opinion piece, he also cautioned that progress required hard work. First he encouraged his readers: "By most any measure, the president's five-and-a-half hour visit to Clarksdale Tuesday—his first to Mississippi since being elected in 1992—was a smashing success. Clinton brought unprecedented exposure, an impressive audience . . . and a timely, crucial message, that contrary to conventional wisdom, the Delta is a great place to do business and that companies, given the right incentives, will invest here, create jobs, and energize the economy."

Then, the editor of the *Press Register* offered this counterpoint: "As the national spotlight follows President Clinton to the west coast, the burden now falls on Clarksdale and its civic, business, and political leadership to seize the momentum and maximize the benefits of this truly historic opportunity. . . ."

Clinton did his part pounding the bully pulpit on behalf of Clarksdale and the Delta. Now the job is ours."[14]

★ ★ ★

At the first stop in Hazard, Kentucky, during his nationwide, whirlwind tour on behalf of his New Markets Initiative, President Clinton addressed the Appalachian community, establishing themes he hoped would reach the halls of Congress. His statements in that initial address were straightforward and concise, and they echoed through each of the stops, including the visit to Clarksdale. Clinton offered these four themes:

1. "This is a time to bring more jobs and investment and hope to the areas of our country that have not fully participated in this economic recovery. We have an obligation to do it."
2. "I came in the hope that, with the help of the business leaders here, we could say to every corporate leader in America: 'Take a look at investing in rural and inner-city America.'"
3. "I believe the government's part is to create the conditions of a strong economy; to give individuals the tools they need to succeed, including education and training; and to give incentives to businesses to take a second look at the places that they have overlooked."
4. "Give people the same incentives to invest in Appalachia or the Native American reservations or the Mississippi Delta or the inner cities we give them today to invest in poor countries overseas, and let the American people show what they can do."[15]

As a result of the campaign for the New Markets Initiative, President Clinton's hoped-for echoes reached not only through the stops of his tour but also to decision makers in the nation's capital. Elements of the proposals became law; for example, the New Markets Tax Credit Program was a part of the Community Renewal Tax Relief Act of 2000. It provided incentives to businesses that, in turn, made nearly $40 billion of investments in impoverished communities during the first ten years of the program.

It could also be argued that the model President Clinton promoted followed him to the Clinton Foundation in his postpresidential years and became a primary vehicle for the work of that charity's efforts on behalf of impoverished communities around the world. Clinton wrote this familiar-sounding description of the organization's mission for a 2016 letter on the website of the foundation: "We started the Clinton Global Initiative to create a new kind of community built around the new realities of our modern world, where problem-solving requires the active partnership of government, business, and civil society."[16]

CHAPTER TWELVE

GEORGE W. BUSH

Forty-Third President of the United States
Republican
Elected 2000 and 2004
Served January 20, 2001, to January 20, 2009

George W. Bush made more visits to Mississippi during his eight years in office than the combined total of the ten presidents who preceded him—nineteen versus sixteen. Of these trips to the state, four were in support of Republican candidates, one was to promote his policy agenda regarding Social Security, and fourteen were related to the state's recovery from the destruction of Hurricane Katrina. Four of his visits included stops in two communities for meetings, tours, or addresses. Thus Bush made a total of twenty-three community stops in Mississippi, seventeen of which were in one of the six southernmost counties, that is, those near or bordering on the Gulf of Mexico.

In view of the workload and responsibilities of the modern presidency, and judging by the total volume of visits by his recent predecessors in the office, nineteen was a remarkable number of trips to Mississippi. Barely eight months into Bush's first term, the nation suffered the terrorist attacks of September 11, 2001, and later that year, he launched the War on Terror with the US invasion of Afghanistan. Nearly eighteen months later, in March 2003, the president ordered the invasion of Iraq. As president, Bush maintained an aggressive legislative agenda—No Child Left Behind (that is, education reform), Medicare, Social Security, and other proposed domestic reforms. In other words, his two terms comprised a busy eight years in office, yet he visited Mississippi regularly on behalf of Republican candidates and to assure the thousands victimized by a devastating hurricane that the federal government was aware of and attending to their needs.

What motivated George W. Bush to spend so much time in a state that is home to less than 1 percent of the nation's citizens is not fully clear, but there are a few reasons that are obvious. First of all, Mississippians voted in his favor by comfortable margins in both of his presidential elections; thus he was visiting and listening to supporters. Second, a year-and-a-half into Bush's first term, Haley Barbour was elected governor of Mississippi, an office he held throughout the remainder of the Bush presidency.[1] Barbour was a familiar face among Republicans, having served as a political operative for Gerald Ford, Ronald Reagan, and George H. W. Bush; chairman of the Republican National Committee; and a cofounder of the lobbying group Barbour Griffith & Rogers, a firm that served the Washington interests of many large corporations with a history of support for the Republican policy platform. Bush and Barbour were close friends and political allies of long-standing, as the president often remarked during his visits. Finally, the frequency of Bush's references to the importance of a compassionate spirit leads unavoidably to the assumption that he was deeply affected by what he saw on Mississippi's Gulf Coast in the aftermath of the nation's most destructive hurricane.

Regardless of his motivations, Mississippians enjoyed more attention from George W. Bush than from any other president. As *Presidential Travel* author Richard J. Ellis points out, Bush was a president who was convinced of the importance of travel, as his on-the-road spending matched predecessor Bill Clinton's expenses of "well over a billion dollars."[2] Thus it was not unusual for him to board Air Force One for trips to those places he or his staff felt would dramatize his policy proposals, further his political agenda, or benefit from his attention to the needs of individuals and their communities.

There are two sections to this chapter, each of which offers information on visits by George W. Bush in chronological order within that section. The first is titled "Campaign and Policy Visits." The second is titled "Hurricane Katrina Visits." This will illustrate the disproportionate balance of time in favor of the president's engagement with disaster recovery efforts. It also allows the reader to better follow themes and emphases in the president's messages.

Campaign and Policy Visits

Campaign trips require particular creativity when it comes to funding, and political parties expect to pay for the costs associated with campaigning. As Ellis relates, this can require walking a fine line: "Campaign travel, according to the Federal Election Commission, includes soliciting, making, or accepting contributions, and expressly advocating the election or defeat of a candidate.... [However,] the rules permit some costs to be shared if the trip has purposes that are not campaign-related." Thus trip planners schedule both campaign and noncampaign stops to allow a sharing of the costs between federal and campaign accounts. For example, "when [President Bush] went to Louisville in February [2004] for a mid-day fund-raiser he first stopped by a local plastic pipe company to participate in what the White House billed as a 'conversation on the economy.'"[3]

This cost-sharing approach explained many of the multipurpose trips President Bush took in the category of "Campaign and Policy Visits." President Bush's staff recognized funding opportunities, and just as administrations before them did, they scheduled trips that included both political and official events. This strategy was obvious and clearly illustrated by several of the presidential visits to Mississippi summarized in this first section of this chapter.

August 7, 2002—Madison and Jackson

Using the financing tactic of coordinating travel expenses, the White House staff planned Bush's first visit to Mississippi as a sitting president. After Air Force One arrived in Jackson, Bush followed a busy schedule that included both political and official events. Everywhere he went, he encountered crowds eager to greet him.

First on the agenda was a brief meeting between Bush and a group of physicians interested in tort reforms to limit damages awarded for alleged medical malpractice or other injury through the civil justice system. In later public remarks during the visit, Bush characterized the physicians at this initial meeting as "the kindest, most decent doctors you can possibly imagine ... people who love their communities, love their profession, [who] are deeply concerned about the future of medicine in this state."[4] Thus, among other emphases, the Mississippi visit became an opportunity for the president to use his public pulpit in the service of humanizing Republican efforts at tort reform. He also established the matter as a federal concern that the US Congress should address because of what Republicans saw as runaway spending on Medicare, Medicaid, and the system of veterans' hospitals.

It was midmorning when the president gave his major address of the trip at Madison Central High School. The next day's *Clarion-Ledger* reported that "scarcely an hour after its doors opened at 8:30 a.m., the gymnasium at Madison Central brimmed at capacity, as an eager crowd of about 2,300 awaited the guest of honor. . . . Never mind the long wait. They greeted him when he walked in at 10:44 a.m. with homemade placards, American flags, and Mississippi hospitality."[5]

At the high school, Bush spoke to representatives from the business community about issues of economic growth and security, while providing a first-person lesson in civics to students. He spoke about what he termed "three important goals for our country." The first was to win the war on terror, the second was to protect the homeland, and the third was to "make it clear that we will not rest until we have economic security for everybody who lives in America."[6]

Characterizing security as "my most important job as the president," Bush assured his audience that he and "a lot of fine folks" were doing everything humanly possible to ensure their protection from "an enemy that hates freedom and therefore hates America." He promoted his proposal for a Department of Homeland Security that would gather under one administrative umbrella more than 100 different federal agencies concerned with national security.

This was a pivotal emphasis for the president. Within three months of Bush's visit to Madison High School, this new cabinet-level department became a reality. Likewise, he warned in his speech to Mississippians, "There are countries which harbor and develop weapons of mass destruction . . . and we owe it to our children to deal with these threats." The United States invaded Iraq based on precisely this rationale—later shown to be inaccurate—on March 20, 2003, barely more than half a year after the Madison High School address.

For the businesspeople present in the public school auditorium, the president assured efforts "to build the economics—the foundations for economic security for our people." He was proud to report that the economy grew, inflation remained low, and worker productivity increased. However, he also had a message for blue collar America: "Listen, so long as anybody is looking for work and can't find work, I think we've got a problem." In turn, he touted his recent efforts with Congress to engineer a "significant tax reduction on behalf of the American people."

Finally, in the Madison High School remarks, the president took the role of spiritual-adviser-in-chief. He encouraged, "Love your neighbor. If you want to help, mentor a child. If you want to help, go see a shut-in and tell them you love them. If you want to help, feed the hungry. . . . You see, America can be saved one heart, one soul, one conscience at a time." This was the first instance, but by no means the last, of George W. Bush using Christian imagery or language in his speeches during presidential visits to Mississippi.

When the president concluded the event at Madison High School, he pro-
ceeded to a luncheon gathering in Jackson at the Hilton Hotel. Mississippi's
Republican Party faithful had gathered at a $1,000-a-plate event intended to
raise funds for the campaign treasury of US representative Chip Pickering.
He was running for the corresponding seat in the recently realigned Third
Congressional District against another incumbent from the US House of
Representatives, Democrat Ronnie Shows. The two had to compete against
one another because of a reapportionment in 2000 that allotted Mississippi
four congressional districts versus the five that were in place since 1960. It was
the first time that the state had fewer than five districts since the Civil War.

Bush was direct about his purpose during his remarks: "You need to
send Chip Pickering back to the United States House of Representatives."
According to the president, Pickering supported spending for a strong military even before the September 11 attack on America by Al Qaida opera-
tives. Bush also reported that Pickering did the right thing by supporting:
the administration's education legislation—No Child Left Behind—which
required teacher accountability for student learning outcomes; the president's
program of tax cuts; and the proposal for tort reform. National security was
on Bush's mind as much in Jackson as in Madison, and he used many of the
same warnings and emphases in both addresses. However, his conclusion to
the Jackson address was different in that he described his hopes not in terms
tinged with religious references, characterizing them rather as a "cultural
change." In other words, he was using terminology first adopted for President
Nixon's Southern Strategy. Furthermore, Bush informed his audience that
he was seeing a shift away from an American culture of self-centeredness to
one of "serving something other than yourself."[7]

When the *Clarion-Ledger* ran its story on August 6 about Bush's visit on
the following day, there was a backstory prediction that the election outcome
between Pickering and his opponent would be a close one. The newspaper
also reported that the president would do more than help with an address
at the fund-raising luncheon: "Mississippi's Republican Party Chairman . . .
said Monday that Bush will attend a smaller $25,000-a-ticket fund-raiser
for the party at an undisclosed time and place. The money will go toward
get-out-the-vote efforts and compiling telephone numbers and voter lists."[8]
Given that Pickering won what was forecast to be a tight election with nearly
64 percent of the vote, it appeared that either the presidential visit gave a
tremendous boost to the Republican candidate or the campaign raised the
specter of a close contest to sweeten fund-raising results.

Regardless, the same edition of the *Clarion-Ledger* offered this edito-
rial comment: "All politics aside, a presidential visit is a special event for

Mississippi and the state welcomes President Bush."⁹ This was an important point to underscore, namely, that despite a campaign agenda compelling a president to travel to Mississippi or any other state, the opportunities the visit offered were important and could not be ignored. On the morning of the presidential visit, *Clarion-Ledger* perspective editor Sid Salter evidenced his understanding of this principle. Directly addressing the president in a column that day, Salter wrote, "As Mississippians, we are so proud of the changes that we have made in our state over the last three decades. . . . Poverty and insularity aren't as visible these days, but when you step to the microphones at the modern, gleaming Madison Central High School this morning you'll still be standing in the poorest state in the union. . . . We need your support to keep federal dollars flowing. . . . The majority of Mississippians gave you their vote in 2000 and appear ready to repeat that commitment in 2004. . . . Mississippi has consistently been Bush country. . . . Our state continues to need your help, Mr. President. . . . That's a lot to ask from a morning's visit. But then again, you're the chief."¹⁰

Clearly, the media understood the significance of a presidential visit, and the public was excited to welcome George W. Bush for his first trip as president to Mississippi. Republican Party leaders were also pleased: "By the end of Wednesday, Chip Pickering had flown on Air Force One, stood next to President Bush to face hundreds of applauding fans, raised at least half a million dollars, and breezed through a $25,000-a-ticket state Republican Party fund-raiser likely to yield another substantial chunk of money for the junior congressman's campaign."¹¹

September 12, 2003—Jackson

When Bush returned for his second visit to Mississippi slightly more than one year after the first, the nation was languishing in the shadow of the events of September 11, 2001, and there was uncertainty about the outcomes of the resulting conflicts in Iraq and Afghanistan. The Ba'athist government in Iraq collapsed in April 2003, but Saddam Hussein, formerly the president, was still at large. According to the Bush administration, fear of Iraqi weapons of mass destruction was a major reason for the US invasion of that country, but such weapons seemed nowhere to be found. President Bush saw his approval rating among the American people fall from a high around 90 percent into a range closer to half that percentage.

Despite his political woes, Bush traveled to Mississippi to campaign for a friend, Haley Barbour, who was running for governor. It was a solidly Republican state generally supportive of the Bush administration in both good and bad times. According to a *Clarion-Ledger* story previewing his arrival, "As [Bush] touches down in Jackson today for a Haley Barbour fund-raising luncheon, there will undoubtedly be the usual cheering crowds and flag-waving fans. And in a conservative state that hasn't voted for a Democratic president since Jimmy Carter in 1976, there might not be much indication his poll numbers have slipped at all."[12] Indeed, Mississippi was welcoming, and Haley Barbour's candidacy was important enough to old friends that three months before this Bush visit, Vice President Dick Cheney appeared on the state's Gulf Coast to address another fund-raising event for Barbour.[13]

On this day, however, it was Bush who addressed a largely supportive crowd at a luncheon that filled the Mississippi Coliseum in Jackson. He began with an endorsement: "If [Mississippians] are interested in good government . . . they need to elect Haley Barbour." And he repeated the campaign's slogan: "Mississippi can do better." From that point forward, many of the domestic policy themes of the Bush speech were his standard fare: if anyone is looking for a job, there is a problem with the economy; tort reform is critical; schools must build on the proposition that every child can learn. Predictably, the president defended the decision to invade Iraq on the basis of an attack suffered by the United States, perpetrated by "coldblooded killers who took our own assets and flew them into buildings." However, he undergirded the defense with a nod to the divine: "Freedom is not America's gift to the world; it is the Almighty's gift to every individual in the world." This gave tacit authority for a mission: "It's so important in the heart of the Middle East that we establish a free society in Iraq."

At that point, Bush returned to his strong endorsement of his friend Haley Barbour, adding the twist that he was "a fellow that when he picks up the phone, the president might just go ahead and answer it."[14] Though President Bush intended this remark as humor, the close relationship between Barbour and Bush became obvious during the months and years of Mississippi's recovery from Hurricane Katrina.

By all appearances, this presidential visit was successful. Journalists reported that the Bush visit generated more than $1.2 million for the Barbour gubernatorial campaign. In return, Barbour praised the president: "As governor, George Bush accomplished in Texas what I want to help accomplish in Mississippi. . . . He defeated a liberal Democrat, put a brake on out-of-control spending, passed serious tort reform, and cracked down on crime. He didn't raise taxes, and he improved the results in education for Texas children."[15]

November 1, 2003—Southaven and Gulfport

Just a few weeks after the campaign visit to Jackson, Bush once again traveled to Mississippi to promote the gubernatorial candidacy of Haley Barbour. This visit bracketed the state north and south with stops in Southaven and Gulfport. As part of the greater Memphis metropolitan area, DeSoto County was the most populous of the northern tier counties in Mississippi. Southaven was the county's largest city, and thus provided a visible setting for the president's visit on behalf of his longtime friend. This was the first visit any US president made to the community, and 10,000 people jammed the DeSoto Civic Center, a large sports and event facility. In fact, by 6:00 a.m.— or nearly four hours prior to the president's scheduled arrival—there were already 3,000 persons in line for the rally.[16]

Referring to Barbour as "the next governor of the state of Mississippi," Bush recalled that his friend had a history in Washington, DC: "He used to run in high circles. I guess in this part of the world, you say he used to pick high cotton." Regardless of this out-of-state success, the president declared, Barbour always "loved to talk about Mississippi," and he "will relate to people from all walks of life." Furthermore, the state would benefit from the prospective governor's "positive view for every single citizen" and his "good values." These included honoring his family, treasuring his relationship with the Almighty, believing in hard work, and recognizing that everyone has worth.

President Bush was proud to report that he and Haley Barbour shared "the same philosophy," and that meant managing a budget and using taxpayer money wisely. Furthermore, the president recalled those times that Barbour—presumably in his role as a Washington lobbyist—"was strong by my side" as Congress considered and passed tax cut legislation. Bush replayed his familiar domestic themes of tort reform and educating every child in the address, and he spoke of the need to "hunt down the enemy," as the search for Saddam Hussein in Iraq continued. "With the advance of human freedom," the president assured the crowd, "the world will be more peaceful and America will be more secure."[17]

Republicans and other attendees from the north Mississippi suburbs of Memphis enthusiastically applauded Bush's speech in Southaven, and after he concluded his appearance, the local campaign organization sent supporters out in buses, vans, and cars to donate an afternoon distributing literature. "By election day, a Barbour volunteer had knocked on nearly every door in the county." This strategy of intensive effort to turn out voters for the Republican candidate was termed the "Seventy-Two Hour Program." A presidential visit and the widespread canvassing paid off for Barbour, who won the DeSoto County with a vote total more than twice that of his Democratic opponent, the incumbent governor, Ronnie Musgrove.[18]

There was a strange occurrence as the president was leaving the civic center. A woman who worked locally as a health care aide, driving with her three children, broke through a barrier and rammed into the facility where Bush delivered his speech. Though police and sheriff's deputies pursued her after she went through the security perimeter, they were unable to apprehend her before she crashed her car. She passed the president's motorcade and jumped a curb before she hit the building. Media reported that there was no evidence the incident was anything but coincidental—no obvious intent to do harm, no weapons, and no health or substance abuse issues.[19]

Having the availability of Air Force One meant that President Bush left the morning rally in Southaven bound not for his scheduled evening appearance in Gulfport—a trip of more than 350 miles—but for Kentucky, where he spoke just before 1:00 p.m. Central Time at the Paducah airport and at 5:00 p.m. Eastern Time at the airport in London. Both of these events were in support of Ernie Fletcher, that state's Republican gubernatorial candidate. It was, after all, less than three days before the polls opened for the fall election.

Finally, the president reboarded Air Force One for his trip back to Mississippi, and he headed for another rally promoting Haley Barbour, this one at 7:00 p.m. Central Time on the coast in Gulfport's Jones Park. The coast's newspaper, the *Sun Herald*, wrote: "[It was] a two-hour campaign rally that included a surprise appearance by Southern-fried rockers Lynyrd Skynyrd. The rally resembled a rock concert at times, except for the armed guards atop protective shields of Dole banana trucks....

"Earlier this year, Bush appeared at a $1,000-a-plate private fund-raiser for Barbour to infuse the campaign with cash. But on Saturday his goal was to provide psychological income to the Barbour campaign, stir the masses, and turn out the vote on Tuesday."[20]

Reports put the crowd size in Gulfport at 4,000. They heard President Bush announce, yet again, that "the right man to be the governor of Mississippi is Haley Barbour." He thanked everyone in attendance—"particularly... the Lynryd Skynyrd Band"—and he urged each voter to meet his or her "obligation to go to the polls ... and to ask friends and neighbors to go to the polls as well." Launching into the meat of the speech, Bush said, "It's important to have the right platform when you're running for governor." This was his lead to repeat the domestic policy and national security themes he had addressed at Southaven. He concluded: "Mississippi can do better, and Haley Barbour will lead Mississippi to that day."[21]

At the end of his long day of four campaign speeches—two each in Kentucky and Mississippi—President Bush boarded Air Force One for a flight to his ranch near Crawford, Texas, a property known during his time in office as the Western White House. Three days later Republican Haley Barbour won the Mississippi governor's office with nearly 53 percent of the vote. On the same election day, Republican Ernie Fletcher won the governor's office in Kentucky.

May 3, 2005—Canton

This was the announcement on the day of the event from the *Jackson Free Press*: "George W. Bush will speak today around noon at the Nissan plant in Canton, Mississippi, where he's expected to address 'fixing the hole in the safety net' of Social Security."[22] *USA Today* reported the backstory: "President Bush said Tuesday that he'll keep campaigning for an overhaul of Social Security despite opposition, and he intensified pressure on reluctant members of Congress to do something to avert big tax increases or cuts in benefits."

The president and other key members of the administration had undertaken what was described as a "Social Security sales blitz" for two months, but their efforts had won few, if any, of the needed Democratic votes in Congress. There were even objections from some Republican leaders, likely because national polling showed that more than half of all Americans disapproved of Bush's proposed changes, which would have affected initial benefit calculations for nearly all workers.[23]

When he arrived around midday at the Nissan plant, nearly 2,200 workers gathered to hear what the president had to say. After introductory compliments to the "highly skilled workforce" at the facility and nods to the dignitaries in attendance, Bush turned his attention to the subject at hand, namely, the reform of Social Security. He said, "The job of a president is to confront problems and not pass them on." Before outlining the problems with Social Security, he was careful to assure current retirees that nothing would change for them. He recognized that Franklin Roosevelt's role in establishing Social

Security had "meant a lot to a lot of people," but he warned of approaching stresses to the system owing to the growing number of retirees beginning with the baby boomer generation. Coupling that population growth with the longer life expectancies of the twenty-first century would mean "a lot of benefits" with fewer "paying into the system," which he described as "pay-as-you-go." According to the calculations upon which he based his reform proposals, Bush told the Nissan workers and other guests that by the year 2041, these stresses would bankrupt the Social Security system. Furthermore, he warned that failure to enact timely reform would mean "a massive tax hike or a 30-percent benefit cut" in the future.

President Bush told the audience that his proposal to correct the problems offered each Social Security participant the opportunity to set up what he termed "a personal savings account." Under the plan, individuals controlled the use of these dollars for investments, which the president suggested would grow at two or more times the rate of government investments, and private ownership of each account meant value passed on to succeeding generations. At this point in his address, Bush introduced a panel of individuals—some of whom had traveled to Mississippi with him and others from within the state—who dialogued with him and offered expertise or testimonials on personal experiences with retirement accounts. Of course, every member of the handpicked panel supported the soundness of the president's proposal for Social Security reform.

In conclusion, the president said, "We have an obligation and a duty to fix this. . . . And I'm going to continue talking to the younger people of America and say that we're going to be wise about how we fix the system. . . . We've got a great opportunity here to show the American people that Washington isn't all politics, that Washington has got the capacity to rise above partisan bickering and solve an important problem once and for all."[24]

Though President Bush and his key advisers spent a great deal of time and political capital promoting their solution to problems they predicted for Social Security, the proposals eventually went nowhere. In a retrospective analysis of these reform efforts, William A. Galston, a senior fellow at the Brookings Institution, wrote that President Bush embarked on "tours crammed with events at which he pitched his plan to the people. . . . [However,] within weeks, observers noticed that the more the president talked about Social Security, the more support for his plan declined. . . . After Hurricane Katrina inundated what remained of the president's support, congressional leadership quietly pulled the plug. By October, even the president had to acknowledge that his effort had failed."[25]

July 1, 2008—Jackson

President Bush's trip to Jackson on July 1, 2008, was his only other visit to Mississippi not scheduled to address the state's recovery from the devastation of Hurricane Katrina, and it was his one remaining stop that was not in a community located on or near the Gulf Coast. In the overall chronology of his travels to Mississippi, this trip to promote a Republican candidate was the eighteenth of nineteen presidential visits. Thirteen of the president's fourteen Katrina-related visits occurred between the stop in Canton profiled in the above paragraphs and this visit to Jackson.

This comment from the *Clarion-Ledger*'s report on the trip neatly summed up the importance of presidential campaign visits: "President Bush's appearance in Jackson on Tuesday helped Republican Senator Roger Wicker secure more money in one lunch than his political opponent raised from January through March."[26] Wicker held the Senate seat beginning on December 31, 2007, when Governor Haley Barbour appointed him upon the resignation of Senator Trent Lott. The special election to fill the seat—scheduled for November 4, 2008—pitted Wicker against Ronnie Musgrove, who was formerly Mississippi's Democratic governor and Barbour's immediate predecessor.

Mississippi's Republican Party used the time-honored format for this event, namely, the $1,000-a-ticket luncheon. Five hundred people came to see the president during his midday, two-hour stop in Jackson. Though the crowd was sizable, a home in the city's Eastover subdivision provided a host site for the event, and the private venue meant that only invitees attended. There were no media representatives allowed, and the public got only glimpses of the president as his motorcade passed through the community. The *Clarion-Ledger* reported that despite the president's low approval rating during this period of his second term, "people lined the roads." Though it was unclear whether the president gave an extended speech or simply made a few comments at the event, journalists reported that "many of those who attended spoke highly of the president's remarks."[27]

When the dust settled in November from the contest between Wicker and Musgrove, Republicans retained the Senate seat. Wicker received nearly 55 percent of the vote.

One final observation from this visit to Jackson related to the earlier mention of cost-sharing for campaign travel. White House staff often partner noncampaign events with those having purely political purposes to justify charging a portion of the costs of such trips to federal budgets. Coverage of this mid-2008 visit by the *Clarion-Ledger* included two photographs that suggest this funding strategy was in play. The first shows President Bush waving with his arm around a woman identified as Cameron Fox of Clinton, a mental health counselor for the American Red Cross. According to the caption, during his visit Bush presented her the President's Volunteer Service Award.[28] The second photograph shows an assembly of the Mississippi Air National Guard with the president passing to review and greet the uniformed members of the military unit.[29]

Hurricane Katrina Visits

Hurricane Katrina formed in the Atlantic Ocean in late August 2005, and as the likely path to landfall became known, most residents of Gulf Coast communities evacuated. It came ashore on August 29 as a Category Three storm (Saffir-Simpson Hurricane Scale) with sustained winds in the range of 125 miles per hour, bringing devastation to a 400-mile stretch of coastline. In the history of the United States, it was neither the strongest storm defined by wind velocity nor the deadliest hurricane in terms of American lives lost,[30] yet it was seen at the time as America's worst weather-related disaster. Less than one month later, an even stronger storm, Hurricane Rita, raged through the Gulf of Mexico. It struck only a glancing blow on the Mississippi coast, but the damage added to the earlier misery. Katrina's destructive effects alone, throughout the Gulf Coast states, were calculated at more than $100 billion.[31]

Persistent and life-threatening suffering for many residents in New Orleans in the aftermath of the storms, owing most of all to the flooding and transportation interruptions, became the focus of media attention. Tens of thousands required rescue by the Coast Guard. Equally large numbers were sick, starving, and stranded either in the Superdome, the indoor stadium where the New Orleans Saints played football, or at the city's Ernest N. Morial Convention Center with almost three million square feet of floor space. Local and state officials looked to the federal government for relief, but there was no immediately available plan or apparent likelihood that the Bush administration would develop a meaningful response in the foreseeable future. Criticism of the president and those who reported to him grew steadily, as the public outrage fed on a widespread belief that Bush had little understanding of the magnitude of the crisis. Unquestionably, the slow and confused federal response to Hurricane Katrina was a low point of the Bush presidency.[32]

Assessing whether President Bush and other federal officials fairly measured the situation and reacted appropriately is beyond the scope of this book; however, the fact that he made fourteen visits to communities on Mississippi's Gulf Coast in the three years of his presidency after August 2005 is notable. Never had the state received such concentrated attention from a president, and his addresses and interviews indicated clearly that he knew Mississippians were suffering no less than the citizens of Louisiana, though the national media remained largely focused on the woes of New Orleans and its surrounding parishes.

When the first of Bush's Katrina visits was imminent—four days after the hurricane's landfall—the front page of the *Sun Herald*, a newspaper serving the residents of Mississippi's Gulf Coast, ran this headline: "Help Trickles In." It was followed by this subhead: "Frustration Mounting as Agencies become Overwhelmed." There was a large photograph running across the page and down to the fold of desperate Gulf Coast residents who waited hours for ice and water at an aid station.

The article minced no words reporting the desperation and suffering. The journalists referred to the affected citizens as "the beleaguered," described long lines awaiting meager help from outside the region, and spoke of the rising death toll. Images were apocalyptic: "Officials feared a massive public health crisis from poor sanitary conditions, including tons of spoiling shrimp and chicken strewn through neighborhood streets."

While the stories in the *Sun Herald* noted that President Bush had asked Congress for $10.5 billion in federal aid on the eve of his announced visit to the coast, those witnessing the devastation firsthand knew that it was "the Federal Emergency Management trucks full of ice, bottled water, and prepared food that most victims of Hurricane Katrina want[ed] to see." There were instances of victims shouting thanks to God at some distribution points, while at other locations soldiers of the National Guard had to control those so desperate that they rushed workers bringing relief supplies. Against this backdrop, Bush planned to survey the destruction by helicopter—first in Mobile, Alabama—dropping to land in Mississippi for a visit in Biloxi.[33]

Republican officeholders understood the need to address the public's concerns about a slow federal response: "The expected arrival of President George W. Bush on Air Force One in Mobile today will be a powerful message to Gulf Coast residents that the full force of the United States government is coming to their aid," said US senator Trent Lott, and he continued, "When the president comes, it's not about him. It's about reassurances to the people."

Lott remembered in his conversation with journalists that the 1969 visit of President Richard Nixon in the aftermath of Hurricane Camille brought hope. The senator, too, needed hope in the wake of Katrina because he lost his home to the hurricane, and he wiped away tears when asked about the loss. "'We've been through a lot,' he said. 'We get knocked down. We do get up.'"[34]

Each of President Bush's Katrina visits to Mississippi received media attention, but the coverage was uneven depending upon the situation and latest developments in the recovery process. Throughout the course of fourteen hurricane-related visits over three years, Bush continually pointed to the effective leadership of his friend Governor Haley Barbour as a principal reason for hope, and he reiterated time and again that his long-standing relationship with the governor prompted his attention to Mississippi's needs. What follows is a chronological list of the dates and places of President Bush's Katrina visits to the state. The entries include information on the context of each visit and brief summaries of the president's remarks and/or interview responses that allow tracking the developments throughout the first three years of the recovery. When Bush visited Biloxi on January 12, 2006, he gave an extended address that provided a summary of federal recovery efforts and offered a defense of his administration's response. That proved to be the most significant of President Bush's Katrina speeches, and Appendix A of this volume includes a verbatim presentation of the address.

September 2, 2005—Biloxi

During his first visit to Mississippi on the fifth day following the landfall of Hurricane Katrina, President Bush took a walking tour of the devastated areas in Biloxi, and shortly after 12:00 p.m., he made remarks and answered journalists' questions. He said to the assembly of relief workers and storm victims that not only was he shocked by the devastation, but he was also inspired by the "spirit here in Mississippi." Among the anecdotes Bush recalled was that of a man standing in the rubble of his childhood home who assured the president that he was doing well because both his mother and he were alive. As he would do in nearly every speech in Mississippi during the years of recovery from Katrina, Bush praised the strong leadership of Governor Barbour, who "set some clear parameters and has followed through on helping calm everybody's nerves."

Bush built a portion of his remarks around the logical scheme of recovery: save lives; stabilize the situation; and mobilize the distribution of water, food, and medicine. His encouragement to the "lots of folks in America that want to help" was to give cash to the Salvation Army and to the Red

Cross, groups that he termed "the armies of compassion." Then there was
a presidential announcement of the "first down payment" of support for
the relief efforts, $10.5 billion, that was in a special bill passed by Congress
and that the president promised to sign immediately. Furthermore, Bush
promised "that out of this rubble is going to come a new Biloxi, Mississippi,"
though he acknowledged that it was "hard to envision it" at that moment.
After making relatively brief remarks and responding to a few questions
from journalists, Bush concluded his visit with thanks to the mayor of Biloxi
for his hospitality.[35]

September 5, 2005—Poplarville

Just three days after his first trip to the hurricane-ravaged Gulf Coast,
President Bush was back in Mississippi for a visit to Poplarville, where he;
his wife, Laura; and Governor Haley Barbour visited with residents. During
the middle of the afternoon, the president and the governor joined several other Mississippi state officials in a meeting at Pearl River Community
College to discuss hurricane relief. Bush was also shown in a photograph
by the *Hattiesburg American* visiting with a crew from the Alabama Power
Company who were in Poplarville helping to restore electrical service.[36]

Records of the president's remarks from the meeting with state officials
are incomplete, but the verbatim portion that survives shows that, once
again, the need for hopeful leadership was very much on Bush's mind. He
said, "Out of this despair is going to come a vibrant coast.... I can't wait to
join you in the joy of welcoming neighbors back into neighborhoods, and
small businesses up and running, and cutting those ribbons that somebody
is creating new jobs. That's what I think is going to happen." He went on
to solicit God's blessings for everyone, and he assured his audience that
federal commitments were for the long term. He ended with these words:
"I understand the damage. I understand the devastation. I understand the
destruction. I understand how long it's going to take. And we're with you.
That's what I want you to know."[37]

September 12, 2005—Gulfport

One week after the visit to Poplarville, President Bush was back in Mississippi.
This time the site of the visit was Gulfport, where he spoke and answered

questions from media representatives in the early afternoon at the Twenty-Eighth Street Elementary School.

On the previous evening, the president flew to New Orleans, and he spent the night aboard a naval vessel, the USS *Iwo Jima*, an amphibious assault ship docked along the city's riverfront that was serving as a command center for recovery efforts. New Orleans flooded when Katrina's fury broke levies, and on September 12 the pumps continued to work on draining the 40 percent of the metro area still under water. Bush toured the city early on that day, while at the same time back in Washington, DC, his appointed head of the Federal Emergency Management Agency (FEMA), Michael D. Brown, resigned after weathering a hailstorm of criticism regarding his handling of the crisis. Bush himself was the target of many accusations of both mismanagement and racism because media reported that the suffering of the African American community in New Orleans was greater than that of other victims. Four military trucks traveling as a convoy provided transport for the president through the devastated neighborhoods.[38]

After his tour of New Orleans, the president flew to Gulfport before returning to Washington, DC. He began his remarks at the elementary school with an awkward compliment to the principal: "She said she lost her school and lost her house, but I told her, she hadn't lost her smile or her will to succeed." Bush noted that the Mexican government sent troops to work alongside US soldiers in recovery efforts. He also reported hearing from the district superintendent that the goal was to have students back in school by the end of October, a sign, he said, that "lives are starting over."

For the first time in Mississippi, the president used this address to establish the boundaries of responsibility for the recovery. This became a significant theme in the months to come. Bush said, "As these communities are rebuilt, they're going to be rebuilt by people from Mississippi. As the coast is replanned and the vision of the coast emerges, it's going to be planned by the people of Mississippi. The role of the people in Washington is to support the governors and support the congressmen." Thus he established limits both as to the expectations and duties of the federal government in the recovery, as well as to his administration's overarching commitment to state and local control over the planning for redevelopment and the actual work of rebuilding.

President Bush took several questions from regional and national journalists following his remarks in Gulfport. Topics of the questions ranged from the resignation of the FEMA director to specific issues regarding funding for rebuilding and insurance details. There was also one question regarding the time required of the president for both hurricane recovery and foreign policy concerns, especially in view of the continuing entanglements in Iraq. Bush responded, "I can do more than one thing at one time."[39]

September 15, 2005—Pascagoula

One of the critical issues of hurricane recovery for the Gulf Coast was restoring access to refined petroleum-based fuels. President Bush's fourth visit to the Mississippi coast following Katrina was to the Chevron refining facility in Pascagoula, where he met for afternoon discussions with Jeet Bindra, Chevron's global refinery president, and Roland Kell, manager of the company's Pascagoula operations. Damages to the facility meant that Chevron was importing refined products to the plant for distribution, rather than refining locally and exporting for use throughout the southeastern states. While at the facility, Bush—traveling with Governor Haley Barbour and Senator Trent Lott—met with regional mayors and business leaders from three Mississippi Gulf Coast counties, Jackson, Harrison, and Hancock. Conversations with the group were termed "frank," and one mayor said that Bush "expressed his remorse and disappointment for the government's tardiness in addressing the problems."[40]

The president made no public remarks during this visit. However, following his stop in Pascagoula, he traveled to New Orleans, where he stood framed by Jackson Square for a televised evening address to the nation on the recovery from Hurricane Katrina.[41]

September 20, 2005—Gulfport

"Every time I come back here, I see progress," said President Bush, as he returned to Gulfport just five days after his last visit to the Gulf Coast. "You know, sometimes when you're so close to the situation, it's hard to really see noticeable change. But this part of the country is changing. You're moving forward."[42]

Governor Barbour named a Commission on Recovery, Rebuilding, and Renewal, and Mississippi businessman Jim Barksdale agreed to accept the governor's appointment to head the new commission. Barbour also invited President Bush to address the commission's meeting in Gulfport, and C-Span judged the event of sufficient national interest to telecast the arrival of the president on Air Force One.[43] Following the 11:00 a.m. meeting in

Mississippi, Bush flew to New Orleans for an update on that city's recovery from Hurricane Katrina. The president spoke in Gulfport at 11:35 a.m., addressing the governor's commission in a tent erected for the occasion at the Prime Outlets Mall.

Recalling what he had announced just a few days earlier in Gulfport, Bush emphasized that Mississippians would create and lead the recovery plan, not federal officials. After yet again praising the state's "can-do spirit," the president said, "You really don't want the federal government telling you how to rebuild. . . . You want a partner, not somebody who is going to tell you what the strategy ought to be." He directed the group's attention beyond the public frustration with slow debris removal and toward the importance of planning for the restoration of the infrastructure, that is, the bridges and highways. Furthermore, he pledged federal help with "plowing through the paperwork requirements as fast as possible so that we can reduce the frustration to you." Then he returned to his primary theme for the commission: "We want the Mississippi people to lay out the Mississippi vision about what this important part of the world is going to look like." And he assured everyone: "We look forward to hearing your vision, so we can better do our job."[44]

October 11, 2005—Pass Christian

About a month and a half after the storm, President Bush visited DeLisle Elementary School in Pass Christian. He made remarks at 11:00 a.m. to journalists and others who accompanied him on the visit. Secretary of Education Margaret Spellings made the trip with the president, as did First Lady Laura Bush, whose civic efforts often focused on the education of children. On the front page of the next day's *Sun Herald* was the headline, "Bush Witnesses Spirit of Rebuilding," but the principal focus of the front page article was on Mississippi's First Lady, Marsha Barbour, and her efforts on behalf of recovery.[45]

President Bush's brief public remarks at the elementary school in Pass Christian were uniquely targeted to education. They provided a slightly different dimension to the previous discussions of hurricane recovery, and thus they are presented here in their entirety:

"Listen, first I want to thank the superintendent for inviting us here. The schools of Pass Christian are blue ribbon schools. And they have been blue ribbon schools before, and they'll be blue ribbon schools in the future.

Part of the health of a community is to have a school system that's vibrant and alive. And in spite of the fact that a lot of equipment was damaged and homes destroyed and teachers without places to live and—this school district is strong, and it's coming back. It's a sign that out of the rubble here on the Gulf Coast of Mississippi is a rebuilding, is a spirit of rebuilding.

"Thank you all for having us. I want to thank the principals and teachers for understanding the quality of education—the quality of the education in a community helps define the nature of the community. And one of the things that's interesting is the high school principal told Laura and me that the—and Madam Secretary—that the high school was deemed to be a blue ribbon high school after Katrina hit. And yet a lot of the students don't know that yet. And so when the high school comes back next Monday, the first thing the principal is going to tell them is that the school that they go to, even though the building is different—the buildings are different—is a blue ribbon high school.

"And the superintendent says, blue ribbon high school last year, this year, and next year. And I appreciate your spirit. Thanks for letting us come by.

"Thank you all. Bye-bye. Good to meet you."[46]

January 12, 2006—Bay St. Louis

President Bush used this visit to Mississippi to offer an extensive accounting of Katrina recovery efforts and a defense of his administration's response. It served as his most comprehensive report on actions of the federal government partnering with local and state governments. Bush spoke at 1:45 p.m. on the campus of St. Stanislaus College in Bay St. Louis, a Roman Catholic academy for male students from grades seven through twelve. The institution's facilities sustained extensive damage during Hurricane Katrina.

Because of the significance and the comprehensive nature of the president's address in Biloxi on this day about four-and-one-half months after the Katrina landfall, Appendix A contains the verbatim record. A sentence near the end of the speech summed Bush's theme: "And so we've done a lot, and there's a lot more to do, but there's a certain optimism and hope that's coming." Also, he was frank in saying, "Obviously, the federal response in parts of this devastated area could have been a lot better." Finally, he assured the region and the nation: "We learned some lessons about how to respond, and we're going to change."[47]

March 8, 2006—Gautier

President Bush paused at two locations while in Gautier. The first was at College Park Elementary School, where he made brief remarks over the lunch hour, referring to his education program, No Child Left Behind. The second was at a new home construction center, where he had a public interaction with Governor Barbour shortly after 1:00 p.m. There was no new information offered at the elementary school, but the president assured everyone that "Laura and I are committed to making sure no child is left behind anywhere in the United States of America."[48]

When Governor Barbour and the president interacted at the home building center, the governor led with thanks to Bush for an extension of the deadline to receive federal funding in support of debris removal and for the recent approval of Mississippi's plan for a homeowner grant program by the Department of Housing and Urban Development that would make $4 billion of Community Development Block Grant money available to the state's citizens. Bush replied: "I really didn't want the plan to be designed by Washington people; I wanted it to be designed by local folks. And Haley has put together a Mississippi plan. He not only put the plan together, but he also came to Washington, D.C., and helped get the plan funded—with the help of two fine United States senators."[49]

April 27, 2006—Biloxi

It was nearing eight full months since the Katrina landfall on Mississippi's Gulf Coast when President Bush made a short afternoon visit to Biloxi. He offered brief remarks first at the Hands-on Gulf Coast Civic Action Center at 3:17 p.m. and then at a BP gas station at 3:33 p.m. As he did on several previous trips to the region ravaged by Hurricanes Katrina and Rita, the president visited not only in Mississippi on this day but also in New Orleans, where he toured homes destroyed by flooding.

Bush spoke for only a moment at the Action Center, just long enough to underscore the compassion among neighbors that he saw during the recovery. He referred to it as a "compassion commune, where people are united by a singular purpose and setting a great example." He told everyone that volunteering would make them feel better and that there were always opportunities to make differences in the lives of others.[50]

While also brief, the president's remarks at the BP gas station had an entirely separate purpose within the context of another of his themes for the day. Ever-ascending gasoline prices were an issue, even as Exxon Mobil and ConocoPhillips announced profits in the billions of dollars. Bush used the visual of this setting in an area that demanded national attention to underscore his message on the nation's energy security. Also on this day, as the president made his remarks in Biloxi, Secretary of Transportation Norman Mineta wrote to congressional leaders supporting legislation for presidential authority to raise fuel economy standards on certain categories of vehicles.[51] Joining the chorus on April 27, officials from the nation's Big Three automobile companies—Ford, General Motors, and Chrysler—announced that they would be meeting with the president to discuss energy. As CNN reported: "The meeting comes at a time when the Bush administration is giving more attention to energy issues due to rising consumer anger over gasoline prices."[52]

President Bush said in Biloxi that paying higher prices for gasoline was "like a tax." He listed the solutions, as he saw them: "make sure nobody is getting cheated"; pass legislation encouraging the expansion of refining capacity in the United States; reduce dependency on foreign oil; and "make sure [light] trucks run on ethanol—and batteries that won't require gasoline." He also asked that Congress give him authority to raise the Corporate Average Fuel Economy (CAFE) standards, which he intended to use for light trucks.[53] Congress first adopted versions of these types of standards in the 1970s during the oil embargo placed on many Western nations by the Organization of Petroleum Exporting Countries (OPEC).

May 11, 2006—Biloxi

President Bush's next visit to Mississippi was for the purpose of speaking at the spring commencement of Mississippi Gulf Coast Community College.[54] This was the first time any sitting president addressed a community college commencement. As he introduced President Bush, the college's president, Willis Lott, said what many Mississippians were feeling about President Bush: "In the aftermath of Hurricane Katrina, we were encouraged by his presence, comforted by his compassion, and inspired by his leadership. . . . President Bush generated the resources that are critical to our recovery in south Mississippi. His presence today is a testimony to his enduring commitment in helping our communities heal and our people prosper against overwhelming odds."[55]

Recognizing that the commencement took place in a stadium still under repair from hurricane damage in a region where "too many lives have been shattered," President Bush said that he was "proud to stand before some of the most determined students at any college or university in America." He brought the campus community a message: "This nation honors your dedication." During his ten visits to Mississippi related to the recovery from Katrina's devastation—prior to and including the trip for this commencement event—Bush said he witnessed a "quiet, unyielding determination" and a "Mississippi spirit that sees hope in adversity." He listed accomplishments: the coastal population almost fully returned; more than 90 percent of the debris cleared; infrastructure repairs under way; homeowners rebuilding; and growth in job availability spurred by recovery projects. He labeled the ongoing work on the Gulf Coast "one of the largest rebuilding efforts the world has ever seen," and he urged the class of 2006 to use their creativity and talents in the service of the region's revitalization.[56]

August 28, 2006—Biloxi and Gulfport

In recognition of the first anniversary of Hurricane Katrina—landfall was August 29, 2005—president and Mrs. Bush, accompanied by Governor Barbour and US senators Trent Lott and Thad Cochran, visited Biloxi and Gulfport, stopping by neighborhoods where Bush first saw the destruction. He spoke at 12:30 p.m. at a luncheon meeting with community leaders in Biloxi, at 2:00 p.m. in a Biloxi neighborhood that was rebuilding, and at 3:30 p.m. at United States Marine, Inc., in Gulfport. The *Sun Herald* reported on the following day that "the Bushes spent much of the day here before departing in the late afternoon for New Orleans. They ate lunch at the Schooner Seafood Restaurant, a popular coast eatery reopened in downtown Biloxi after Katrina washed away both of the owner's restaurants at the city's eastern tip.... Inside [the restaurant], the president heard about issues coast residents are dealing with today: insurance, the need for affordable housing, and economic recovery."[57] Clearly, significant issues remained at the time of the first anniversary.

At the luncheon in Biloxi, President Bush commented on "how clean the beaches look, and that wasn't a given a year ago." He saw it as a hopeful sign, as he recalled the debris and garbage that cluttered those same beaches a year earlier. He assured his hearers that the federal government would not forget them and their needs as time passed, but he also reminded them that "the ultimate future for this region down here depends on the people of Mississippi."[58]

When the president and First Lady toured the same Biloxi neighborhood he saw a few days after the storm's landfall, Bush said, "It's amazing, isn't it? It's amazing what the world looked like then and what it looks like now." Recognizing what he termed "a sense of renewal," the president congratulated the local residents for their courage and perseverance. "There are still challenges," he empathized, "[but] I feel the quiet sense of determination that's going to shape the future of Mississippi." As he had at the luncheon, Bush expressed that federal commitment was firm through the completion of the Gulf Coast's recovery.

After his more personal remarks directed at local residents, the president chose this setting to make a one-year anniversary report on the recovery efforts, knowing that journalists traveling with him would give the message national visibility. Though much had been done toward recovery from the devastating hurricanes, as Bush reminded residents and his broader audience, there was still uncertainty, frustration, and anger. For example, Ray Suarez of Public Broadcasting's *News Hour* reported on this day from Biloxi: "Out of the $110 billion in federal funds approved by Congress to help rebuild the Gulf Coast, so far some $22 billion in aid has been allocated to the state of Mississippi. But much of the money has yet to be distributed. Some 35,000 Mississippi families are still living in FEMA trailers."[59]

However, the president was determined in his remarks to strike a chord of optimism. He characterized Katrina as "one of the strongest hurricanes to ever hit America," with "devastation and debris [that] were unimaginable." Mississippians were heroic in saving lives, and they were committed to rebuilding. Progress was significant. Federal support remained strong. Local and state officials set the directions for recovery. He said, "We all have roles to play." And he continued, "I'm here to thank you all for showing the country how to respond to natural disaster." There was presidential praise for the commission appointed by Governor Barbour: "You've got a sound strategy." Finally he expressed thanks to the thousands of volunteers and donors, or, as he called them, "the armies of compassion that conducted the millions of acts of kindness." It was there, the president said, that one could see "the true strength of the United States of America."[60]

President and Mrs. Bush, along with accompanying dignitaries, left Biloxi to travel the fifteen or so miles to Gulfport, where the party visited a high-performance boat manufacturing facility, United States Marine, Inc. Following his tour, President Bush made brief remarks and then took questions from journalists. In his opening comments, he highlighted the shortage of workers on the Gulf Coast, offering the encouragement that "if people are looking for work, they should come." Also, he made it clear that he knew there was more work to be done: "This is an anniversary, but it doesn't mean it ends. Frankly, it's the beginning of what is going to be a long recovery." During the time allowed for questions, a journalist asked how long the president anticipated it would be before the area was fully rebuilt. Bush responded, "I would say years, not months." Someone also asked whether the $110 billion appropriated for the recovery by Congress would be the end of the necessary spending. His answer was: "Hopefully that will work. Hopefully that's enough. . . . Mississippi's up and running. . . . The governor stepped up, and he put this fantastic commission together, and they developed a plan. Now that plan has been funded."[61]

March 1, 2007—Long Beach and Biloxi

As the disaster receded into history and the hard work of recovery became more and more of a routine for the people of Mississippi's Gulf Coast, the interval between presidential visits to the region lengthened. The visit of March 1, 2007, was slightly more than six months after the trip to mark the one-year anniversary. On this day, President Bush took a midmorning tour of five houses still being reconstructed in Long Beach, Mississippi, where he used the home of Cheryl and Ernie Woodward as a setting for brief remarks. Later in the morning, he met with elected officials and community leaders for forty-five minutes at the Biloxi City Hall, and at 11:40 a.m. he spoke to the group.

The Woodwards used federal grant funds to rebuild, and the president presented them with an American flag to hang outside of their home.[62] Standing on their front lawn, Bush recalled his first visit and the "piles of rubble" with "debris stacked upon debris." He said that it was hard for him to believe then that he would be able to visit a home one day: "I had trouble visualizing it." He spoke of the federal dollars and the state and local officials who facilitated the distribution of those funds, so that "today we are able to sit in the Woodwards' home." The common phrase, "Welcome to my home," had a "special ring to it on the Gulf Coast," he added. As always, the president offered assurance of continuing the federal commitment to the recovery, even as he congratulated "the good folks in this part of the country for their resilience."[63]

Mississippi's Democratic Party chose the backdrop of this presidential visit to the coast to issue a press release criticizing the federal bureaucracy and the "painfully long" recovery process that left behind "thousands of Mississippians [who] continue to live in FEMA trailers waiting for financial help to piece their lives back together." The press release accused President Bush of overlooking those residents—terming them "homeless"—and asking him how he would help the "people who continue to suffer one-and-a-half years after Hurricane Katrina struck our state." Also targeted for criticism by the Democratic Party was the Mississippi Development Authority (MDA), the state's economic development agency responsible for managing the federal grant funds for recovery. Though nearly 18,000 people applied, the press release said, MDA awarded just over 11,000 grants. The chairman of the Mississippi Democratic Party asked, "Why is this process taking so painfully long?"[64]

When he spoke in Biloxi to the leadership of the Gulf Coast communities, it is uncertain whether Bush knew of the press release of the Mississippi Democratic Party. However, he clearly heard the criticism that echoed throughout the Katrina-damaged states regarding the slowness and insufficiency of the federal response. Mixed into the Biloxi speech, along with his typical themes about Katrina recovery, was this acknowledgment: "One of the things I've heard loud and clear is that there's a continued frustration with the slowness of federal response at times." The president pledged that he and others working on recovery at the federal level would "do what the people expect us to do to respond to the needs of the people in Mississippi."[65] Also on March 1, the White House released an extensive document titled "Fact Sheet: Working with State and Local Leaders to Help Rebuild the Gulf Coast." The document enumerated in detail all the federal dollars—along with the various programs and other commitments—that went toward helping with Katrina recovery by that date.[66]

August 29, 2007—Bay St. Louis

On the second anniversary of Hurricane Katrina, President Bush visited what he referred to as "Ground Zero." He spoke in the early afternoon at Our Lady of the Gulf Parish Community Center at Bay St. Louis, and following the speech he traveled to New Orleans for more scheduled events related to hurricane recovery.

The drumbeats of criticism heralding what many considered federal mismanagement still sounded quite clearly in both Mississippi and Louisiana. Yet the president stuck to his recognizable Katrina themes: there was devastation, but the progress was remarkable; Governor Haley Barbour provided outstanding leadership; much work remained, but the federal government was there for the duration; and the recovery was a responsibility of local and statewide leaders with federal support.

Bush reminded everyone that the federal financial commitment was strong—$114 billion as of the second anniversary. As evidence of progress, he cited the rebuilding of the Bay St. Louis Bridge "in record time," and he reported that 31,000 families relocated from temporary housing into permanent homes. There was presidential praise for the relatively swift reopening of schools following the storm, and the president, once again, spoke positively of the "Mississippi spirit."[67]

August 20, 2008—Gulfport

Seven weeks after a visit to the state capital to campaign for Senator Roger Wicker (see the first section of this chapter) and one year after his last trip to the Gulf Coast, George W. Bush made his final Katrina visit as president to Mississippi in recognition of the hurricane's third anniversary. He had dinner with local leaders at Vrazel's Fine Foods in Gulfport and made remarks at 6:30 p.m. As was generally the case whenever Bush visited Mississippi, Governor Barbour was at his side. Though the president said in his brief comments that it was "not the farewell dinner," this visit to Gulfport turned out to be the last of his nineteen presidential trips to Mississippi. His second term ended five months later.

There were no new themes or messages in Bush's relatively brief address on this occasion. He brought with him US Marine general (Ret.) Doug O'Dell, whom he appointed as the Gulf Coast coordinator four months previously. The president said he wanted people to share any concerns with the general.

Bush seemed to be in a reflective mood, perhaps prompted by the approaching terminus of his presidency. He said, "I remember what it looked like right after the storm. I remember what it looked like in the first anniversary right after the storm. I remember what it looked like last year, governor." He shared his satisfaction that there was remarkable progress.

Yet he declared that he knew there were "still people wondering about their futures," and there were "other issues to deal with, like cleaning out some of the bureaucracy so that the housing issues can get solved quicker." All in all, he concluded that "things are better here on the Gulf Coast of Mississippi." Finally, there was one final presidential promise that the region would be "even better six months from now than it is today."[68]

★ ★ ★

When a US president travels to a state one or two times during that individual's term of office, there are observations to make—political and otherwise—that may help to interpret the significance of the visit(s). However, when the number of trips made to a particular state by a president totals more than the sum of all visits made by his or her immediate ten predecessors in the presidential office, one must search for reasons and a lesson or two to be learned. George W. Bush traveled nineteen times to Mississippi in his eight years as president; the men who served between the middle and end of the twentieth century—Harry Truman, whose term began in 1945, through Bill Clinton, whose term ended in 2001—visited the state a combined total of sixteen times.

Some reasons seem quite obvious for President Bush's frequent visits. First, Mississippi became a solidly Republican state during the last quarter of twentieth century, and it awarded Republican George W. Bush a near 20 percent majority of its votes in 2000 and 2004. Party leaders obviously wanted to reward that success and to cultivate its continuation. Also, when the president visited to promote his policies, he was reasonably assured of an enthusiastic reception. Second, there are precipitating events that demand presidential visits; in this case, it was the terrible devastation of Hurricane Katrina that brought Bush to Mississippi's Gulf Coast fourteen times between 2005 and 2008. Indeed, so connected to the event was the forty-third president that he accepted an invitation to return to Gulfport for a remembrance ceremony on the storm's tenth anniversary in 2015. Third, relationships matter in the affairs of states and the nation. Thus the longtime friendship and political alliance of President George W. Bush and Governor Haley Barbour not only added to the appeal of visiting Mississippi, but many observers both during the recovery and during its aftermath suggested that the close personal ties were a significant factor in Mississippi's recovery versus the struggles of surrounding states.

Among the lessons teased from the many visits to Mississippi by George W. Bush, one stands as the most obvious: when the perception is widespread that a leader failed the expectation of a bold and timely response to any challenge, gaining back public trust is a near impossibility. Hurricanes Katrina and Rita ravaged the Gulf Coast communities in multiple states beyond the capacity of any nation to assure recovery in the short term. As days and weeks passed following the storms, there were provocative media images—government-constructed levees that could not hold floodwaters, victims wandering with nowhere to go, and children and the elderly starving and dying in public facilities with no relief in sight—all sharpening the sense that those charged with marshaling help were disorganized and powerless. Though George W. Bush personally visited Mississippi fourteen times over three years and provided leadership for the distribution of more than $100 billion in federal recovery funding, the sense that he and his administration failed the nation in a moment of extreme crisis was always floating within an arm's length of this president.

CHAPTER THIRTEEN

BARACK OBAMA

Forty-Fourth President of the United States
Democrat
Elected 2008 and 2012
Served from January 20, 2009, to January 20, 2017

During his eight years of service as president of the United States, Barack Obama made only one trip to Mississippi, that being in 2010 during the man-made disaster created by the massive petroleum spill into the Gulf of Mexico following the explosion of the Deepwater Horizon oil well. It was not a surprising record of visits in light of the margins of victory Mississippians had given Obama's Republican opponents in 2008 and 2012—13 and 12 percent, respectively—but it certainly represented an abrupt change in presidential attention from the George W. Bush years. However, the situation brought on by the environmental catastrophe mandated a visit by the president to the Mississippi Gulf Coast, where communities experienced dramatic upsets in many aspects of daily life and reversals in all elements of their regional economy.

Eleven workers lost their lives when the Deepwater Horizon well exploded on April 20, 2010. For eighty-seven days the ruptured wellhead spewed crude oil into the Gulf of Mexico, destroying or severely damaging both the aquatic and coastal ecosystems. Commercial fishing, tourism, and other drivers of the region's business community were at a standstill, as federal agencies and BP, the corporate owner of the well, worked to stem the flow of raw petroleum. President Obama visited Mississippi on the fifty-fifth day of the wellhead's unabated gushing into the waters of the gulf.

June 14, 2010—Gulfport

Headlining the front page of the *Sun Herald*—serving the Gulf Coast and published out of Biloxi, Mississippi—on the day of President Obama's visit were words in large type that suggested he needed a reminder of the magnitude of the disaster: "Here's Our Story, Mr. President." It was a long report that left little unsaid and laid bare the region's uncertainty and anger. Local journalists termed the Deepwater Horizon spill the "worst natural disaster in U.S. history" as well as "the worst manmade disaster in U.S. history." They also wrote that it caused the "worst economic recession in generations."

Pouring out of the *Sun Herald* story were images of extreme frustration over a situation that brought unfamiliar circumstances: "Resilience is being put to the test. . . . We know hurricanes—how to prepare, how to dig out . . . and get to work on recovery. . . . With massive oil leaks—not so much."

Fingers pointed in several directions: "Government projections on when and where oil might land appear to be about as effective as BP's efforts to stop its wellhead from gushing. . . . [Local leaders] haven't been allowed much input into plans. . . . [It is] a disaster in need of some leadership."

Perhaps scariest of all for local folks was the perceived rush by public and private sector officials to push the disaster onto someone else's desk: "Government officials, from Washington on down, say cleanup and all its costs and financial damages to people and industry are BP's responsibility. . . . Environmentalists have suggested federal and state leaders should have stepped in more, taken charge, and provided more oversight of BP's handling of the disaster. . . . Both [Mississippi governor Haley] Barbour and you, Mr. President, have caught some flak for not taking stronger roles in riding herd over BP."

Answers to the most important questions seemed nowhere to be found: "The extent of the ecological damage the Deepwater Horizon disaster will cause in Mississippi and the gulf at large is unclear. . . . Some experts say fisheries and marine life will be devastated and take years to recover. Others say the warm gulf waters teeming with microorganisms will deal with even large amounts of light-sweet Louisiana crude rather quickly."[1]

When the *Clarion-Ledger* announced that President Obama planned a visit to Mississippi, Alabama, and Florida, the report said that he already made three trips to Louisiana to address the Deepwater Horizon disaster and visited in the White House with relatives of the workers who lost their lives. Haley Barbour's spokesman said the governor would join Obama in Gulfport and that Mississippi officials were worried about "the impact of national news coverage showing the Gulf Coast area ankle deep in oil." Also, the story noted that at the time about one-third of the Gulf was closed to fishing.[2]

In anticipation of the three-state visit, the Obama administration issued a statement directing those negatively affected by the oil spill to a website, a toll-free number for damage claims, and another toll-free number for reports to the United States Coast Guard (USCG), should interactions with BP prove unsatisfactory. The White House statement—"Message to the Gulf Coast from the President"—ran in newspapers throughout the area directly affected by the disaster. It read, in part:

"In the days since the BP oil spill began, the failure to stop the leak has caused incredible anger and frustration—especially for the people of the Gulf Coast struggling to survive one of the worst environmental disasters in our nation's history.

"During the last few weeks, I've visited the gulf and met with people directly impacted by this tragedy. . . . These people don't want excuses—they want results. They want the leak stopped, the coastline protected, and the water cleaned. They want their lives to go back to normal, and their communities to be made whole again.

"This is an assault on our shores. An American way of life is at stake. And we are doing everything in our power to repel this assault. . . .

"This leak is an unprecedented catastrophe and a technical challenge unlike any we've ever seen. That's why we're pressing for every possible remedy to keep it from flowing into the gulf, and to capture as much as we can while relief wells are drilled that will permanently stop the leak."

[Note: at this point, the president's statement detailed statistics on the thousands working on the cleanup, as well as the amount of oil captured, burned, and skimmed from the surface of the gulf. It also announced a Justice Department criminal investigation into the explosion and a Department of Interior plan for greater oversight of the oil drilling industry.]

"I understand the frustration and anger that the people of the Gulf Coast are feeling. I share it. But instead of allowing feelings of anger and frustration to overwhelm our efforts, we must stay focused on the work at hand. We must not slow down or lose focus until this leak is capped and the communities that have been devastated by this catastrophe are restored. We owe it to the people of the gulf to bring this ordeal to an end, and we owe it to the American people to make sure it never happens again."[3]

During his visit to Gulfport, President Obama made a late morning visit to the Coast Guard station, where he received a briefing and made a few remarks. He then went to The Chimneys Restaurant for lunch with local residents. The meeting included a discussion with participants, and the president made brief comments. Obama recognized both Governor Haley Barbour of Mississippi and Governor Bobby Jindal of Louisiana who traveled to the Mississippi coast for the presidential visit. During both of his addresses in Gulfport, Obama mentioned Admiral Thad Allen, the twenty-third commandant of the USCG, who accepted appointment to the role as national incident commander of the Unified Command for the Deepwater Horizon Oil Spill in the Gulf of Mexico. Allen earned recognition among Gulf Coast residents for directing federal efforts during a previous disaster recovery. His statement upon accepting the new appointment said, in part: "This is a continuation of longstanding relationships that I have had in the Gulf Coast for nearly ten years, and also reflects the ability to interact with the folks down there as I did during the assignment as the principal federal officer for Hurricane Katrina."[4]

Speaking at the Coast Guard station, President Obama thanked Mississippi governor Barbour and his wife, Marsha, for hosting the presidential visit, as well as Governor Jindal of Louisiana and various elected and appointed officials for joining him. He also recognized Admiral Allen and indicated that the admiral's report, along with suggestions from attendees, would be of value as the recovery proceeded. Coordination of skimmers on Coast Guard vessels in the Gulf arose in the conversation, as participants sought assurance that this equipment would be used to prevent or slow the oil before it reached the shoreline.

Unlike many presidential addresses, Obama asked more technical or administrative questions of the group: "There is a range of issues having to do with communications. Are there—do they—some of these smaller vessels have radios on them? Have we done an effective inventory of which ones are large enough and have enough trained personnel that they can actually lay boom or they can engage in skimming? Which ones should be deployed more as sentinels to identify where, in fact, the oil may be coming in?" The president turned to the local incident commander, Captain Steve Poulin (USCG), for implementation of the suggestions.

President Obama spoke to the process of clarifying the role of BP in the recovery: "We also talked about claims to make sure that people here in Mississippi, but throughout the region, are going to be adequately compensated for the damages and the losses that they're experiencing right now. There are still problems with them. I think as everybody is aware, I'm going to be meeting with the chairman and other officials from BP on Wednesday. And so we're gathering up facts, stories right now so that we have an absolutely clear understanding about how we can best present to BP the need to make sure that individuals and businesses are dealt with in a fair manner and in a prompt manner."

Finally, the president recognized that many in the room expended tremendous personal effort toward engineering solutions to address the tragedy: "Folks around the table here have been working twenty-four/seven. The governors [have] been on a constant state of full alert and have been putting in a lot of time and a lot of energy working with Thad Allen [USCG] to make sure that [we are] dealing with this disaster." Then he stated clearly the goals: "We are minimizing the short-term impacts and we're making sure that we've got the resources to fully recover."

As almost an addendum, the president showed that he heard the concerns of state officials and local residents regarding tourism: "Here in Mississippi—but it's true in Florida, it's true in Alabama, and it's true in portions of Louisiana—there's still a lot of opportunity for visitors to come down here, a lot of beaches that are not yet affected or will not be affected. We just want to make sure that people who have travel plans down to the gulf area remain mindful of that, because if people want to know what can they do to help folks down here, one of the best ways to help is to come down here and enjoy the outstanding hospitality."[5]

There are no complete and publicly available recordings of President Obama's address at The Chimneys Restaurant, nor of what he said at the outset to the assemblage of local leaders. However, the material that does exist once again showed that he viewed the crisis at a technical level not often expected of senior leadership. He said, for example, "This stuff had been tested with a much smaller amount of oil. . . . We really have never seen up to a million gallons of dispersant put out there. And so we already provided some waivers, because our attitude was, given the toxicity, given how toxic the oil was already—it's a matter of the lesser of two evils—it was better to go ahead and put that out. We tested it for safety, and the EPA [Environmental Protection Agency] has been involved in that."

He continued: "The technologies generally—whether it's dispersants, booms, skimming devices—they really haven't developed much over the last thirty or forty years. We're using the same stuff—the industry is using the same stuff that the industry was using forty years ago. And we've got to—part of the review that we're doing involves making sure that whether it's private industry or a public-private partnership that people start developing better mechanisms to respond to this kind of disastrous situation."

Addressing the concerns of the businesspeople in the room, the president referred to the "spectacular beach" and to two individuals, one of whom owned the Edgewater Inn and the other owned the Blow Fly Inn. They told him business was off by 40 percent since the Deepwater Horizon disaster began. He said to the press pool, "It gives you a sense of the kind of potential economic impact that a crisis like this can have on individual business owners. Obviously, they've got to make payroll, and they've got employees, and it trickles down and has an impact on them as well." He pledged: "We are going to be working with business owners like this, with governors and mayors to make sure that they are made whole as a consequence of this crisis."

Also, he recognized that "the full effects of this may not be known immediately. They may not be known three months from now and may not be fully known for another six months or a year. We just want to make sure we've got structure in place so that people . . . are adequately dealt with. That's going to be a top topic of mine when I meet with the BP officials on Wednesday."[6]

★ ★ ★

Presidents Barack Obama and George W. Bush were different in many aspects of their leadership, not the least of which was their approach to disaster response, illustrated by two major incidents that affected Mississippi. After some early organizational stumbles in the aftermath of Hurricane Katrina, President Bush lavished Mississippi with his frequent appearances and his expressions of personal concern (see previous chapter). Visit after visit, he praised his friend Mississippi governor Haley Barbour and the people of the state for their spirit and steadfast efforts at recovery. President Obama, on the other hand, traveled to Mississippi one time in the shadow of the Deepwater Horizon explosion and oil spill, and his entire focus seemed to be on the technical details of the cleanup and the establishment of financial responsibility to get funding into the hands of those who suffered losses.

When CNN carried a story on June 15, 2010—one day after the presidential visit to Mississippi—concerning Obama's efforts toward the Deepwater Horizon recovery, the report stated, "The president . . . has faced criticism that he hasn't been fully engaged in the crisis." As an example, there was a quote from "Gulf Coast resident Jim Hall," who told the reporter: "Looking at the overall picture, I wish he would take more assertive power in what's going on as far as protection of our environment. My property values have probably dropped 30 or 40 percent in the last fifty days." Presidential adviser David Axelrod responded that any slowness had to do with negotiations between the federal government and BP.[7]

In an address to the nation on the evening of the CNN report, President Obama charged Ray Mabus, secretary of the navy and a former governor of Mississippi, with developing "a Gulf Coast restoration plan in cooperation with states, local communities, tribes, fishermen, conservationists, and gulf residents." Also, the president said that he had "authorized the use of 17,000 National Guard members to help with the cleanup," even as he reported that the governors of Mississippi, Alabama, and Louisiana actually dispatched very few of the troops. Finally, he levered public pressure toward Congress by suggesting that their inaction stemmed from the interventions of "oil industry lobbyists."[8]

Two other disasters that affected Mississippi also spoke to President Obama's approach to disaster response. These were the remaining tasks related to Katrina recovery when he took office, and a smaller-footprint, but still devastating flood that touched the state in 2016.

Though the recovery from Hurricane Katrina was not, by any means, complete when he took office in January 2009, President Obama did not choose to make an immediate visit to the Gulf Coast to view the challenges that remained. Eight months later, when he recognized the fourth anniversary of the storm on his weekly radio address from Washington, DC, on August 29, 2009, he said that he would visit New Orleans in the months ahead. There was no mention of visiting Mississippi.[9]

According to a 2009 report by journalists at WDAM-TV 7, the president chose to send cabinet members to the Gulf Coast during the early months of his presidency, all of whom were focused on hurricane recovery. A news release by the White House said, "President Obama's commitment to Mississippi's recovery is demonstrated by his tireless work to cut through the bureaucratic red tape and improve coordination among federal agencies and local partners. . . . As a result, public assistance projects that had been stuck for years have moved forward since the start of the administration." Noting that the administration obligated $160 million for Mississippi recovery and announced another $2.5 billion in Recovery Act funds for the state, the press release said, "The Obama Administration knows challenges remain and has taken steps to learn from the mistakes of the past."[10]

On August 27, 2015, Obama visited New Orleans to commemorate the tenth anniversary of Hurricane Katrina. He traveled with Craig Fugate, the

FEMA administrator, and the two met with New Orleans mayor Mitch Landrieu and residents of neighborhoods hit by the storm. Fugate also visited hurricane recovery sites in Mississippi and Texas as part of the trip, but Obama did not join him.[11]

Another disaster hit in August 2016: southern Louisiana and Mississippi received more than two feet of rain in forty-eight hours. Six counties in Mississippi sustained damage to roads and homes. However, most of the property damage and all of the loss of life occurred in Louisiana, and when the president traveled to the flooded areas several days after the cleanup began, he chose to visit neighborhoods in that state where the devastation was tremendous. In East Baton Rouge, for instance, the preliminary estimate was that 400,000 cubic yards of debris required removal. More than 60,000 homes showed some level of water damage, and 115,000 of Louisiana's citizens sought federal disaster assistance.[12] As he had in 2009 and in 2015 during trips related to lingering issues from Hurricane Katrina, once again in 2016 President Obama chose not to visit Mississippi communities affected by this natural disaster.

Both Bush and Obama suffered criticism for their approaches to disaster recovery in Mississippi, though each steered federal efforts to benefit the state with determination to help those affected. Surely the most striking difference between the two was their readiness to make trips to Mississippi to visit with victims of the devastation and to show by their presence that they were working toward solutions. Much of the difference in readiness to visit could likely be explained by the varying nature and scope of the events, as well as the party affiliations of the two presidents. George W. Bush, Republican, visited a state that voted overwhelmingly for his candidacy in 2000 and 2004. Barack Obama, Democrat, lost the state in 2008 and 2012, just as Democratic candidates did in every election—except the election of 1976—from 1960 onward.

CONCLUSION

When William McKinley traveled to Mississippi in the spring of 1901, he became the first US president to visit the state while in office. Twenty-four men served as the nation's chief executive prior to McKinley; none of them included Mississippi in their travel plans. Zachary Taylor provided the closest event in Mississippi to a visit from a sitting president in the nineteenth century when he stopped by Vicksburg in 1849 for a brief celebration as president-elect on his way to the nation's capital for the presidential inauguration.

Some of the earliest presidents made rather extensive journeys despite the hardships for travelers in those days. George Washington, for instance, visited several of the states that existed while he was in office, and President James Monroe even made a goodwill tour of eight southern states in 1819, but he stopped short of Mississippi and headed northward after visiting Alabama.

Presidents holding office in the twentieth and twenty-first centuries have a better record of paying attention to Mississippi; thirteen of the nineteen from McKinley to Obama visited the Magnolia State. The six from this more recent era who didn't make it to Mississippi while they occupied the White House were Warren Harding, Calvin Coolidge, Herbert Hoover, Harry Truman, Dwight Eisenhower, John Kennedy, and Lyndon Johnson. It is worth reporting that most, if not all, of these men set foot in the state at one time or another during their lifetimes (see Appendix B).

As this book reports, there were forty-five presidential trips to Mississippi between 1901 and 2016, and thirty-three of the state's communities hosted one or more of the sixty-nine stops the presidents made during those visits. This suggests that during this period of 115 years, there was a presidential presence in the state on average approximately every two-and-one-half years. Of course, such a measure misrepresents the reality of the history. There was a period of no presidential visits stretching twenty years between Woodrow Wilson's first-term vacation on the Gulf Coast and Franklin Roosevelt's three whistle stops in 1934. Even longer, after FDR's final trip to Mississippi in 1942, twenty-seven years passed before Richard Nixon paid the next visit. At the other end of the spectrum, George W. Bush traveled to the state nineteen times during his two terms in office. While this calculates to a Bush visit every five months, again the reality varied from the average. During his presidency the two shortest intervals between visits were actually just three days apiece, and the longest interval was eighteen months.

While there were several factors that determined why some presidents visited frequently and others not at all, historical context explained much of the variance. For instance, fourteen of the nineteen trips to Mississippi during the eight years served by the forty-third president were directly related to Gulf Coast recovery from the devastation of Hurricane Katrina. In fact, of the forty-five visits made to Mississippi by presidents, the primary reason for eighteen of them was disaster assessment and recovery. Participation in political campaigns, either for a president's own reelection or for the election of candidates from the president's party, accounted for eleven visits. Promotional efforts on behalf of policy proposals brought presidents to Mississippi eight times. Presidential recreation accounted for three trips to the state. Finally, in a catchall category one might label "Other" are five trips when presidents exercised the role of commander in chief at in-state military installations, spoke at postsecondary commencement ceremonies, or simply sought goodwill or general public support.

Because of scheduling pressures and expense, presidential visits purely for goodwill are rarely made these days to any state. Most often such visits occur when a president is on a purposeful trip elsewhere and Mississippi—or any other state—is a relatively convenient, added stop along the way. Extended presidential tours around the nation to grip and grin with the citizenry over a period of several weeks, or even months—a fairly common practice into the first quarter of the twentieth century—are no longer useful or desirable given modern transportation and communication technology.

Of course, the categories of visits above are not exclusive of one another. Though there is a primary reason for each trip on a president's schedule, there are often add-on items for the agenda that blur the lines between categories. Presidents have spent hours in Mississippi promoting policies before audiences of voters, only to stop by political fund-raising events before leaving the state. At other times, the political campaign purpose was primary, but at the airport there was a ceremonial review of a military unit by the commander in chief before he departed. Scheduling efficiency makes multipurpose trips a smart strategy, but the tactic also allows the sharing of expenses between official federal travel accounts and the coffers of political parties.

At least as important as why particular presidents traveled to Mississippi or how they paid for the trips are questions regarding what each of the visits accomplished. If White House staff chose a particular location for its potential to dramatize the need for a president's preferred program or policy proposal, did follow-up analyses suggest that the president's trip turned the tide? If a president was the headliner at a political event appealing for donations to the party, were the right people in attendance and were goals met for the number of gifts and the dollars contributed? If the president's intention was to endorse a party hopeful in a pivotal race for the governor's office or a seat in Congress, was the candidate elected? If a natural or manmade disaster brought widespread devastation to an area of the state, did the president's presence hasten recovery, offer a measure of comfort to the victims, and enhance the presidential image of concern for the well-being of the citizens he served? Indeed, the question of public image attaches to any presidential appearance anywhere regardless of the announced purpose for the visit; the political nature of the office punishes any chief executive who overlooks that basic principle for even a moment.

Many people asked and answered such questions after each of the presidential visits to Mississippi, especially staff members at the White House. But there were also analyses by officials serving at the national and state headquarters of the president's political party. Journalists used their stories and opinion pieces to address the questions for their readers, and, most important, voters who witnessed a visit assessed everything from the likability of the president to the quality of the event and the substance of the spoken and unspoken messages. These attendees, in turn, shared their impressions within their circles of influence, and those with whom they spoke passed the news to others. In other words, though presidential visits to Mississippi are relatively rare occurrences, they are always impactful events freighted with significance regardless of their scheduled purposes.

This means that for each trip the primary responsibility of the president's staff is to make careful preparations, and some staffers generally arrive onsite several days in advance of the visit to assure that no controllable detail is left to chance. Security is always a primary concern, but it is just one issue among many for those planning a president's travel.

Presidential trips to Mississippi demonstrated that outcomes inform the question whether the effort and expense of such visits accomplish intended goals. For example, when George W. Bush visited the Nissan Plant in Canton, Mississippi, on May 3, 2005, he and other senior officials of his administration were on a two-month sales campaign to build public support for his proposal to address predicted shortfalls in the Social Security Trust Fund by creating individual accounts that were quasi-private for account holders to personally invest in during their active working lives. It was a solution that he and others in Republican leadership circles embraced because they believed it would stimulate the economy and generate greater investment earnings for Social Security dollars, while at the same time it forestalled increases in Social Security taxes. Though the highly visible program at the factory in Canton included the president's encouraging pitch for the changes, as well as testimonials from several other officials, Bush's proposal for sweeping Social Security changes went nowhere. The public seemed fearful of losing benefits, and Congress could not be persuaded. This presidential visit to Mississippi and other events during the two-month sales blitz were not successful.

One example of an opposite result is Bill Clinton's earlier visit to Clarksdale, Mississippi, on July 6, 1999. Again the event site was a manufacturing facility; this time it was the Waterfield Cabinet Company. The president and the entourage of administration officials and special guests traveling with him were on a nationwide tour of communities challenged by poverty. They visited Hazard, Kentucky, in the Appalachian Mountains before traveling to Clarksdale in the heart of the Mississippi Delta. Also scheduled for visits after Clarksdale were the inner city of East St. Louis, Illinois; the Pine Ridge Indian Reservation in South Dakota; and a Hispanic neighborhood in Phoenix, Arizona. In advance of congressional consideration of the president's proposed federal budget for the next fiscal year, Clinton was stumping for his New Markets Initiative, a collection of programs offering federal incentives to lever private investments for the benefit of the nation's economically underserved areas. Unlike Bush's preferred Social Security changes described above, some of the presidential proposals within Clinton's New Markets Initiative became part of a budgetary package adopted by Congress. In retrospect, it is reasonable to say that Clinton's Mississippi stop contributed to a successful outcome.

Assessing presidential visits for the purpose of political campaigning is more of a straightforward exercise. When Gerald Ford visited Jackson on July 30, 1976, he sought the support of the Mississippi delegation to the Republican National Convention in his bid for the party's nomination versus the challenger in that year, Ronald Reagan. Ford successfully secured the nomination. When Reagan visited Gulfport on October 1, 1984, he campaigned for his own reelection to a second term. He won local, statewide, and national majorities. President George H. W. Bush visited Jackson on March 6, 1992, in the middle of a difficult primary election campaign. He sought renomination versus the challenge of right-winger Patrick Buchanan. While he captured the nomination and won Mississippi in the general election, his bid for reelection fell short against Bill Clinton. George H. W. Bush's visit to Gulfport on October 12, 1989, likewise had an unsuccessful outcome. He promoted the candidacy of Republican Tom Anderson against Democrat Gene Taylor for a seat in the US House of Representatives. Though Bush's popularity in the state likely meant a boost for Anderson, the eventual result of the balloting was the election of his opponent, the Democratic candidate. Media accounts that raised questions about unreported gifts of travel for the Republican and a perception that the Democrat was the candidate with local interests at heart carried the day, despite Bush's best efforts.

These examples of presidential visits for the purpose of political campaigning show mixed results—some wins, some losses, and some situations beyond the president's control. Perhaps less obvious, but just as certain, is that these examples and others that could be listed demonstrate that for the last sixty years Mississippi has been a Republican stronghold. Only one sitting Democratic president, Jimmy Carter, has ever visited Mississippi on behalf of his own candidacy for reelection, and none has visited on behalf of an in-state Democratic candidate running for office. Carter won the state and national balloting in 1976, but he lost both to Ronald Reagan in 1980. Thus all but one of the results from the eleven presidential visits to Mississippi for campaigning—whether positive or negative—are Republican results. At times, these outcomes have been both positive and negative, as when George H. W. Bush campaigned in Mississippi for his own reelection, carried the state, but lost the national election.

As for the most common type of presidential travel to Mississippi—that is, for visits related to damage assessment and recovery from natural or manmade disasters—fourteen of the eighteen were made by George W. Bush between 2005 and 2008, the years following the landfall of Hurricane Katrina on the state's Gulf Coast.[1] Other presidents visiting for disaster assessment and recovery were Richard Nixon after Hurricane Camille in 1969 and after flooding on the Mississippi and Yazoo Rivers in 1973, Jimmy Carter after Hurricane Frederic in 1979, and Barack Obama after the Deepwater Horizon explosion and oil spill in 2010.

Public expectation that a president will respond immediately and with total commitment in the aftermath of a disaster appeared to grow exponentially in recent years. Notice that Nixon and Carter each visited Mississippi only once following two devastating storms. Hurricane Camille (Nixon) brought destruction to five states, with Mississippi suffering the highest estimated total of damages, as well as fifteen deaths. Hurricane Frederic (Carter) was also devastating, with sixteen counties in Mississippi declared eligible for federal disaster aid, as many counties involved to this degree as there were combined in the other two affected Gulf Coast states, Alabama and Florida. However, the public criticism of George W. Bush and his administration following Katrina brought him to the region time after time, stained him with charges of racism and mismanagement, and contributed significantly to a legacy of flawed leadership. Likewise, Barack Obama suffered public disapproval for not visiting Mississippi early in his presidency to pick up the reins of Katrina recovery efforts, for too-slow and inadequate response to the Deepwater Horizon disaster, and for failing to visit the state when flooding hit Louisiana and Mississippi in 2016.

Whether the expectations of presidents downwind from natural and manmade disasters will continue to grow is uncertain, but it is a likely outcome in a day when technology has enabled journalists' coverage of such events to quicken and expand, even as social media bring second-by-second, worldwide immediacy to the communication of individual experiences in these situations. These developments mean that not only are the broad sweep and the human details of each disaster event conveyed instantly across the nation and beyond its borders but also that the public assessments of presidential responses from both informed and uninformed sources are broadly distributed. Regardless of where breakdowns occur in rushing assistance to victims of major disasters—policy, bureaucracy, or human failures at national or local levels—observations over the past decade made it clear that in these media-driven times, sitting presidents should expect to endure the lion's share of the criticism and ultimately to shoulder the blame.

Of course, there is a flip side to this equation, namely, that the advent of new technology brings positive opportunity as well as the potential for downside criticism. We have witnessed the expansion of various social media as factors in presidential elections over this same decade, and logic suggests that both the use and influence of these technologies will grow. It will be interesting to watch this development in national politics.

Likewise, it will be interesting to see how the use of social media and other communication and transportation technologies affect presidential visits to Mississippi and other states. Will actually shaking hands with a president or listening to his or her remarks in a shared physical space remain the normative, personal experiences with the chief executive, or will the live image of a president on one's handheld device with interactive opportunities become a suitable substitute? After all, we long ago accepted televised candidate debates in place of the in-person format Lincoln and Douglas used in the nineteenth century. Also, as recently as 1934 Franklin and Eleanor Roosevelt traveled hundreds of miles by train from Washington, DC, to Mississippi, speaking first at Corinth, where they overnighted in their railcar, and then proceeded the next day to Tupelo and Amory for appearances. By the time they made additional stops in other states and returned to the nation's capital, they had lived out of suitcases for days. Less than seventy years later, in 2003, George W. Bush woke up one morning in the White House, flew on Air Force One to northern Mississippi for a speech, departed on the presidential airplane for speeches at two locations in Kentucky, flew to southern Mississippi for another speech, and then returned to Washington, DC, to sleep in his own bed—all of this travel on the same day.

Thus it is reasonable to conclude that future developments in communication and transportation will again alter dramatically the travel of the nation's chief executives, as well as the expectations citizens have for their presidents to visit them in Mississippi or any other state. Exactly what changes will occur and on what timetable are left to conjecture.

ACKNOWLEDGMENTS

Questions can come unexpectedly, and this one certainly did. John had just submitted his manuscript for a book on Theodore Roosevelt's campaign for the vice presidency (*American Cyclone*), and a new opportunity arrived out of the blue. Would we write a book on the visits of US presidents to the state of Mississippi? It was not a topic we had considered, and one good reason to say no immediately occurred to us. We hadn't a clue whether a comprehensive and definitive list of such visits was available to launch the research. We asked. It wasn't. We have learned in life, however, that the quick answer is most likely regretted, and our request to think about the idea for a little while was granted.

That little while turned into several months, as each of us began looking at a couple of other projects. Along the way, we kept coming back to the offer to create a useful reference work that didn't exist but really should. We eventually surprised ourselves by saying yes.

Our initial concern was that we would have to spend seat time going through 200 years of newspapers to find reports on presidential visits one at a time. That turned out not to be true. The Mississippi Department of Archives and History maintained a file on the subject, and though it was a mishmash of handwritten notes, clippings, and other loose sheets of paper with an incomplete record of visits, it proved to be a good starting point. We are grateful to the archivists with that agency for stuffing items into the file over many years and for providing it to us as a resource.

We wrote to the archivists at the National Archives and Records Administration, who were cordial and quick to respond with a list of colleagues at the various presidential libraries and museums where one was more likely to find travel records. Such facilities, complete with staff, exist for all presidents since Herbert Hoover who have completed their terms. Again, responses were reasonably quick and helpful, generally referring us to resources where we might find answers to our questions. Thanks to all archivists who provided assistance.

We remain a bit mystified by the response from the George W. Bush Library. The archivist said we would have to fill out paperwork to pursue our inquiry through the intricacies of the federal Freedom of Information Act process. Since we had requested a simple list of President Bush's visits to Mississippi, the requirement seemed over the top. Thus we decided to look elsewhere to avoid what we suspected would be months of delays. (Perhaps George W. Bush made a highly classified visit to Mississippi during his presidency? If that is the case, we didn't find any evidence in publicly available documents. It is possible, we suppose, because we discovered that Franklin Roosevelt traveled to Mississippi under a cloak of secrecy to inspect Camp Shelby during World War II.)

Journalists and the media outlets they serve were a primary source of information, and we thank them for writing the first draft of history. Among the various resources consulted, two books were particularly valuable in developing a context for the presidential visits: Jere Nash and Andy Taggart's *Mississippi Politics* and Richard J. Ellis's *Presidential Travel*. Also, this book could not have been written without the information available through the American Presidency Project, a comprehensive, online resource created and maintained at the University of California, Santa Barbara by Gerhard Peters and John T. Woolley. Nowhere else are presidential addresses and other documents so conveniently available.

Thanks to Leila W. Salisbury, formerly the director of the University Press of Mississippi (UPM), for offering us the opportunity to take on this project and initially guiding its development. Also, thanks to Craig Gill, currently the director of UPM, who reliably steered us through the revisions, encouraging us all the way and making this a much better book. Craig and the other staff of the press are unfailingly cordial, responsive, and helpful. Historians who read and reviewed drafts of the manuscript offered editing suggestions, additional resources, and corrections that made this a much better book. Collaborating with the staff at UPM, Robert Burchfield of Doghouse Editing and Research Services in Iowa City, Iowa, patiently and effectively moved us through the tedium of copyediting.

While John is retired and enjoys the freedom to research and write to his heart's content, Zach serves as a faculty member at Virginia Commonwealth University, and he appreciated the support his colleagues showed as he worked on this project.

Most important, thanks to Pat Hilpert, John's wife, herself a creative thinker and writer, for her ideas, encouragement, editing assistance, and help with the illustrations. And to Sandy Flemming, Zach's wife, who understands him well and generously offers him the environment he needs to be productive.

Writing this book became quite an adventure, as we sorted through leads and a variety of sources to discover one-by-one the journeys made by US presidents to Mississippi. Frankly, presidential visits to this state began at a later point in history than we supposed, and there were more of them than we estimated.

As we followed the trail of history, we grew in appreciation of how critical it is that there be a worthwhile purpose for each presidential appearance. Such trips require detailed planning, jealously guarded time, and generous budgets to transport the traveler in chief, along with White House staff, other senior officials, security personnel, and special equipment, including vehicles. Thus we attempted to provide in each case the underlying history and reason the president visited, rather than simply relating what happened during the time he was in Mississippi.

Finally, we thank you, the reader, for your interest and your time. We hope this book serves you well.

APPENDIX A

Four Addresses Delivered by US Presidents While Visiting Mississippi

Among the many speeches, brief comments, and interview responses delivered by sitting presidents of the United States during visits to Mississippi, a few spark greater interest because of their historical context. The coauthors of this book identified four instances when one president or another addressed—directly or indirectly—nationally significant issues or events while in the Magnolia State. When considering the importance of presidential visits as this book has, we believe it is also vital to consider just how Mississippi's role as a setting for presidential addresses, in a few key instances, shaped the presidents' own thoughts and proclamations.

Setting plays a significant and often symbolic role in the pronouncements made by American presidents. Some of the most well known backdrops for presidential speeches became familiar because of the historic weight their looming presence carries. On somber occasions when a president directly addresses the American people, the Oval Office transforms into a television studio to broadcast his words into millions of homes. Images of the president standing at the dais in the House Chamber are familiar to anyone who watches presidential State of the Union addresses, and the White House Rose Garden is familiar as the site to announce new political and judicial appointments of national import. One president after another returned to familiar settings in instances where tradition imbued a space with particular meaning.

When the president makes public remarks away from these most common settings, it is often because the setting itself is wrapped up in the meaning of the moment. On multiple occasions, Mississippi hosted noteworthy speeches by presidents who recognized that the state itself was central to the symbolism of their remarks. One of the first nationally important addresses by a sitting president speaking in Mississippi was Theodore Roosevelt's speech in Vicksburg on October 21, 1907, wherein the visiting president paid homage to the state's soldiers in the Civil War, an acknowledgment of Confederate gallantry by a Republican and a northern-born president. William McKinley, Roosevelt's predecessor in the Oval Office, initiated the theme of national unity during his visit to Mississippi in 1901, when he said in Jackson, "We stand as one people." Advancing and expanding the concept, Theodore Roosevelt, addressing Mississippians gathered in Vicksburg in 1907, sought to strengthen Washington's bond with the South by championing the mission to develop the Mississippi River's economic potential at the dawn of the twentieth century. This president stepped from a steamboat onto the soil of Mississippi—where racial hatred and mistrust of the federal government persisted—and he embraced the state as a vital participant in a public works project that would benefit the nation, including local citizens and their commercial interests.

Mississippi was an important setting for the championing of economic plans by the other President Roosevelt as well. In the case of Franklin Roosevelt's address in Tupelo on November 18, 1934, the president chose to speak at a site symbolic of one of the greatest achievements to that point in his presidency: the creation of the Tennessee Valley Authority (TVA). Speaking in the first town to draw electricity from the TVA, Roosevelt addressed in person many of the people who built and would benefit from the TVA, while also bringing reporters to see the program's success for themselves. An enthusiastic crowd on the ground in Mississippi helped frame positive press across the country, and so Tupelo played host to Roosevelt's historically significant celebration of this early New Deal success.

The state also hosted significant speeches by sitting presidents that took place against far less celebratory backdrops as well. On April 25, 1974, as the storm clouds of the Watergate scandal gathered, President Richard Nixon addressed the Mississippi Economic Council (MEC) in Jackson amid the series of military, economic, and political crises that soon resulted in his resignation. Nixon took the stage at the Mississippi Coliseum to trumpet the accomplishments and opportunities of his presidency, giving a remarkably rambling and unfocused address that provides readers a window into the mind of a president under siege. The defensiveness and self-aggrandizement on display that day in Jackson, especially in front of a presumably friendly crowd—the MEC invited him to speak, after all—unmistakably showed that Nixon saw Mississippi as a refuge in the midst of a storm.

Real, catastrophic storms occasionally demanded a presidential presence in Mississippi as well. When Hurricane Katrina devastated the Gulf Coast in 2005, President George W. Bush made repeated visits and delivered several speeches on the ground in Louisiana, Mississippi, and Alabama. Particularly significant to this volume of presidential messages was Bush's address in Bay St. Louis on January 12, 2006. It came at a key moment in the recovery process, when the federal government finally and firmly settled in to help the rebuilding challenges of Mississippians and other Gulf Coast residents. These extensive remarks were both a summary of federal efforts and a defense of his administration's commitment. Bush made clear the government's dedication to continued participation in the recovery process, and he sought to reassure the audience that, despite initial setbacks and errors in Washington's response, no one should harbor any doubt about his personal support for sustained action. Taken as a snapshot of Washington's interactions with Mississippi in the hurricane's aftermath, Bush's speech in Bay St. Louis intended to portray that he and his administration were on the ground in affected areas, a message meant not only for the hard-hit victims in Mississippi but also for viewers across the country, many of whom were critical of the president's response.

We present these four speeches in full on the following pages, and we invite the reader to consider them within the contexts explained here. As this record makes evident, the settings of presidential addresses are often just as significant as the spoken words.

Theodore Roosevelt's Address in Vicksburg—October 21, 1907

It is indeed an honor for me to be today the guest of Vicksburg and of Mississippi, and I was inexpressibly touched by the greeting over that great arch of cotton bales, as I came up from the boat which said, "Mississippi Greets the President." I should not be fit to be president at all if I did not, with all my might and main, with all my heart and brain, seek to be, in the full sense, the president of Mississippi, the president of every state in this union. I am glad to be here in this historic city, this city forever memorable of the conflicts in which victor and vanquished alike showed such splendid courage, such splendid fealty to the light as it was given to each.

Even before the Civil War, Mississippi's sons had shown that they knew how to fight. It was from Vicksburg that a company [came] of the famous Mississippi regiment which won undying renown in the Mexican War under the gallant leadership of its colonel, who afterwards became the favorite son not only of Mississippi but of all the South, Jefferson Davis.

I have twice been down in this alluvial delta of the Mississippi; in each case I came primarily for bear.

The last time I got 'em; the first time, all I can say, is that the bears and I broke even. I got as many of them as they did of me. But on each occasion I learned a lot that had nothing to do with the bear hunting, and it seems to me that no American president could spend his time better than by seeing for himself just what a rich and wonderful region the lower Mississippi valley is, so that he may go back, as I shall go back to Washington with the set purpose to do everything that in me lies to see that the United States does its full share in making the Mississippi River practically a part of the sea coast, in making it a deep channel to the great lakes from the gulf.

And as an instance of building the levees for the lower part of that great river, I wish to see them so built as to remove completely from the minds of the dwellers of the lowlands all apprehension of a possible overflow.

Mr. Williams [Congressman John Sharp Williams], it has been suggested to me that we need to construe the constitution broadly in order to get power to do what I want. I think I heard you mention that you are a good federalist. I heard a man say once, a man whom I have never seen afraid of anything, that he was afraid of the Mississippi, that he should be afraid to dwell by it and feel that it might overwhelm the land on which he might live. I wish to see the federal government build a system of dikes, of levees, down the course of the Mississippi which shall make the farm, the plantation of the man that lives by the Mississippi, as safe as if he had a plantation by the Illinois, or the Hudson or the Red River of the North.

I advocate no impossible task, no difficult task. The people of Holland, a little nation, took two-thirds of their country out from under the ocean, and they live behind the dikes now and have lived behind them for centuries in safety. With one-tenth of the effort we, an infinitely greater nation, can take the incomparably rich bottom lands of the lower Mississippi out from all fear of ever being flooded or ever being overflowed by the Mississippi. While I do not like to say in advance what I intend to do, I shall break my rule in this case and say that in my next message to Congress I shall advocate as heartily as I know how that the Congress now elected shall take the first steps to bring about the deep channel-way and the attendant high and broad levee system which will make of these alluvial bottoms the richest and most populous and most prosperous agricultural land not only in this nation but on the face of the globe, and, gentlemen, here is one of my reasons why I am particularly glad to be able to advocate such a policy. I think that any policy which tends to the uplifting of any portion of our people in the end distributes its benefit over the whole people.

But it is far easier, ordinarily, to put into effect a policy which shall at the moment and direction help the people concentrated in the centers of population and wealth than it is to put into effect a policy whose first and direct benefit will come to the man on the farm, the man on the plantation, the tiller of the soil, the man who makes his fortune out of what he grows on the soil. We are now digging the Panama Canal and it is being well done. One reason why the work is being handled well is that we refused to go into it until after careful study, so that we should know we did not make any false steps—in other words, we acted on Davy Crockett's principle, "Be sure you are right, then go ahead."

I want—when we start on this great work this epoch-making work of the improvement of the Mississippi—I want to be sure that we start on principles that will prevent mistake, extravagance, and misapplication of effort. Now I shall have no small difficulty, men and women of Mississippi, in persuading some people—some people in my own locality—of the wisdom of a policy such as that I advocate, a policy that means the expenditure of an immense sum of money, a policy which must continue over a long course of years. If that policy is tainted in any way by jobbers or folly, it will make it immeasurably more difficult to carry it through, and what we should look out for is the action of men—probably well-meaning men—who in their anxiety to serve some particular district will try to divert what should be a national effort.

Ultimately, I believe there can be an enormous spread of the activity of the national government in the care of our waterways; ultimately, I believe that the national government, for instance, can do an immense amount of irrigation through certain portions of the southern states not affected by the project for the deepening of the Mississippi, of which I am now speaking. I am confident that in most of the southern states the loss to the farmer by the washing away of the soil of his farm, by the fact that the streams are not at one period destructive torrents and at another period dry, is infinitely the heaviest tax the famers have to pay, and I believe that through the cooperation of the national government much can be done in the way of irrigation to relieve their condition in certain of the southern states, just as much as has already been done by irrigation in the far west.

I believe that ultimately we shall be able to canalize, to deepen, a large number of streams and waterways in the nation, but take the big rivers first, take the Mississippi, and its most prominent tributaries first.

Now, my friends, I have spoken to you only of the things affecting our material well-being. They are of the utmost importance. It is as important for a nation that there shall be a foundation of material prosperity as it is important for an individual that there should be such a foundation. I distrust the man in private life who is filled with enthusiasm to reform mankind but who cannot support his own wife and family. Let the man first pull his own weight; let him support himself and those dependent upon him.

He will find it at times a good deal of a job; let him do that and if he does that he has then laid the foundation for permitting himself to become a useful citizen in broader aspects. Now, with a nation it is the same thing; we must have a basis of material prosperity on which to build; but woe to the nation which never rears on that foundation the super-structure of a higher life.

Gentlemen, you and those who fought beside you and those who fought against you are enshrined imperishably in the hearts of the people of the entire nation because when the time came which called for you to risk all that you had—prosperity life, and all—for fealty to your ideal, you gladly spurned every other consideration, treating all else as naught compared to the chance to show your manhood on the field of battle.

We honor you and those who fought under you; we honor those who fought against you because they had that fine capacity to ignore everything else, life included, when honor called. But we need to have that spirit shown in civic life just as much as in military life. If ever our people become so sordid as to feel that all that amounts to money—prosperity, ignoble well-being, ease, and comfort—then this nation will perish, as it deserves to perish, from the face of the earth.

Mr. Williams has said that for a day we can sink all mere party differences. Since I have been president I have found that most of the time I have needed to sink them because the differences of party are of small importance compared to the great fundamentals of good citizenship upon which all American citizens should be united. We can afford to differ on the first questions only so long as we remember that the differences on those questions never must be allowed to obscure our identity of feeling on the other and infinitely greater questions.

We as a nation have great and terrible problems to confront us in the century that is now opening. I do not believe that there is any other nation with a future as great as ours, but I believe in that future primarily because I believe that the average American citizens will bring to the solution the political problems which confront us the three cardinal virtues of honesty, courage, and common sense, and we shall need all three. In our highly complex industrial civilization of today we are confronted with certain abnormal tendencies which must be overcome, not by indifference, not by a foolish optimism which is but one degree more foolish than a foolish pessimism, but by a resolute purpose to face the evil, to recognize it, and to overcome it.

Gentlemen, our nation has a wonderful future. We are seated upon a continent; we front two great oceans; we can realize our future only upon condition that we do what I know we will do; that we conduct our policy as among ourselves in accordance with the immutable law of righteousness, trying to get for each man and exact from each man justice, no more and no less; giving to each individual the largest possible liberty of individual action that is consistent with reason, provided that he does not wrong other individuals; and in external affairs we will proceed upon the principle of so bearing ourselves as to avoid all causes of quarreling with any other nation and yet so bearing ourselves that it shall be to the interest of all other nations to avoid forcing an unjust quarrel on us.[1]

Franklin Delano Roosevelt's Address in Tupelo—November 18, 1934

Senator Harrison, Governor Conner, Mr. Mayor, my friends:

I shall not make a speech to you today because we are assembled on this glorious Sunday morning more as neighbors than as anything else.

I have had a very wonderful three days; and everywhere that I have gone, the good people have come as neighbors to talk with me, and they have not come by the thousands—they have come literally by the acres.

This is the first time in my life that I have had the privilege of seeing this section of the state of Mississippi. Many, many years ago, when Pat Harrison and I were almost boys, I became acquainted with his stamping ground down on the gulf. Today I am especially glad to come into the northern part of the state.

Two years ago, in 1932, during the campaign, and again in January, 1933, I came through Kentucky—through the Tennessee Valley—and what I saw on those trips, what I saw of human beings, made tears come to my eyes. The great outstanding thing to me for these past three days has been the change in the looks on people's faces. It has not been only a physical thing. It has not been the contrast between what was actually a scarcity of raiment or a lack of food two years ago and better clothing and more food today. Rather it is a something in people's faces. I think you understand what I mean. There was not much hope in those days. People were wondering what was going to come to this country. And yet today I see not only hope, but I see determination and a knowledge that all is well with the country, and that we are coming back.

I suppose that you good people know a great deal more of the efforts that we have been making in regard to the work of the Tennessee Valley Authority than I do, because you have seen its application in your own counties and your towns and your own homes; and, therefore, it would be like carrying coals to Newcastle for me to tell you about what has been done.

But perhaps in referring to it I can use you as a text—a text that may be useful to many other parts of the nation; because people's eyes are upon you and because what you are doing here is going to be copied in every state of the union before we get through.

We recognize that there will be a certain amount of rugged opposition to this development, but I think we recognize also that the opposition is fading as the weeks and months go by—fading in the light of practical experience.

I cite certain figures for the benefit of the gentlemen of the press, who have come hither from many climes. I am told that from March of this year, when you started using TVA power, the consumption of power for residential purposes has risen from 41,000 kilowatts to 89,000 kilowatts—an increase of 26 percent [sic]. I understand that from the financial point of view, in spite of various fairy tales that have been spread in other parts of the country, your power system is still paying taxes to the municipality. That is worth remembering. I understand that, as a whole, it is a remarkable business success.

I talk about those figures first, for it has been so often wrongly alleged that this yardstick which we are using could not be applied to private businesses, because a government yardstick receives so many favors, because it is absolved from paying this and paying that and paying the other thing. Well, we are proving in this Tennessee Valley that by using good business methods we can instruct a good many business men in the country.

And there is another side of it. I have forgotten the exact figures and I cannot find them in this voluminous report at this moment, but the number of new refrigerators that have been put in, for example, means something besides just plain dollars and cents. It means greater human happiness. The introduction of electric cookstoves and all the other dozens of things which, when I was in the Navy, we used to call "gadgets," is improving human life. They are things not especially new so far as invention is concerned, but more and more are they considered necessities in our American life in every part of the country.

And I have been interested this morning in seeing these new homesteads—not just the buildings, not just the land that they are on, not just the excellent landscaping of the trees among which those homes have been set, but rather the opportunities that those homes are giving to families to improve their standard of living.

And finally, my friends, there is one significant thing about all that you are doing here in Tupelo, that others are doing in Corinth, in Athens and Norris, and the various other places where accomplishment can be seen today—aye, the most important thing of all I think is that it is being done by the communities themselves. This is not coming from Washington. It is coming from you. You are not being federalized. We still believe in the community; and things are going to advance in this country exactly in proportion to the community effort. This is not regimentation; it is community rugged individualism. It means no longer the kind of rugged individualism that allows an individual to do this, that, or the other thing that will hurt his neighbor. He is forbidden to do that from now on. But he is going to be encouraged in every known way from the national capital and the state capital and the county seat to use his individualism in cooperation with his neighbors' individualism so that he and his neighbors together may improve their lot in life.

Yes, I have been thrilled by these three days, thrilled not only in the knowledge of practical accomplishments but thrilled also in the deep-seated belief that the people of this nation understand what we are trying to do, are cooperating with us, and have made up their minds that we are going to do it.

And so, in saying "good-bye" to you for a short time—because I am coming back—I ask all of you, throughout the length and breadth of the Tennessee Valley and those areas which form an economic portion of that valley, to remember that the responsibility for success lies very largely with you and that the eyes of the nation are upon you. I, for one, am confident that you are going to give to the nation an example which will be a benefit not only to yourselves, but to the whole 130 million of Americans in every part of the land.[2]

Richard Nixon's Address in Jackson—April 25, 1974

Governor Waller, all the distinguished guests on the platform, all of the distinguished guests in this audience, and all of those who, I understand, are outside and are able, not to be here, but can hear on the loudspeakers:

In answer to that very generous introduction by the governor of this state, I can only say that I am proud to be the first president in history to address the Mississippi Economic Council, and after this kind of a reception, I am sure I won't be the last one to do it.

As a matter of fact, as I looked at this huge auditorium, I thought I had never spoken in a place where I had so many people behind me.

And I want to pay tribute, incidentally, not to only the members of the council who are going to have lunch, I understand, if I don't speak too long, but also to your many guests, I understand, from the high schools, the colleges, the other fine institutions. Particularly, I thank the Mississippi State University band for playing "Hail to the Chief."

Just so I don't get in any trouble with some of the other colleges and universities— I know places like Millsaps—I went to school with a fellow from Millsaps. And believe me, as a Washington Redskins fan, I know what Archie Manning did to us in the New Orleans Saints game. And to all of those in this great state, whether it be from Ole Miss or

Mississippi State or one of the other universities or colleges, let me say, if you ever find a good quarterback who can throw and who can run and who is young, call me, not George Allen. We need that kind of a quarterback or fullback.

This also gives me an opportunity, in responding to the governor, to pay tribute to the Mississippi delegation in the Congress of the United States. Sometimes, those who are served by their senators and congressmen have to be told by someone from outside what really great men they are.

I want you to know that having served with these men for five years—most of them—I can say that no state in the union is represented by men in the Congress of the United States who more vigorously speak up for their states and for the nation than has the state of Mississippi.

Senator Jim Eastland, the President pro tem of the Senate, as you know [holds] the fourth ranking office in all of this great country.

Senator John Stennis. When they write profiles in courage, he will be there.

And since I can't mention all of the bipartisan delegation in the House of Representatives, I will just refer to my good friend, Sonny Montgomery. And having said "bipartisan," let me tell you something about this delegation that I have seen through the years. I have found that we have had many very, very strong, tough votes and debates over these years when America's power was being tested, but more important, America's character and America's will and its determination and its sense of destiny. And I can assure you that whenever the issue was the honor of America or the strength of America or respect for America, Mississippi spoke as one voice for America and not for any one party.

And in these times, that is the kind of representation that we need in the Congress, in the senate—be it Democrat or Republican. In these times, you can be proud that you have that kind of representation.

I realize that this is an anniversary for you. This is the twenty-fifth anniversary, I understand, of the Mississippi Economic Council. And on such an occasion, a proper theme, therefore, is for me to not only look back but also to look forward to the next twenty-five years.

And particularly for those who are younger, those who will be the new senators and congressmen fifteen, twenty, [or] twenty-five years from now, for all of those who have your lives ahead, let's look back a moment and see where we have come and where we have been and how we have withstood the trials that we have been through.

I remember the end of World War II. We came out of that war, and we thought, with the United Nations, with all that the world had been through, that this would be a new era of peace, and yet it was not. In these past twenty-five years, this nation has gone through two very difficult and very unpopular wars—first in Korea and then in Vietnam. And in these past twenty-five years, this nation has gone through five recessions—not depressions, but recessions—in which the economy did not produce at full production.

And in this period of time, particularly in the years of the sixties, this nation has gone through a period of unrest—social unrest, racial unrest—in which, at times, there were explosions on our college campuses and our university campuses and in our cities. And over and over again in those twenty-five years, if you read the newspapers and the magazines and listened to television, you would hear those who said, "America has seen its greatest days. America cannot see itself through this crisis. We cannot go on to be a great nation. We are tearing ourselves apart."

Those were the pessimists, but they were wrong. They were wrong then, and they are wrong today. America's greatest days are ahead of us, because it is not the easy times that test either an individual or a nation, it is the hard times. And America has withstood the hard times and has come through even stronger each time.

And so today, I want to address this great audience on two subjects—one of which is particularly of interest to you because of the nature of your organization—where our economy is and where it is going. And the other, which should be of interest to all of you because of our concern about the future of our young people and of the next generation, and that is, what are the chances to keep the peace that we now have after so many years of war.

Let me look at the economy a minute with you. And I am sure out here in this audience we have lots of experts who may have differing views about it. I can only give you the best judgment that I have from the economic advisers, not only from the administration but from outside, who look at the American economy today, analyze it, and wonder where we are going. Let me put it in perspective by saying this:

When we talk about the difficulties America has been passing through, the energy crisis, the inflation that we have had, due primarily—two-thirds of it in 1973 was as a result of higher food prices and higher energy costs—when we look at those difficulties, we think we are the nation that has the most difficult time, and they are difficult times in that respect.

But when I was in Paris just a couple of weeks ago, I had the opportunity to meet the leaders of great nations and small nations, the Prime Minister of Great Britain, the President and Prime Minister of Italy, the Chancellor of Germany, the President then of France, who succeeded temporarily, until the new election is held, President Pompidou, and of course, the President of the Soviet Union, Mr. Podgorny, and in addition thirty-five other heads of government and heads of state. And as I talked to each of them, I want to tell you I learned one thing: we have problems, but there is not one of them who would not trade his problems for whatever problems we have.

America today has more opportunity, more prosperity, more freedom than any nation in the world.

Now, ladies and gentlemen, that does not mean that we look at the problems of inflation, the problems of energy, the others which confront our nation and say, "Well, whatever they are, there are other nations that have it worse than we have."

That isn't enough. That isn't the American way, because when we have problems, we analyze them and we do something about them. That is the American spirit. It is what made this country in the beginning, has kept us going throughout our 200 years, and will keep us even greater in the future.

So, let us examine, first, the problem of the economy, where it is. As we know, in the first quarter of this year, we have had an economic downturn, primarily related to the problems of energy and also characterized by inflation, inflation which began in 1973 due primarily again to energy, as I have indicated, and to higher food price costs.

Under these circumstances then, as we look at our economy, we wonder, what is the prospect for the second quarter, for the third quarter, for the fourth quarter? And here it is as we see it today:

First, the problem of inflation is a most nagging one. That problem, however, is not going to be solved by putting this economy under the straitjacket of government controls from Washington. That would be an awfully easy answer for a president to give.

But we have tried that way, not only this administration [but] others. It works for a time, but in the end we pay a bigger price in higher prices. That problem also is not going to be solved by simply spending more, because while you can spend yourself into an inflation, you can't spend yourself out of inflation.

So, that means as we look at the problem of inflation, that whenever we make decisions in Washington with regard to what your government spends for the federal budget that affects your family budget. We must spend what is necessary to keep our economy on the move. We must spend what is necessary to deal with such problems as disasters that the governor has referred to and we will. But I can assure you, too, that we will be responsible—responsible because we must remember that a sound policy in Washington, where the government spends only what is necessary and not more, is essential if we are going to be able to control the fires of inflation that presently are eating away at us.

What, then, is the answer, long-term, as far as inflation is concerned? You know what it is: more production—more production of food—and here the prospects are good. A record agriculture year in which Mississippi, a great agriculture state, now primarily an industrial state—which is an indication of a change in twenty-five years that has occurred in this state—Mississippi is playing its great role in that respect. And so, that means that as we have more production of food, that the rise in food prices will tend, as we go through the balance of the year, to level off. That is one good sign for the future.

And then the other problem is that of energy. Here again, it is a problem of whether or not we have the supplies to meet the demand.

The other day I was talking to the Chancellor of Germany. I was asking him how much it costs for a gallon of gasoline in Germany. He said, "$1.40 and we are willing to pay it." Now, of course, as far as we are concerned, we believe the prices we pay for gasoline are too high now because of what we have been through in the past, and they are.

We believe that some of the profits that are made are windfall profits and that the Congress should tax them, as I believe the Congress eventually will, but let us remember this, too: The answer to getting our energy prices under control is to produce more, and that is why it is essential for the Congress to deregulate natural gas so that we can have more gas all over this country and reduce the price of energy for all Americans.

That is why we have also called upon the Congress to change the environmental restrictions, temporarily at least, but long enough so that the investment will be worthwhile, so that we can extract and use the resource [of] which we have two-thirds of the free world's [supply], our coal resources, which are in the ground. They are there, they should be mined, they should be used, and that will help on the energy problem. That is why we should move forward, not only in these two obvious areas but in also developing our own oil and gas reserves, wherever they may be, on federal property or otherwise.

And that is why, looking down the road, we should develop our great sources of nuclear power which, in the years to come, will replace some of these other elements of power. We, the nation that found the secret to the breaking of the atom, are far behind in this area. It is time for us to go forward on it, because the generation of the future will bless us for having done so.

That is why we must go forward with legislation that will allow the development of deepwater ports so that when we import, we can import adequately, at adequate prices and reasonable prices, the fuel that we need.

Now, I do not say this to lecture my friends in the Congress who are behind me, because I believe all of them support these proposals that I have made. I do not say this in order to lecture the Congress, but I only say this: we have a great goal in mind . . . let America never go through again what it did in October or November last year when some other nation was able to cut off our energy. Let us be independent of any other nation where that is concerned.

That does not mean that we won't be glad to purchase their energy at proper prices in the years ahead and we shall. But it does mean that a nation that has the resources in the ground, that has the resources also in its technology—I am referring to nuclear power, for example—that when we have the resources to be independent of any other nation, let's say that we shall be independent in 1980, and we will do it. That is a great goal for America and one we can achieve.

Now an economic prognosis for the balance of the year: First quarter showed a dip, primarily energy-related. Second quarter predictions are we will level off. Third quarter, fourth quarter, the economy will begin to move forward again.

What is this based on? It is based on the fact that except for two very major items, automobiles and housing, this economy is enormously strong. It is strong, for example, in the agriculture area. It is strong in many other consuming and producing areas. But in automobiles and housing, we have had the downturns to which I have referred and which are a primary cause of the problem we presently have.

But what are we finding now? Automobile production is beginning to go up, not fast, but the predictions toward the end of the year are for a good automobile year—not the best, but a good one. Housing starts are beginning to go up, not as much as we would like, but I will announce within weeks programs of federal activity in this area which I think will stimulate that industry which is so essential to a strong and prosperous America.

So, that is why today I will say to you in making the prognosis on the economy, we have been through what I believe is the lowest point in the downturn. We now can look forward to the leveling off. Toward the last half of the year we will see this economy moving forward again and moving upward.

The major problem is inflation. That we will all have to fight together. And we shall fight it through more production, we shall fight it by keeping down the costs of government where we can, and we shall fight it also through responsible policies in the dealings between labor and management. And I see the year 1974, at the end—and now it is very difficult for us to look that far ahead—but at the end that we will look back and say 1974 was not our best year, as were 1972 and 1973, but it was a good year. I will say and I will flatly predict that 1975 will be a very good year. And I say today that 1976, the 200th anniversary year for America, will be the best year in America's history, the most prosperous, the most free, not only in terms of prosperity, however, and freedom and opportunity for all of our people—a great goal that you are working for here in Mississippi and that we must all dedicate ourselves to—but it will be a year in which America will not only be prosperous but will have prosperity without the cost of war, and that is a great goal. We can achieve it by the year 1976.

Now, having referred to prosperity without war, let us take an overview of the world for a moment, see where we have been, where we are, and where we are going.

We have just ended the longest war in America's history, twelve long, difficult years. For the first time in twenty-five years, no young American is being drafted for the armed services, and everyone is indeed thankful for that.

But let me say, I would hope that Mississippians, who have been in the forefront always in fighting the battles for this country as volunteers, will, many of them, make the decision to serve as volunteers in our armed forces, the peace forces. We need you, and it is a proud service to be in, whether it is the Army, the Navy, or the Air Force of the United States of America.

And finally, with regard to the long and difficult war through which we have been, how we ended it was important. I know that sometimes people say it didn't make any difference, just get it over. But America had to end it in a way that we did not lose the confidence of our allies, the respect of those who were our adversaries, and at least some feeling of respect from those who were the neutrals. And that is why ending it in a way that the people of South Vietnam have an opportunity to choose their own way without having a communist government imposed upon them against their will—that was right. We can be proud of it.

We can be proud of the young men who served for that cause and achieved it, and we can be proud, too, that for the first time in eight years, every American POW has returned from abroad and is at home. And as one of them said when he came home, standing tall and erect—he said, "Thank God we came home on our feet and not on our knees." We can be proud of that fact as well.

But ending a war is not enough. That has been the American failure in this century. We fight wars and fight them well when we have to do so, although we love peace. But we ended World War I, and then we thought we were going to have peace, and the sons of those that fought in World War I had to fight in World War II.

And then we thought we had peace after that long and difficult war. And the younger brothers and even the sons of some of those who fought in World War II fought in Korea.

And then when that war was ended by President Eisenhower in 1953, we thought, "Well, now this must be the last one in this century." But the younger brothers of those that fought in Korea, and even some of their sons, fought in Vietnam.

We must not let this happen again and that Governor Waller, as you said so eloquently in your introduction, is what our foreign policy is about today.

Why do we talk to the Soviet Union leaders? Why do we talk to the leaders of the People's Republic of China? Because we agree with their philosophy? No, they don't like our philosophy; we don't like theirs. But talking, for example, [to] China—one-fourth of all the people in the world live in China—they are among the ablest people in the world. They are not a super power today. They will be, fifteen years from now. And far better to have the United States talking to them now than waiting until then. That is why the opening to China is so important to peace in the world—not just now but in the generations to come.

Why do we talk to the leaders of the Soviet Union when we are both now approximately equal insofar as our nuclear power is concerned? Not because we agree in all of our interests around the world, because some places they are adverse to each other, and not certainly, as I have indicated, because our philosophies are the same, because they are not, but because both sides recognize a simple fact of life: that the leader of America—whoever he is—and the leader of the Soviet Union—whoever he is in the foreseeable future—if he ever resorts to the use of nuclear war, will be committing, in effect national suicide for his own country.

This must not happen, and that is why we are negotiating a limitation on nuclear arms. That is why we are trying to negotiate, in addition, a limitation on and a reduction of forces in Europe, on a mutual basis.

Having referred, however, to these things, let me say that in order for the United States to play this role, a great and a proud role of peacemaker in the world, in order, for example, for us to play the role that we are laying in the Mideast, where in that troubled area of the world that has not known peace for twenty-five years—they have had four wars in twenty-five years; as a matter of fact, it probably hasn't known it for 1,000 years—the chances that our initiatives there to bring an era of peace to that troubled area of the world will depend on America's leadership.

And let me tell you what that leadership entails. First, it entails strength. I refer, first, to military strength. By that, I do not mean military strength in terms of the arrogance of power in which we attempt to push others around. That is never the way we want to use it. We can be proud that in the wars that we have fought in this century, we have never used our strength to destroy freedom, but only to defend it. We have never used our strength to break the peace, but only to keep it. And the other nations of the world know it. Strength in the hands of America is a good thing for those who love peace in the world, and let's keep America strong.

And I would strongly urge, never send an American president to the conference table with any other leader of the world as the head of the second strongest nation in the world. Let that be a goal for Americans to remember, too.

It requires also, if we are to exert this kind of leadership that will build a generation of peace, economic strength. I have referred to that already. And that economic strength is going to come. It is going to come from depending not on government enterprise—government plays a role—but on private enterprise. That is why, for example—if I may use just one example in a field not completely related to your businesses—as far as medical care is concerned, we need a new program, one in which everyone in this country who needs it will have health insurance, but in which no one is forced to have it if he doesn't want it.

But also, let's have a program that does not raise taxes. Let's have a program that is not run by the federal government, because when I have a doctor, I want that doctor working for me and not for the federal government.

Putting it in larger perspective, let's look at energy. You have heard about our government energy program. It will cost $15 billion. We are going to put at least that much in it over the next three to five years, and that sounds like a very big program.

That is bigger, we can say, than the Manhattan Project. It is as big as the space project. But that isn't really the whole of it. It is only the tip of the iceberg. Because, while the government will be spending $15 billion, did you know that over the next ten years, private enterprise, to achieve our goal of becoming independent as far as energy is concerned, private enterprise will be spending $500 billion. That is many times bigger than the Manhattan Project and the space project put together. It will give an enormous boost to the American economy.

So, the prospects for the future, as I say, for those who are young and look ahead for jobs, for more opportunity, they are good. They are good because this nation has the right kind of an economic system. Let's never forget that, and let's never displace it. They are good because this nation is strong in terms of its vision, and I believe this is true about the future. And that brings me to the third element of strength that is so important.

As you look over the pages of history and see what has happened to the great civilizations of the past, an ironic fact stands out and is repeated over and over again: the great civilizations of the past, and you have seen, many of you, the ruins in Athens, you have walked, as I have, at night in the Forum at Rome, and you wonder, why did it happen? And whether it was Rome or Greece or some of the other great civilizations, the ironic thing is that they decayed and they fell not when they were poor, but when they were rich; not when they were supposed to be weak materially, but it was at a time when they were strong. In other words, the time of greatest danger for a great country and society is when it is very wealthy, as we are, when it is very strong, as we are, because the tendency then is for a country to become soft, to become complacent, to turn inward from the thrust toward greatness that brought them where they were.

We must not let this happen to America. And I will tell you why it cannot and it will not happen. It cannot and it will not happen because in addition to our military strength and economic strength, the character of the American people, the spirit of the American people is strong.

I can assure you that is the case, whatever the handwringers and the doom criers say. It is strong all over this country, and it is strong here in Mississippi.

What kind of a spirit is it? The governor referred to that visit to Gulfport. I remember it very well. It was in 1969. I was returning from California. The war then in Vietnam had just reached its peak, and we were beginning to develop the long process that finally brought it to an end. And someone from Mississippi, I think the two senators and congressmen, called and said, "Can't you stop down at Gulfport and give those people a lift?" And so our plane dropped down at Gulfport. I remember it was in the dusk of the evening, and there were tens of thousands of people there.

And you know what? They told me I was supposed to give them a lift. They gave me a lift. They were wonderful people. I remember one man I talked to—you know, you would like to talk to everybody, but you can only talk to a few. As I went down the line, shaking hands—he was a young man, a farmer, obviously. He was holding his little girl in his arms.

She was about six years of age. I will tell you how I can guess. She had two teeth out in front. And I said to him, "Well, how are you doing?" He said, "Well, I lost my home. I lost my barn. I lost my car. I lost my tractor, but," he said, "I got my wife, I got my little girl." And he said, "I love my country, and I love my state, and I am going to see it through. We are going to come back." That is the spirit of America.

My final remarks I address not to the older generation, who are here in such great numbers, but primarily to your sons and your daughters and to the younger generation represented in the balconies and behind me as well.

We often think that we live in the worst of times. We often think, wouldn't it be better if we lived someplace else or were born at a different time? Let me say to this younger generation, don't ever buy that, not about America, not about yourself, and not about the time in which you live, because you have a great future.

Our country is going to be and will continue to be the most prosperous. Our country will continue to have more progress and more opportunity for every person in this country, whatever his background, whatever his color or race or creed.

Our country is going to continue to have more freedom than any other country, but it has more than that. When an individual lives only for himself, he cannot be a great individual. When a nation lives only for itself, it loses whatever opportunity it has to be great.

President de Gaulle once said to me in 1963, when I visited him when I was out of office, he said, "You know, France is never her true self unless she is engaged in a great enterprise."

America today—and I say to our young people—we, you, are engaged in truly a great enterprise, not the works of war, but the works of peace. In your hands, in our hands, is the key to peace for America and for the world for generations to come. What we do or fail to do will determine the future of Americans, but also of three billion people on this earth.

And the question is, will America, with all of its wealth, with all of its strength materially, will we have the spiritual strength, the character, the stamina, the vision to lead as we must lead whether it is in negotiating a peace in the Mideast, whether it is in negotiating a reduction in the burden of armaments in the world, whether it is in developing a dialog with those who are our adversaries, as well as with our friends? America, in order to do that, and an American president, in order to have that kind of leadership, must have the backing of a strong and a united American people.

Let me say to you, my friends, that today that is the challenge we face. Our challenge, then, is not just for ourselves alone. Our challenge is about the whole human race.

That is not original with me. Thomas Jefferson said it much better when America was very young and very poor and very weak. At the time of the signing of the Declaration of Independence, he said we act not just for ourselves alone, we act for the whole human race.

That was not true then, but he believed it. And Lincoln believed it, Andrew Jackson believed it, and I am sure Robert E. Lee believed it, and I am sure, too, Woodrow Wilson did, the other presidents through the years.

What I am saying today is that today, it is true, there is no other nation in the free world of the great nations that has the strength, militarily and economically, to give the leadership which must be given if we are to build a world of peace.

And so, it is all in our hands, and the question is: will we fail or will we succeed? And the answer is in your hands, and I say that the answer will be: we shall not fail. We cannot fail, because Americans are a great people. We would not have come so far all across the prairies and clear over to the Pacific, we could not have survived so many disasters unless we were a good people and a strong people.

And so today, we will be strong not only materially but spiritually. And in the leadership that we will provide to the world, we will be strong, we will meet that challenge, and a day will come—I can see it now—twenty-five years from now a President of the United States, I trust, may be standing in this very place. It will be the year 2000, a new year that comes only once in 1,000 years, and he will look back to this critical generation of ours and he will say, "They did not fail when the going was very difficult and when American leadership was so important to the world."

But even more than that, when that year 2000 comes, if we meet the challenge that destiny has placed upon us, and if we meet it not as a burden, but as an opportunity, gladly, if we meet that challenge, then three, or probably four billion people on this earth will look at America, will look at what we have done, and joining with us, they will say, "God bless America."[3]

George W. Bush's Address in Bay St. Louis—January 12, 2006

Thank you all. Please be seated. Haley [Mississippi governor Barbour] said that it's protocol not to introduce the president. Well, that shows what he knows about protocol. He just introduced me. Thanks for having me back. My first observation is, it's good to see—to be able to look in people's eyes and not see them all bloodshot.

I can remember coming here, the times I came and looked hard in people's eyes and saw a sense of desperation and worry and deep, deep concern about the future. I'm sure there is still concern about the future, but the eyes have cleared up. There's a sense of optimism. There's a hope. There's a little bounce in people's step. I'm not surprised; the people down here have showed incredible courage. And I want to thank you for showing the rest of our country what it means to survive an incredible hardship with high spirits.

Your governor has done a magnificent job. He went up to Washington. You know, it's nice of him to give me the credit to sign the bill. It's nice of him to compliment Congressman [Gene] Taylor who deserves to be complimented, and compliment Congressman Chip Pickering, both of whom are here, and I thank them for coming. It's wise of him to compliment Senator [Trent] Lott and Senator [Thad] Cochran. And he's right to compliment them. But the truth of the matter is, the person who deserve the biggest compliment, in my judgment, is [Haley Barbour] who brought the will of the Mississippi people, the needs of the Mississippi people up to Washington, DC, and fashioned one heck of a piece of legislation for the people of this important state. Thank you, governor, for your hard work.

And I want to thank Marsha [Barbour] for being here as well. I don't know how you put up with him for all these years. You must be a patient soul. But he married well, just like me. And speaking about that Laura [Bush] sends her best wishes to all of you all. She's looking forward to coming back down here. She's not going to believe the difference between the last time she was here and today.

It's hard sometimes, unless you've got a perspective. I have the perspective of having spent some time here but not all my time. And I can remember what was and now what is, and I can see what's going to be too. And it's going to be a better Gulf Coast of Mississippi.

I want to thank Roy Bernardi, who is deputy secretary of HUD [Department of Housing and Urban Development]. He's going to have some stuff to do to make sure this part of the world rebounds. I like your mayors. They're down-to-earth people. They are good, solid people—Mayor Eddie Favre. You know, one time a buddy of mine said, when the baseball players and owners couldn't figure out an agreement and they went on strike and quit Major League Baseball, he said, "I'm never going back to a baseball game for ten years." And I said, sure, you know. And he's a great baseball fan. And, sure enough, last year was his tenth year, and he finally went to a game. The reason I bring that up is Eddie said, "I'm not going to wear long pants." And I'm saying to myself, "One of these days, the president is going to show up, and Eddie sure enough will put on long pants." I didn't know him very well. I arrived here at this important school, and he's got short pants on. Eddie, I like a man who sticks to his guns. Thanks for hosting us.

And so I'm standing in the White House at a Christmas reception, and in walks Tommy Longo. He's the mayor of Waveland, of course. And he had on a fantastic suit. I nearly fell out. Longo in a suit? I said, "Where did you get that thing?" He said, "It's amazing what you can find in the rubbish."

I've learned something about the mayors up and down the Gulf Coast. You've got some young mayors east of here who have been in office, what, three or four months, and the storm hit. They were incredibly tested—Pascagoula and other places. You got some veterans who have been around for a while, never dreamt they'd see a day like the day they saw. But whether they're veterans or rookies, all of them have stood strong. All of them have rallied with the first-responders. All of them have shown great compassion to the people. I am proud of your local mayors, your local governments, people like Rocky Pullman of the Hancock board of supervisors, the people working in these counties. You got some good folks down here. And one of the reasons why I'm confident about your recovery is because you've elected good people to take on the job.

Finally, I want to thank Brother Talbot and Brother Hingle of this fantastic school. Thanks for hosting us. Tommy Longo was in the class of 1975. I hope that means you didn't lower your academic standards in that year. He and old Doc Blanchard went here, they told me. Doc Blanchard went here, in case you didn't know it, the Heisman Trophy winner who carried the leather for West Point. And one of the things the Brother told me, he said, "We wanted to make sure we saved the Heisman Trophy that Doc Blanchard had made sure was housed here at this facility." But I do want to thank you all for letting us come by. Thanks for your being in education; really an important part of the future of this state and this country, to make sure people get a good education.

I stood in Jackson Square early on in—after the storm hit, and I said, "We're not just going to survive, but thrive." By that I meant, it's one thing to kind of ride it out; it's another thing to take out of the harm that came, convert this into a better life. I said, "We're not just going to cope, but we'll overcome." I meant what I said. I couldn't have said that if I didn't have confidence, though, in the people in the local area that have such a spirit to be able to do so.

I'm here to report to you some of the progress made and to let you know that people in faraway places like Washington, D.C., still hear you and care about you. Signing all the legislation I've signed, the federal government has committed $85 billion so far to helping folks and to help rebuild the Gulf Coast of our country. Of that $85 billion, about $25 billion has been spent. So $85 billion is available; $25 billion of it is already in the pipeline. That's $60 billion more coming your way.

Part of the strategy to make sure that the rebuilding effort after the recovery effort worked well was to say to people like Haley and the governor of Louisiana and the mayor of New Orleans, "You all develop a strategy. It's your state. It's your region; you know the people better than people in Washington. Develop the rebuilding strategy. And the role of the federal government is to coordinate with you and to help."

I thought that was an important first statement to make when people began to wonder what life would be like after the storm hit. My view is, and a lot of my political philosophy is based on, the local folks know better than the folks in Washington, D.C. I remember when Haley invited me down, and he said—I think we were in a tent at that time, and there wasn't a lot of electricity—it was like an old-time daytime revival without electricity. It was hot in the tent. It was the first meeting, I think, at least the first called meeting, of the commission headed by Jim Barksdale. Citizens from all walks of life, all occupations, all aimed at one thing: putting together a strategy that will help this part of the world become even better than it was before.

I have an obligation to make sure that the federal government responds and coordinates and stays in touch with not only the commission and the governor but local folks as well. And I picked a fellow that I trust, a person who's had a lot of experience, a person who understands rural life, and he knows the importance of county commissioners; you call them county supervisors, I guess. He's a guy who's a good listener, and he's got my full confidence. And that's my friend Don Powell who's with me today. He's going to be the federal coordinator. His job is to come down here and listen and report back.

I recognize there are some rough spots, and I'm going to mention some of them here in a minute, and we're going to work to make them as smooth as possible. The first challenge we had after the storm hit was to take care of the people that were displaced, millions of people, or over a million people evacuated and scattered. It was an amazing period in our history, when you think about it. One day people's lives are turned upside down, and they're looking for help, and they're looking for compassion, and they found it. People found it in churches, in synagogues, in community centers, and in private homes. It's an amazing part of our history, when you think about it. It's like there's a great capacity to absorb hurt in our country, because we've got individuals that are so decent and honorable.

The government had a role to play, and that was to get money in people's pockets. I mean, when you have to evacuate, you don't have time to plan. And so one of the first things we did was, we got $2,000 in people's pockets as quickly as possible, to help them. In other words, it was a response geared toward the individual. We had a special designation for all evacuees, so they can become available for Medicaid or family services or the federal programs. The idea was to get a response as quickly as possible to people who are scattered all over the country so they could—to help get their feet on the ground.

We gave waivers to states. In other words, we kind of deregulated the system so states could respond quickly to the people who needed help. We provided 700,000 households with rental help. In other words, the goal is for people to be back in their homes, in a home they call their own. That's the goal. But in the meantime, we had to deal with people evacuated and people without homes. And so a part of the plan has been to provide temporary housing with rental vouchers; $390 million went out as HUD vouchers for a group of people that qualified.

I can remember people hollering for trailers. We became the largest consumer of trailers probably in the history of mankind. And I know it was slow to begin with. The production needed to be ramped up, and, frankly, the government crowded out other purchasers in order to set priorities for people down in this part of the world. We've now put out 61,000 trailers, and there are more in the pipeline. I was asking Haley, does he have a feel for how many more we need, and he said, "We're getting close to the end, but there's still a need." And we understand that. And the manufacturing is making—we put cruise ships out at one point to help people house on a temporary basis, particularly in New Orleans, so that we could get the police and the firefighters a place to stay so they could do their job.

People ended up in hotel rooms. At one time there was about eighty-some-thousand people in hotel rooms. It's now down to 25,000 families in hotel rooms. We're in the process of trying to locate every single family and provide the rental assistance help for them, so they can move from the hotel into rental housing, all aimed, by the way, at providing some kind of housing until the permanent housing market takes off. We're trying to bridge from being an evacuee to a person in a place until their own home gets ready to move into.

And so what can we do? Well, first thing is, we can focus on repairing homes. That's not going to do you very good down here in Waveland. I understand that. Tommy and I and the governor and Marsha just drove by; there's no homes to repair. It's just been flattened. That's what the people of America have got to understand. Sometimes hurricanes go through, and, you know, there's a home and a structure you can maybe put a roof on or do something—not here. Our fellow citizens have got to know when this hurricane hit, it just obliterated everything. It just flattened it.

But in parts of the hurricane zone, there's repairs that can be done. FEMA [Federal Emergency Management Agency] assistance will help with that. SBA [Small Business Administration] loans have gone out to about—for about two-point-one-billion dollars to help people repair their homes. Now, the most innovative approach, however, to getting the homes rebuilt is the CDBG [Community Development Block Grant program] grants that Haley Barbour negotiated on behalf of the people of Mississippi. That's government initials for, direct money to help people who weren't able to get their insurance to pay them off.

I remember being down in Biloxi. I think it was my first trip. And it was hot, and it was steamy. An old lady walked up to me and said to me—I said, "How are you doing?" And she looked at me and she said, "Not worth a darn." And I said, "Well, I don't blame you." She said, "I've been paying all my life for my insurance. Every time that bill came, I paid it, every single month. And all of a sudden the storm hit, Mr. President, and I came time to collect, and they told me no." And she was plenty unhappy, and she was looking for anybody she could be unhappy with, and I just happened to be the target. I think Gene was with me then; I might have shared the story with Gene about that.

One way to handle the issue—I know you got a lawsuit here; I'm not going to talk about the lawsuit. But Haley did something innovative, which was take the CDBG, a lot of money for Mississippi and going to help the people do the job that many think the insurance companies should have done in the first place.

Having said that, the government has paid out twelve-billion dollars in flood insurance. For those who had flood insurance, the government is making good on its—on the bargain with the people. If you got an FHA [Federal Housing Administration] loan, your loan will be forgiven for a year. In other words, there is an attempt to try to make sure that things are being done so that we can—people can get back in their homes, and people can get to be rebuilding.

There's going to be a building boom down here; there just is. It's going to be an exciting time for people. One of the real challenges is whether or not people are going to have the skill set necessary to be able to meet the needs of the people. Are there going to be enough electricians, enough plumbers, and enough roofers? But you're going to have yourself a building boom; you watch. There's going to be work; people are going to be working hard here.

Don Powell and I, to this end, met with a group of leaders in Washington, D.C., from building trade unions and businesses, and the whole idea was to come up with a strategy to make sure people have got the skills necessary to fill the jobs which are going to exist. See, our goal, and I know it's the governor's goal, is to make sure the jobs first go to Mississippi people—when it comes to rebuilding—and Mississippi businesses. We want this opportunity to be an opportunity where minority-owned businesses and women-owned businesses have a chance to flourish. An ownership society has got to be a part of a new vision, where people from all walks of life can say, "I'm owning my own business. I'm operating my own business. I'm owning my own home."

It's a fantastic opportunity, but it's not going to work unless people have the skill set necessary to be able to fill those jobs and to be able to provide for consumer demand. So the idea is to work with your community college system or the building trades and have centers where people can go to learn how to get the skills necessary to fill the jobs which are coming. They're coming. It's going to be an exciting time down here, just so long as you're able to get enough material and enough labor.

One of the important—and by the way, speaking about jobs, not only do we got to make sure people have the skills necessary to fill the jobs, the federal government has got a lot of facilities down here, and there's a lot of federal employees in this part of the world. We're going to rebuild the federal facilities so that the people will be able to work.

This recovery is going to be led by the private sector. However, the federal government is going to help, and $85 billion is a good—I would call that help—so far. But the truth of the matter is, the jobs and the quality of life, the recovery, is going to be led by the private sector. I was asking Haley about some of the industries down here, and he told me, for example, at the year-end, a casino opened. I mean, it's remarkable. If you'd have seen what I saw I'm sure you saw what it looked like up and down this coast, and all of the sudden, there's businesses, and people are thriving. People are beginning to work. It's happening. It's the private sector that's going to carry much of the recovery.

Congress did a smart thing, in my judgment, [it] was to provide tax incentives for businesses who are in this part of the world. They provide tax incentives for small businesses to expenses up to $200,000 of investment and private—and incentive for all businesses to provide a 50-percent bonus depreciation for investment made. What I'm telling you is, it's kind of economic talk for saying, if somebody spends money in an investment in this part of the world, they get a tax incentive to do so. In other words, if you're able to make the tax code attract capital so people invest, it means you're more likely to be able to find work here. It goes on. It's a smart idea, and again, I want to thank the members of Congress for working on that. I think it's going to make a big difference.

If you're a small-business owner—we just met today, by the way, with some small-business owners in New Orleans. And one of the things that became loud and clear to me was that because a lot of people haven't moved back into the area, and if you're a small-business owner, there's no customers, so you have no cash flow, which makes it awfully difficult to survive. There are SBA loans for this, and I understand for some the word "SBA" means "slow bureaucratic paperwork." I hear it loud and clear. I will tell you that SBA has put out about $470 million worth of SBA loans. In other words, the loans are going out.

But this small agency has been overwhelmed. And so Don Powell is working on an interesting idea, and that is to work with the local bankers, people who understand the local customer, as to how to become the agent for the SBA to get money out the door to help small businesses manage their cash flow needs until the customer base comes back.

The other thing that happened quickly—and I'm real proud of you folks down here—was that the energy sector rebounded unbelievably fast. This part of the world is really important for national security and economic security of the United States of America. Remember, when the storms hit, a lot of folks were really worried about the price of crude oil and gasoline. We, fortunately—we just did two things I thought were wise.

One, we suspended reformulated gasoline rules, which enabled us to import gasoline from Europe, which helped to take the pressure off the market. And the price of gasoline, although it went up, didn't go up nearly as high as a lot of people thought, and is now heading back down, thank goodness, for people who are working for a living. And the price of crude oil stayed reasonable because we opened up the Strategic Petroleum Reserve. I was confident in being able to do that because I knew how fast this industry could move if just given a chance. The suspension of some regulations to help these refineries and these gas processing plants get up on their feet was important. In other words, if you can get government out of the way, amazing things can happen sometimes in the private sector.

And so, I want to thank those of you who work in the energy industry for doing what you're doing. I remember going to the plant in Pascagoula. We had people there camped out there working as hard as they could to get the refineries up so that our citizens from all around the country would be able to have gasoline at a reasonable price. And these people worked hour after hour after hour and did the nation a great service. In the meantime, we did our part, tried to do our part to make sure that we cleaned out the waterways so that the ships could move better. Our Coast Guard, by the way, provided invaluable service here in this part of the country.

Part of the recovery of this part of the world is going to be when you get your infrastructure up and running. And I can remember first choppering over here and seeing the incredible devastation done to the bridges and highways. First of all, there has been some incredible construction done. The Slidell Bridge there, to the west of you, got up in record time. It's amazing what happens when you provide a completion bonus for people doing work.

And I know you're concerned about the I-10 Bridge, but they're getting ready to start on it, as I understand. And the bills I've signed provide $2.3 billion for repair of highways and bridges in this part of the world. That's going to provide not only jobs, but it's going to make the quality of life come back to what it was. You're dependent upon good highways and good bridges in this part of the world. The government recognized that and put the money out there, available for reimbursing the states when they get these highway projects moving.

One of the really interesting things that happened was education, how the country responded for the kids who have been moved around. School districts all over America took children from Louisiana and Mississippi and helped educate them. It was really remarkable to watch the education system rise to the challenge. In the bill there is $2.6 billion worth of operating money. It was money to help these schools stay afloat; it was to reimburse school districts for taking in the children who had evacuated to their part of the world. That's in addition to the federal commitment to replace every school. In other words, part of the commitment is that if your school got destroyed, the federal government will help rebuild the school or will rebuild the school.

Plus, we understood that there was a lot of kids that were going to higher education and these—higher education institutions were affected by the storm, obviously, and they were allowed to retain their federal aid, even though children weren't going to school. In other words, we made a concerted effort to help these schools to cope with the crisis. We're going to make a concerted effort to help the schools deal with the long-term reconstruction as a result of the crisis.

Ninety-three percent of the schools here in Mississippi are up and running, and it's an amazing feat in four months' time. It's a great credit, again, to your governor and your education institutions but more importantly, it's a great credit to the teachers and superintendents and principals of your local schools.

Finally, the first issue I was confronted with as the president was debris. I remember the meeting very well when the mayor showed up and said, "We can't possibly say to our people things are going to bet better so long as we got piles of debris lying around." It was not only a practical issue, but it was a psychological issue. And I can understand—I mean, I understood right off the bat what they were talking about. And we had a slow start, because we had an issue of how to get debris off of private property. Thankfully, there was some creative work done here at the local and state level, and with the federal government, as to how to deal with the liability issue.

I don't want to go into the law; I'm not even a lawyer. Got too many of them up there in Washington, anyway. But my point is, is that by listening to the local folks and by being flexible about how to deal with an important issue like debris, we're making pretty good progress. Out of forty-two million cubic yards of debris, twenty-seven million have been removed.

Now there's still debris. It's estimated about fifteen million cubic yards of debris left. But there's a certain momentum that's gathering. Haley believes that by the end of March, we can get most of the debris off of the public property. In other words, they're making progress.

Don Powell's job is, to the extent that the federal government is contracting out—we want to make sure that they just don't hustle when the president shows up, that they're hustling all the time, because the rebuilding and rebirth of this area is really going to depend in large measure to getting these lots clean, to getting your public access roads cleaned up, getting that debris out of people's sight. There's something—there's a certain confidence to be gained when you see this beautiful countryside cleared of the damage of Katrina. Things have changed a lot when it comes to debris. It looks a lot different, a whole lot different. And we got more work to be done, and we're going to stay on it until it gets done.

And so we've done a lot, and there's a lot more to do, but there's a certain optimism and hope that's coming. I hope you feel that. You've come a long way in four months. Seems like an eternity to you, I know. Seems like a lot of time for a lot of people to have gone through what you went through. Four months is not all that long, and a lot has happened in that four-month period. And a lot more is going to happen in the next four months, and then the next four months. I can't wait to come back, and keep coming back and seeing the progress that's being made.

We've learned some lessons from Katrina, and we're going to analyze every lesson learned. Obviously, the federal response in parts of this devastated area could have been a lot better. We want to know how to make them better. We want to make sure that when there's a catastrophe of any kind, this government, at the federal level, is capable of dealing with it, in conjunction with the state and local governments.

There's going to be some lessons learned about having agencies that get overwhelmed by a size of a storm, agencies whose job it is to help people get on their feet and maybe aren't able to do it quite as efficiently as some would like. Those are the lessons we're going to continually analyze. That's what you ought to expect of those of us who have been given the high honor of serving you, to constantly look for ways to do things better. And I just want to assure you, we are. We are.

But there's some other lessons learned where we don't need to change: the lesson of courage. We saw great courage. I'll never forget going to the hangar to see those Coast Guard kids that were flying those choppers. I think it's something like 30,000 citizens were saved by rescue efforts by Coast Guard men and local responders. And the people here on the frontlines of saving lives showed great courage during Katrina.

I remember seeing the determination of our citizens. One of the lessons learned is when people are determined, they can get things done. At the Pass Christian school system, for example, this is a place where they consolidated all the schools at the elementary school. It was kind of inconvenient, when you think about it, but the inconvenience didn't bother the people in charge of that school system. As a matter of fact, they viewed it as a fantastic opportunity to be able to come together and share—and that school was up and running, with broken windows—but there wasn't a broken heart, and their spirit wasn't broken.

One of the lessons, of course, is the compassion of our fellow citizens. Think about lonely folks being sent out, having all their property, their material goods destroyed, wondering what the future meant for them, and there's a loving family saying, "I love you, brother. I love you, sister." Think about a country where the compassion is so strong that a neighbor in need can find a stranger that wants to help them get their feet back on the ground.

One of the lessons of this storm is the decency of people, the decency of men and women who care a lot about their fellow citizens, whether they be elected officials or just folks on the ground here just trying to make somebody else's life even better than it was before. So we learned some lessons about how to respond, and we're going to change. But some of the lessons shouldn't change, and that is the decency and character of the American people.

It's been an amazing experience for you. You just got to know, though, that a lot of people in this country, many of whom have never been down here, care for you; they pray for you, and they're pulling for you. God bless.[4]

APPENDIX B

Visits by US Presidents before or after Their Terms in Office

Early in the process of defining this research project, the coauthors made the decision that the best strategy was to narrow its focus to visits by presidents of the United States while in office, thus making the book an authoritative resource for historians, journalists, government officials, teachers, students, and others interested in the topic. This choice to limit the scope was based largely on the premise that it would be nearly impossible to compile a list inclusive of all visits by individuals who would be or had been presidents. Who could say, for instance, whether or when Jimmy Carter's family vacationed on the Mississippi Gulf Coast during his childhood years? Who would think to check whether the Wolverines played a football game in Mississippi during Gerald Ford's time on the University of Michigan team? How could one unearth whether Andrew Johnson took a steamboat trip down the Mississippi River in retirement with a stop in Vicksburg or Natchez? Obviously, the reasonable decision for this book was to limit the scope to the visits of sitting presidents.

However, as we pursued the research, we found various sources that spoke of visits to Mississippi by one or another individual who held the presidency, but at a time in the person's life when he was not in office. Among the sources providing such records were handwritten notes or typewritten sheets mined from an accumulated, never organized file titled, "Presidential Visits," held by the Mississippi Department of Archives and History. Few of these scattered references offered useful clues as to the origin of the information. Other mentions of these sorts of visits showed up in books or scholarly journals. Then there were the occasional, always incomplete newspaper accounts written to summarize presidential visits to the state. In each case, we jotted a note and pressed onward.

As we later considered these notes—sketchy as the sources often were—we realized that even an unverified list of visits by individuals before or after their years in the presidential office might provide leads for other scholars with their own research goals. Perhaps such a list would simply benefit the generalist interested in Mississippiana who could use the information as a launch point for a more detailed search. Some references appear to represent local legends or family stories—for example, William Henry Harrison delivering an address in Rodney, Mississippi. Others are clearly based on historical fact—for example, Herbert Hoover as secretary of commerce visiting in the Mississippi Delta during the Great Flood of 1927. Thus we caution readers to recognize that records of visits during the prepresidential years are especially subject to distortions resulting from pride of place or the vagaries of memory. Any individual's presence in the state before his years of national prominence would rarely be notable. In other words, a single report of a spotting in Mississippi decades prior to a particular man's term of office—for example, Lincoln traveling the Natchez Trace in the 1820s—deserves skepticism and close scrutiny.

In the end, we decided to include in this appendix all references we discovered to individuals who served as president and who purportedly visited Mississippi prior to or following their years in office. Obviously it is not offered as an exhaustive accounting; there may have been other visits during the lives of those men listed, or visits by other presidents whose names did not appear as by-products to our principal research. Some of the items are labeled as "date uncertain"; others report a year, or even a month and year, if that information showed up in our sources. Those entries seemingly based on thin evidence generally include such wording as, "said to have," or "rumored to have." Thus we offer this list to the reader with all appropriate disclaimers and warnings to look further before accepting the veracity of any reference. If there are similar items that should be included in this list, please consider sending a note to either of the authors or to the publisher for inclusion in a future edition.

Andrew Jackson

1791	Said to have married his wife, Rachel Donelson Robards, at a plantation near Fayette in Jefferson County.
1814	Stopped in Mississippi Territory prior to his participation in the Battle of New Orleans; said to have camped near the Kiln Road in Hancock County, on his way from Mobile to Louisiana.
Date uncertain	Said to own and frequent a home in Coahoma County.
January 1828	Delivered campaign speeches in Natchez and Jackson.
January 1840	Stopped in Vicksburg during a river voyage to New Orleans.
January 1840	Visited Jackson as a retired president where he addressed the state legislature in the old capitol building.

William Henry Harrison

Date uncertain	Said to have delivered a speech in Rodney.

James Polk

Date uncertain	Owned a plantation near Coffeeville; whether he ever visited is undetermined.

Zachary Taylor

1820   Commanded the infantry unit that built a road from Pearl River to Bay
                St. Louis.
1847   Following his victories in the Mexican War, Mississippians wined and
                dined him in Pass Christian and Pascagoula, where he bought and
                frequented a summer home. His widow eventually died at the home.
1848   Campaigned for the presidency in Bay St. Louis where a poorly con-
                structed speaker's stand collapsed under him.
February 1849   Visited as president-elect his Jefferson County Cypress Bend plantation
                and stopped at Vicksburg on the trip to the nation's capital for his
                inauguration.

Millard Fillmore

March 1854   Stopped on the steamer *R. J. Ward* in Natchez.

Abraham Lincoln

1828   Rumored to have traveled the Natchez Trace, though a biography dis-
                putes the claim.

Ulysses Grant

May to July 1863 Led the Vicksburg Campaign of the Civil War.
Spring 1880   Delivered a political speech in Vicksburg while unsuccessfully seeking
                  a third presidential nomination by the Republican Party.

James Garfield

Date uncertain   Served in Mississippi as a Union soldier during the Civil War.

Theodore Roosevelt

March 1911   Made a hunting trip to the Mississippi Delta.
1915   Vacationed in Pass Christian, stayed with a friend, and fished the
                Chandeleurs.

Calvin Coolidge

Early 1930s   Said to have been observed standing on a train platform in the Gulf
                   Coast region of the state.

Herbert Hoover

April 1927   Visited the Mississippi Delta as secretary of commerce to view the de-
                   struction caused by the flooding Mississippi River; provided super-
                   vision for recovery efforts; photographed on the levee in Greenville.

Franklin Roosevelt

1917   Visited the Mississippi Gulf Coast as assistant secretary of the navy to
                   inspect the ports.

Harry Truman

1933   Made the first of a series of family vacation trips to the Mississippi Gulf
                   Coast. During the 1933 trip, the Trumans stayed in a rental cottage
                   for six weeks and then sought a reservation for the following spring.
1944   Delivered a campaign speech in Gulfport as the vice-presidential
                   candidate.
1956   Made a postpresidential trip to the Mississippi Gulf Coast to visit his
                   daughter, Margaret, who was sent to the area to recuperate from
                   an illness.

Dwight Eisenhower

July 1947   Presented the keynote speech at Vicksburg's Carnival of the Confed-
                   eracy, where he answered a journalist's question about his willing-
                   ness to serve as president with an affirmative response, reportedly
                   for the first time. He stopped in Jackson on the previous day before
                   journeying to Vicksburg.

John Kennedy

October 1957   Visited Jackson as a US senator to address a meeting of the Young
                   Democrats; spent the night at the governor's mansion.

Lyndon Johnson

1953	Campaigned in Jackson, as the minority leader of the US Senate.
June 1957	Visited Greenville to serve as godfather for Margaret Wynn, daughter of a family friend from Texas; Johnson was US Senate majority leader at the time.
1960	Made campaign whistle stops in Meridian, Laurel, Hattiesburg, and Picayune as the vice-presidential candidate on the Kennedy/Johnson ticket.

Richard Nixon

| September 1960 | Stopped in Jackson during his first campaign for the presidency. |
| November 1978 | Gave a postresignation address for Veteran's Day at the Mississippi Coast Coliseum in Biloxi. |

Gerald Ford

| August 1974 | Delivered political speeches as vice president in support of Mississippi candidates just prior to assuming the presidency following Richard Nixon's resignation. |
| February 1981 | Spoke at a Republican fundraiser for Gil Carmichael. |

Jimmy Carter

| September 1976 | Traveled the Gulf Coast to kick off the general election campaign in Mississippi; he was accompanied by Senators Eastland and Stennis. |

Ronald Reagan

| August 1980 | Made a political speech at the Neshoba County Fair. |

George H. W. Bush

| May 1984 | Visited as vice president to speak at Delta Council's annual meeting in Cleveland and at a GOP fund-raising event in Greenville at the Washington County Convention Center. |
| December 1994 | Joined the guests for a gala evening in Jackson to honor the state's economic progress, termed the "Mississippi Miracle." Mrs. Bush accompanied him. |

April 1998   Attended the funeral in Jackson of retired Episcopal bishop John Allin.
                  Met briefly with Governor Kirk Fordice.

Bill Clinton

Dates uncertain   Periodically visited Mississippi during his terms as governor of Arkan-
                  sas, including a stop in Cleveland, Mississippi, to serve as speaker at
                  the Delta Council annual meeting. During the visits, he was rumored
                  to occasionally enjoy the steaks at Doe's Eat Place in Greenville.

George W. Bush

August 2015   Visited Gulfport for the tenth anniversary of Hurricane Katrina to
                  honor police and firefighters who saved lives. His wife, Laura, ac-
                  companied him.

June 2017   Spoke in Jackson at a fund-raising reception for US senator Roger
                  Wicker. Event was held at a private home, and couples paid up to
                  $20,800 to attend.

Barack Obama

March 2008   Campaigned for the Democratic presidential nomination on the cam-
                  pus of Jackson State University.

September 2008   As part of the 2008 national election, debated Republican candidate
                  John McCain on the University of Mississippi campus in the first of
                  three such meetings sponsored by the Commission on Presidential
                  Debates. The other two presidential debates were in October 2008
                  on the campuses of Belmont University in Nashville, Tennessee, and
                  Hofstra University in Hempstead, New York.

Donald Trump

August 2016   As the Republican nominee for president, visited Jackson for a private
                  fund-raising event, followed by a public rally in the evening at the
                  Mississippi Coliseum.

NOTES

William McKinley

1. Olcott, *William McKinley*, 2:300ff.

2. *Greenville Times*, May 4, 1901, 4.

3. Busbee, *Mississippi*, 190.

4. *San Francisco Call*, April 30, 1901, 1.

5. *Kansas Agitator*, May 3, 1901, 4

6. *Billings Gazette*, April 30, 1901, 1.

7. *Minneapolis Journal*, May 1, 1901, 1.

8. *Daily Corinthian*, September 21, 1977, 1.

9. Ibid.

10. *Vicksburg Post*, May 6, 2001, 1.

11. *New York Times*, May 1, 1901, 1.

12. *Clarion-Ledger*, May 16, 1977, 3G.

13. *Minneapolis Journal*, May 1, 1901, 1.

14. *Pascagoula Democrat-Times*, May 10, 1901, 1–2.

15. Ibid.

16. Ibid.

17. *National Historic Landmark Registration Form*, https://www.nps.gov/history/nhl/news/lc/fall2015/msstatecapitol.pdf, 22.

18. *New York Times*, May 2, 1901, 1.

19. *Clarion-Ledger,* May 16, 1977, 3G.

20. Mississippi Department of Archives and History, File: *Presidential Visits.*

21. *Macon Beacon*, May 11, 1901, 1.

22. Ibid.

23. Ibid.

24. *Pascagoula Democrat-Times*, May 10, 1901, 2.

25. *Macon Beacon*, May 11, 1901, 1.

Theodore Roosevelt

1. Hilpert, *American Cyclone.*

2. Morris, *Theodore Rex*, chapter 12.

3. Harbaugh, *Power and Responsibility*, 171.

4. *Indianapolis Journal*, November 10, 1902, 1.

5. Ibid.

6. Morris, *Theodore Rex*, chapter 12.

7. Roosevelt, *Hunting the Grisly and Other Sketches*, chapter 2.

8. *St. Louis Republic*, November 16, 1902, Part III, 29.

9. Bernard and McIlhenny, *Tabasco*, 75.

10. *Rock Island Argus*, November 19, 1902, 1.

11. *New-York Tribune*, November 19, 1902, 1.

12. King, "History of the Teddy Bear."

13. Lower Delta Partnership, *Great Delta Bear Affair*.

14. Boyd and Chen, *History and Experience of African Americans in America's Postal Service*.

15. Gatewood, *Theodore Roosevelt and the Art of Controversy*, 75.

16. Ibid., 78.

17. *Aberdeen Weekly*, November 21, 1902, 1.

18. See *Columbus Commercial*, October 12, 1905, 4. Also *Minneapolis Journal*, October 22, 1905, 1.

19. *Greenville Times*, October 6, 1907, 1.

20. *Herald and News*, October 22, 1907, 1.

21. *Natchez Democrat*, August 27, 1979, 1.

22. Ibid.

23. *Evening Star*, October 22, 1907, 11.

24. *Nashville Globe*, November 27, 1908, 6.

William Taft

1. Ellis, *Presidential Travel*, 6.

2. *Aberdeen Weekly*, June 4, 1909 1.

3. Ellis, *Presidential Travel*, 150ff.

4. Ibid., 212.

5. Ibid., 172ff. Theodore Roosevelt traveled to Panama in 1906 to inspect progress on the construction of the canal crossing the isthmus.

6. *Columbus Commercial*, October 31, 1909, 1.

7. Ibid.

8. St. Louis Business Men's League, *Down the Mississippi River*, 4.

9. *Pensacola Journal*, October 30, 1909.

10. Lakes-to-the-Gulf Deep Waterway Association, *Report on the Fourth Annual Convention, New Orleans, October 30 to November 2, 1909*, 29–32.

11. *Daily Press*, October 29, 1909, 1.

12. *Calumet News*, October 28, 1909, 1.

13. *Daily Press*, October 29, 1909, 1.

14. *Rock Island Argus*, October 29, 1909, 1.

15. *Topeka State Journal*, October 29, 1909, 1.

16. Ibid.

17. Ibid.

18. *Pensacola Journal*, October 30, 1909, 1.

19. *New York Times*, October 30, 1909, 6.

20. As a member of the state senate prior to his time as Mississippi's governor, Edmond Noel authored and guided the passage of a statute that defined political parties as private organizations legally allowed to limit those who participated in party activities. By this action, the state's legislature excluded African American voters from primary elections, despite the assurances of the Fifteenth Amendment to the US Constitution. It was a strategy widely imitated in the South, and it nearly always meant that whites-only primary elections produced party-preferred winners in the general elections.

21. *Rock Island Argus*, November 1, 1909, 1.

22. *Forest Republican*, November 3, 1909, 1.

23. *Aberdeen Weekly*, August 27, 1909, 2.

24. *Forest Republican*, November 3, 1909, 1.

25. Ibid.

26. Ibid.

27. Ibid.

28. *Columbus Commercial*, July 18, 1909, 1.

29. *Columbus Commercial*, July 25, 1909, 1.

30. *Columbus Commercial*, August 8, 1909, 2.

31. *Columbus Commercial*, September 9, 1909, 2.

32. *Columbus Commercial*, September 26, 1909, 2.

33. *Columbus Commercial*, October 31, 1909, 1.

34. *Columbus Commercial*, November 4, 1909, 1.

35. *Cairo Bulletin*, November 3, 1909, 1.

36. *Columbus Commercial*, November 4, 1909, 1.

37. Jacob M. Dickinson was a native of Columbus, Mississippi, whose career as attorney, judge, law professor, government official, and railroad executive took him to Tennessee and Illinois before he was named Taft's first secretary of war, serving in the president's cabinet from 1909 to 1911.

38. Mississippi gave Republican William Taft only 6.5 percent of its votes in the general election of 1908. Democrat William Jennings Bryan carried the state with more than 90 percent of the votes.

39. *Columbus Commercial*, November 4, 1909, 1.

40. *Columbus Commercial*, November 7, 1909, 1.

41. *Macon Beacon*, November 6, 1909, 4.

42. *Okolona Messenger*, November 10, 1909, 4.

Woodrow Wilson

1. *Washington (DC) Times*, December 20, 1913, 1. Grip—or grippe—suggested influenza.

2. Boudreaux, *Legends and Lore of the Mississippi Golden Gulf Coast*, 132.

3. *Sun Herald*, January 11, 1998, 1E.

4. *Evening Star*, December 20, 1913, 1.

5. Boudreaux, *Legends and Lore of the Mississippi Golden Gulf Coast*, 133.

6. *Sun*, December 21, 1913, 7.

7. Ibid.

8. *Evening Star*, December 28, 1913, 1.

9. Ibid.

10. Compare to Boudreaux, *Legends and Lore of the Mississippi Golden Gulf Coast*, 134.

11. *Punta Gorda Herald*, January 1, 1914, 1.

12. Boudreaux, *Legends and Lore of the Mississippi Golden Gulf Coast*, 134.

13. *Times Dispatch*, January 10, 1914, 1.

14. Ibid.

15. *Sun Herald*, January 11, 1998, 1E.

16. Boudreaux, *Legends and Lore of the Mississippi Golden Gulf Coast*, 135. The Confederate veteran's pledge read: "If I ever disown, repudiate, or apologize for the cause for which Lee fought and Jackson died, let the lightning of Heaven rend me and the scorn of all good men and true women be my portion; sun, moon, stars, all fall on me when I cease to love the Confederacy. It is the cause, not the fate of the cause that is glorious."

Franklin D. Roosevelt

1. Morris, "Rural Electrification of Northeast Mississippi."

2. Ibid.

3. Roosevelt, *Remarks at Corinth, Mississippi, November 17, 1934*, www.presidency.ucsb.edu.

4. *Northeast Mississippi Daily Journal*, May 18, 2008, Opinion Section.

5. Morris, "Rural Electrification of Northeast Mississippi."

6. Smith, "Tupelo Homesteads," 85–112.

7. Ibid., 102.

8. As a young child in 1936, Johnny Cash—who eventually gained national fame as a singer and songwriter—moved with his parents into a federally sponsored subsistence homestead located in the Dyess Colony of the Arkansas Delta. Brown, *Back to the Land*, 151.

9. Roosevelt, *Remarks at Tupelo, Mississippi, November 18, 1934*, www.presidency.ucsb.edu.

10. *Northeast Mississippi Daily Journal*, May 18, 2008.

11. Roosevelt, *Remarks at Tupelo, Mississippi, November 18, 1934*, www.presidency.ucsb.edu.

12. *House Bill No. 77 (As Approved by the Governor)*, Regular Session 1936 of the Mississippi Legislature.

13. *Amory News*, November 22, 1934, as included in an article in the *Amory Advertiser*, April 26, 1997, 12C.

14. *Amory Advertiser*, April 26, 1997, 12C.

15. *Franklin D. Roosevelt Day by Day*, a project of the Pare Lorentz Center at the FDR Presidential Library, April 27, 1937.

16. Givens, *Roosevelt Went Tarpon Fishing*.

17. *Franklin D. Roosevelt Day by Day*, April 29, 1937.

18. Roosevelt, *Informal, Extemporaneous Remarks of the President from the Rear Platform of the Presidential Special Train, Gulfport, MS, April 29, 1937*, catalog.archives.gov.

19. *Sun Herald*, January 11, 1998, E1.

20. *Press-Register*, April 22, 1937.

21. *Franklin D. Roosevelt Day by Day*, September 1942. Map showing the president's itinerary for this inspection tour from September 17 to October 1, 1942.

22. *Jackson Daily News*, March 22, 1953, in Letters to the Editor.

23. *Franklin D. Roosevelt Day by Day*.

24. Schultz, *85th Division in World War II*.

Richard Nixon

1. Moore, "Richard Nixon," 291.

2. Ellis, *Presidential Travel*, 196.

3. Nash and Taggart, *Mississippi Politics*, 49.

4. Ibid., 41.

5. Pielke, Simonpietri, and Oxelson, *Hurricane Camille Project Report*.

6. *New York Times*, August 19, 1969, 1.

7. Ibid., 1.

8. *New York Times*, September 9, 1969, 1, 35.

9. *Richard Nixon's Daily Diary September 1–30, 1969*, entry for September 8.

10. Nash and Taggart, *Mississippi Politics*, 303.

11. Nixon, *Remarks Following Aerial Inspection of Damage Caused by Hurricane Camille in Mississippi, September 8, 1969*, www.presidency.ucsb.edu.

12. Nixon, *Presidential Daily Diary September 1–30, 1969*, entry for September 8, Appendix D, www.nixonlibrary.gov.

13. Nixon, *Statement Following an Inspection Flight over Flooded Areas in Mississippi, Arkansas, and Louisiana, April 27, 1973*, www.presidency.ucsb.edu.

14. Nixon, *Remarks at the Dedication of the John C. Stennis Naval Technical Training Center, April 27, 1973*, www.presidency.ucsb.edu.

15. Ibid.

16. Ibid.

17. Nixon, *Remarks at the Annual Convention of the Mississippi Economic Council, April 25, 1974*, www.presidency.ucsb.edu.

18. See study at http://www.gallup.com/poll/116677/presidential-approval-ratings-gallup-historical-statistics-trends.aspx.

19. Nixon, *Remarks at the Annual Convention of the Mississippi Economic Council, April 25, 1974*, www.presidency.ucsb.edu.

Gerald Ford

1. *New York Times*, August 6, 1974, 1, 19.

2. *New York Times*, August 5, 1974, 15.

3. Ibid.

4. Witcover, *Marathon*, 441–442.

5. Ibid., 444ff.

6. Nash and Taggart, *Mississippi Politics*, 63.

7. Witcover, *Marathon*, 487ff.

8. Hoover's 1928 campaign employed this slogan: "A chicken in every pot and a car in every garage."

9. *Jackson Daily News*, July 30, 1976, 1.

10. Ford, *Remarks at a Republican Party Reception in Jackson, MS, July 30, 1976*, www.presidency.ucsb.edu.

11. Ford, *Exchange with Reporters in Jackson, MS, July 30, 1976*, www.presidency.ucsb.edu.

12. *Jackson Daily News*, September 27, 1976, 1.

13. Ford, *Remarks in Bay St. Louis, MS, September 25, 1976*, www.presidency.ucsb.edu.

14. Ford, *Remarks in Gulfport, MS, September 25, 1976*, www.presidency.ucsb.edu.

15. Ford, *Remarks in Biloxi, MS, September 25, 1976*, www.presidency.ucsb.edu.

16. Ford, *Remarks in Pascagoula, MS, September 25, 1976*, www.presidency.ucsb.edu.

17. Nash and Taggart, *Mississippi Politics*, 71.

Jimmy Carter

1. Nash and Taggart, *Mississippi Politics*, 57.

2. For additional information on Governor Finch, see Sansing, "Charles Clifton Finch."

3. Nash and Taggart, *Mississippi Politics*, 70–71.

4. Ibid., 6

5. Ibid., 68.

6. *New York Times*, July 21, 1977, A1, A6.

7. Wooten, *Dasher*, 373.

8. Witcover, *Marathon*, 580ff.

9. Nash and Taggart, *Mississippi Politics*, 69.

10. *New York Times*, July 21, 1977, B1, B7.

11. Ellis, *Presidential Travel*, 223.

12. Carter, *Remarks on Arrival at Allen C. Thompson Airport in Jackson, MS, July 21, 1977*, www.presidency.ucsb.edu.

13. Carter, *Remarks and a Question-and-Answer Session at a Public Meeting in Yazoo City, MS, July 21, 1977*, www.presidency.ucsb.edu.

14. *New York Times*, July 23, 1977, A6.

15. Carter, *Remarks and a Question-and-Answer Session at a Public Meeting in Yazoo City, MS, July 21, 1977*.

16. *Commercial Appeal*, August 26, 1977.

17. *Jackson Daily News*, July 20, 1978, 1A.

18. *New York Times*, September 15, 1979, 1.

19. *New York Times*, September 14, 1979, A1.

20. Ibid.

21. Carter, *Remarks Following an Inspection Tour of Areas Damaged by Hurricane Frederic, Pascagoula, MS, September 14, 1979*, www.presidency.ucsb.edu.

22. See discussion in Nash and Taggart, *Mississippi Politics*, 115ff.

23. Ibid.

24. *New York Times*, October 31, 1980, A16.

25. Reagan, *Reagan Quotes*, pbs.org.

26. *New York Times*, November 1, 1980, A1, A9.

27. Witcover, *Marathon*, 562.

28. Noted by J. J. Feinauer in an opinion piece for the *Deseret News*, November 13, 2014, deseretnews.com.

29. Carter, *Remarks at a Rally with Area Residents, Jackson, MS, October 31, 1980*, www .presidency.ucsb.edu.

Ronald Reagan

1. Widmer, *Campaigns*, 306–307.

2. Ellis, *Presidential Travel*, 239.

3. Nash and Taggart, *Mississippi Politics*, 7.

4. Ibid., 313.

5. Ibid.

6. Wills, *Reagan's America*, 377.

7. *Neshoba Democrat*, transcription of the *Speech of Ronald Reagan at the Neshoba County Fair on Sunday, August 3, 1980*.

8. Reference for this quotation and all those from this address in the following paragraphs: Reagan, *Remarks at a Mississippi Republican Party Fund-raising Dinner, Jackson, MS, June 20, 1983*.

9. This phrase may have originated in published descriptions of Massachusetts politician Benjamin Butler during one of his fiery speeches during the post–Civil War era in the US House of Representatives. It became common in describing political speakers who talked forcefully about martyrdom or taking up arms on behalf of the nation or a just cause. The reference remained current in 1887, when the periodical *Puck* ran a cover illustration showing a wild-eyed John Sherman (Republican politician from Ohio) waving a blood-stained shirt in a graveyard and shouting, "To arms! The war ain't half over yet!"

10. WLOX-TV coverage of the Ronald Reagan rally in Gulfport, Mississippi, on October 1, 1984, available on YouTube.com. It is filed as *WLOX Memories: President Reagan Visits the Coast 1984*.

11. *New York Times*, October 3, 1984.

12. Reagan, *Informal Exchange with Students from Bayou View Elementary School, Gulfport, MS, October 1, 1984*, www.presidency.ucsb.edu.

13. This is a version of the question Ronald Reagan asked as he delivered concluding remarks at his debate with President Jimmy Carter during the 1980 presidential election. He asked voters viewing across the nation on their television sets, "Are you better off now than you were four years ago?" It was a telling moment in a campaign waged during a devastating recession for the US economy.

14. Reagan, *Remarks at a Reagan-Bush Rally, Gulfport, MS, October 1, 1984*, www.presidency .ucsb.edu.

15. Wayne Weidie, *Ocean Springs Record*, carried in the *Clarion-Ledger*, October 7, 1984, on the Opinion Page.

16. Caemmerer, *Preaching for the Church*. Much of Caemmerer's classic book is structured to teach the goal, malady, means paradigm.

George H. W. Bush

1. Ellis, *Presidential Travel*, 9.

2. Ibid., 239.

3. Ibid., 226.

4. Ibid., 196.

5. Nash and Taggart, *Mississippi Politics*, 205.

6. Ibid., 205–206.

7. White House Transition Project, *The President on the Road: International and Domestic Travel, 1977–2005 (Report 2009-05)*, 20.

8. Alcorn State University is also classified as a land-grant institution by the federal government.

9. *Los Angeles Times*, May 9, 1989, section: Newsmakers. articles.latimes.com.

10. *Philadelphia Inquirer*, May 14, 1989. articles.philly.com.

11. This reference and those below from the two university commencements described in the text are from one of these sources: George H. W. Bush, *Remarks at the Alcorn State University Commencement Ceremony, Lorman, MS, May 13, 1989*; or George H. W. Bush, *Remarks at the Mississippi State University Commencement Ceremony, Starkville, MS, May 13, 1989*, both www.presidency.ucsb.edu.

12. W. B. Montgomery managed a successful ammunition plant in Montgomery, Alabama, for the Confederate forces during the Civil War. Montgomery, Ballard, and Piper, *Sonny Montgomery*, 8.

13. *New York Times*, October 14, 1989.

14. Ibid.

15. Ibid.

16. Laura Parker, *Washington Post*, October 15, 1989.

17. G. H. W. Bush, *Remarks at a Fundraiser for Congressional Candidate Tom Anderson, Gulfport, MS, October 12, 1989*, www.presidency.ucsb.edu.

18. For details and commentary, see *Los Angeles Times*, October 18, 1989, section: Nation in Brief, articles.latimes.com.

19. Nash and Taggart, *Mississippi Politics*, 256–257.

20. Wehrum, "How I Did It."

21. *Commercial Dispatch*, December 4, 1991, 1A, 11A.

22. Ibid.

23. G. H. W. Bush, *Remarks to Peavey Electronics Employees, Meridian, MS, December 3, 1991*, www.presidency.ucsb.edu.

24. *Clarion-Ledger*, March 3, 1992, 3B.

25. *Clarion-Ledger*, March 7, 1992, 1A, 11A.

26. Peter Applebome, "The 1992 Campaign: Far Right; Duke's Followers Lean to Buchanan," *New York Times*, March 8, 1992.

27. *Clarion-Ledger*, March 7, 1992, 1A, 11A.

28. Ibid.

29. For instance, Nash and Taggart, *Mississippi Politics*, 47, cite an earlier work that said of Clarke Reed, a Greenville businessman and Mississippi Republican Party chair, that his "political influence [would become] unequalled by any other non-officeholder in the South." Bass and DeVries, *Transformation of Southern Politics*, 214.

30. *Clarion-Ledger*, September 20, 1992, 1A.

31. The 1902 reference in the *Clarion-Ledger* was to the legendary bear hunt of Theodore Roosevelt near Smedes in Sharkey County, Mississippi, one of the eighteen counties generally included in the region known as the Mississippi Delta (see chapter 2). In fact, there were also stops in Vicksburg in Warren County and Mound Bayou in Bolivar County by Theodore Roosevelt in 1907 and a stop by William Taft (Vicksburg) in 1909, as well as a 1977 town meeting with Jimmy Carter at Yazoo City in Yazoo County—Bolivar, Warren, and Yazoo are traditional Delta counties. (See chapters 2, 3, and 8.) For additional information on the Mississippi Delta, see the website of the Mississippi Delta National Heritage Area at msdeltaheritage.com.

32. *Delta Democrat Times*, September 20, 1992, 1A.

33. *Delta Democrat Times*, September 21, 1992, 1A.

34. *Delta Democrat Times*, September 22, 1992, 1A.

35. *Delta Democrat Times*, September 23, 1992, 1A.

36. Ibid.

37. Ibid., 5A.

38. Ibid., 4A.

Bill Clinton

1. White House, *Biography of William J. Clinton*, WhiteHouse.gov.

2. Nash and Taggart, *Mississippi Politics*, 242.

3. Ellis, *Presidential Travel*, 159.

4. Ibid, 248.

5. Avila, *Decade of Economic Development*, 89.

6. Clinton Digital Library, *President Clinton's Daily Schedule*, clinton.presidentiallibraries.us.

7. Cobb, *Most Southern Place on Earth*.

8. Ibid.

9. White House Announcement, *President Clinton's New Market's Tour: Tapping America's Potential*. This announcement provided "background on the Clinton-Gore Administration's community development record" as well as outlining the new initiative. It is available on-line from the National Archives and Records Administration at clinton2.nara.gov.

10. Clinton, *Remarks in a Roundtable Discussion on Investment in the Mississippi Delta Region, Clarksdale, MS, July 6, 1999*, www.presidency.ucsb.edu.

11. Ibid.

12. Clinton, *Interview with Ron Insana of CNBC's "Business Center" in Clarksdale, MS,
July 6, 1999,* www.presidency.ucsb.edu.

13. *Clarksdale Press Register,* July 7, 1999, A-1.

14. Ibid., A-4.

15. Clinton, *Remarks to the Community in Hazard, Kentucky, July 5, 1999,* www.presidency
.ucsb.edu.

16. Clinton, *Empowering People to Build Better Futures for Themselves, Their Families,
and Their Communities,* Letter from President Bill Clinton, Founder, Clinton Foundation,
August 22, 2016, clintonfoundation.org.

George W. Bush

1. Nash and Taggart, *Mississippi Politics,* 303, on the career path of Haley Barbour: "Helping with the arrangements for Nixon's visit (September 8, 1979) was Haley Barbour, then
a twenty-one-year-old sometime student at the University of Mississippi and a budding
Republican operative. By the time Barbour welcomed President George W. Bush to the Gulf
Coast thirty-six years later to witness the destruction of Hurricane Katrina, he was not only
governor of Mississippi, but his career had mirrored the rise of the Republican Party in the
state he was now serving as its chief executive officer."

2. Ellis, *Presidential Travel,* 158.

3. Ibid., 159–160.

4. G. W. Bush, *Remarks at Madison Central High School, Madison, MS, August 7, 2002,*
www.presidency.ucsb.edu.

5. *Clarion-Ledger,* August 8, 2002, 9A.

6. Source for this quotation and others from Madison, MS, that follow is: G. W. Bush,
Remarks at Madison Central High School, Madison, MS, August 7, 2002, www.presidency
.ucsb.edu.

7. G. W. Bush, *Remarks at a Luncheon for Representative Charles W. Pickering, Jackson,
MS, August 7, 2002,* www.presidency.ucsb.edu.

8. *Clarion-Ledger,* August 6, 2002, 5A.

9. Ibid., 6A.

10. *Clarion-Ledger,* August 7, 2002, 11A.

11. *Clarion-Ledger,* August 8, 2002, 1A.

12. *Clarion-Ledger,* September 12, 2003, 1A, 7A.

13. *Jackson Free Press,* June 9, 2003.

14. G. W. Bush, *Remarks at a Luncheon for Gubernatorial Candidate Haley Barbour, Jackson, MS, September 12, 2003,* www.presidency.ucsb.edu.

15. *Clarion-Ledger,* September 13, 2003, 1A, 2A.

16. Nash and Taggart, *Mississippi Politics,* 307.

17. G. W. Bush, *Remarks in Southaven, MS, November 1, 2003,* www.presidency.ucsb.edu.

18. Nash and Taggart, *Mississippi Politics,* 307.

19. CNN report, November 1, 2003, cnn.com.

20. *Sun Herald,* November 2, 2003, A-1, A-2.

21. G. W. Bush, *Remarks in Gulfport, MS, November 1, 2003,* www.presidency.ucsb.edu.

22. *Jackson Free Press*, May 3, 2005.

23. *USA Today*, May 3, 2005.

24. G. W. Bush, *Remarks in a Discussion on Strengthening Social Security, Canton, MS, May 3, 2005*, www.presidency.ucsb.edu.

25. Galston, *Why the 2005 Social Security Initiative Failed.*

26. *Clarion-Ledger*, July 2, 2008, 1A.

27. Ibid.

28. Ibid., 3A.

29. Photograph clarionledger.com.

30. National Oceanic and Atmospheric Administration, *Hurricane Katrina*, ncdc.noaa.gov.

31. History Channel, *Hurricane Katrina*, history.com.

32. For a comprehensive review of the response to Hurricane Katrina in Mississippi, see Barbour and Nash, *America's Great Storm.*

33. *Sun Herald*, September 2, 2005, 1, 10.

34. Ibid.

35. G. W. Bush, *Remarks Following a Walking Tour of Areas Damaged by Hurricane Katrina and an Exchange with Reporters, Biloxi, MS, September 2, 2005*, www.presidency.ucsb.edu.

36. *Hattiesburg American*, September 5, 2005, photo gallery of President Bush's visit to Poplarville, hattiesburgamerican.com.

37. G. W. Bush, *Remarks to the Community in Poplarville, MS, September 5, 2005*, www .presidency.ucsb.edu.

38. King and Malveaux, *Bush Gets Ground Tour of Katrina Damage.*

39. G. W. Bush, *Remarks on the Aftermath of Hurricane Katrina and an Exchange with Reporters, Gulfport, MS, September 12, 2005*, www.presidency.ucsb.edu.

40. *Mississippi Press*, September 16, 2005, 1-A, 4-A.

41. See G. W. Bush, *Address to the Nation on Hurricane Katrina Recovery, New Orleans, LA, September 15, 2005*, www.presidency.ucsb.edu.

42. G. W. Bush, *Remarks to the Governor's Commission on Recovery Rebuilding, and Renewal, Gulfport, MS, September 20, 2005*, www.presidency.ucsb.edu.

43. C-Span, *Presidential Arrival in Gulfport, September 20, 2005*, c-span.org.

44. G. W. Bush, *Remarks to the Governor's Commission on Recovery Rebuilding, and Renewal, Gulfport, MS, September 20, 2005*, www.presidency.ucsb.edu.

45. *Sun Herald*, October 12, 2005, 1.

46. G. W. Bush, *Remarks to Reporters, Pass Christian, MS, October 11, 2005*, www.presidency .ucsb.edu.

47. G. W. Bush, *Remarks on Gulf Coast Reconstruction, Bay St. Louis, MS, January 12, 2006*, www.presidency.ucsb.edu.

48. G. W. Bush, *Remarks on Recovery Efforts in the Areas Damaged by Hurricanes Katrina and Rita, Gautier, MS, March 8, 2006*, www.presidency.ucsb.edu.

49. G. W. Bush, *Remarks on New Home Construction, Gautier, MS, March 8, 2006*, www .presidency.ucsb.edu.

50. G. W. Bush, *Remarks during a Visit to the Hands-on Gulf Coast Civic Action Center, Biloxi, MS, April 27, 2006*, www.presidency.ucsb.edu.

51. CBS News, *Bush Calls for Better Gas Mileage*, April 27, 2006, cbsnews.com.

52. CNN Money, *Bush Said to Meet with Car Chiefs*, April 27, 2006, money.cnn.com.

53. G. W. Bush, *Remarks during a Visit to a BP Gas Station, Biloxi, MS, April 27, 2006*, www.presidency.ucsb.edu.

54. Note that this George W. Bush visit to Biloxi on May 11, 2006, was to serve as the commencement speaker at Mississippi Gulf Coast Community College. Because this trip was clearly related to the series of Katrina visits as was obvious from the date, the location, and the theme of his remarks, it is included here in the category with his other disaster-related visits.

55. *Sun Herald*, May 12, 2006, A-9.

56. G. W. Bush, *Commencement Address at Mississippi Gulf Coast Community College, Biloxi, MS, May 11, 2006*, www.presidency.ucsb.edu.

57. *Sun Herald*, August 29, A-1.

58. G. W. Bush, *Remarks Following a Lunch Meeting with Community Leaders, Biloxi, MS, August 28, 2006*, www.presidency.ucsb.edu.

59. Suarez, "President Bush Visits Gulf Coast for Katrina Anniversary."

60. G. W. Bush, *Remarks on Hurricane Katrina Recovery Efforts, Biloxi, MS, August 28, 2006*, www.presidency.ucsb.edu.

61. G. W. Bush, *Remarks Following a Tour of United States Marine, Inc., and an Exchange with Reporters, Gulfport, MS, August 28, 2006*, www.presidency.ucsb.edu.

62. Conroy, *Bush Tours Katrina-Ravaged Areas*.

63. G. W. Bush, *Remarks Following a Visit with Gulf Coast Grant Recipients, Long Beach, MS, March 1, 2007*, www.presidency.ucsb.edu.

64. Mississippi Democratic Party, *Bush Overlooking Suffering on Coast*, msdemocrats.net.

65. G. W. Bush, *Remarks Following a Meeting with Elected Officials and Community Leaders, Biloxi, MS, March 1, 2007*, www.presidency.ucsb.edu.

66. G. W. Bush, *Fact Sheet: Working with State and Local Leaders to Help Rebuild the Gulf Coast, March 1, 2007*, www.presidency.ucsb.edu.

67. G. W. Bush, *Remarks on Gulf Coast Reconstruction, Bay St. Louis, MS, August 29, 2007*, www.presidency.ucsb.edu.

68. G. W. Bush, *Remarks Following a Dinner with Elected Officials and Community Leaders, Gulfport, MS, August 20, 2008*, www.presidency.ucsb.edu.

Barack Obama

1. *Sun Herald*, June 14, 2010, 1A, 2A.

2. *Clarion-Ledger*, June 11, 2010, 1B, 4B.

3. *Sun Herald*, June 14, 2010, 11A.

4. Allen, *Thad Allen Named National Incident Commander for Deepwater Horizon Spill*.

5. Obama, *Remarks Following a Briefing on the Oil Spill in the Gulf of Mexico, Gulfport, MS, June 14, 2010*, www.presidency.ucsb.edu.

6. Obama, *Remarks during a Discussion with Community Members, Gulfport, MS, June 14, 2010*, www.presidency.ucsb.edu.

7. CNN Breaking News—Politics, *Obama "Gathering Up Facts" on BP Compensation*, June 15, 2010, CNN.com.

8. "In Oval Office Speech, Obama Calls for New Focus on Energy Policy," *New York Times*, June 15, 2010.

9. Obama, *Weekly Address on August 29, 2009: Marking the Fourth Anniversary of Hurricane Katrina*, whitehouse.gov.

10. WDAM-TV, *President Obama Bypassing Mississippi on his Gulf Coast Visit*, wdam.com.

11. White, *Obama to Visit New Orleans on Tenth Anniversary of Hurricane Katrina*, time.com.

12. WLOX, *Louisiana Flood Victim Surprised by Obama Visit*, wlox.com.

Conclusion

1. The George W. Bush visit to Biloxi on May 11, 2006, was to serve as the commencement speaker at Mississippi Gulf Coast Community College, a purpose that would normally set this visit into the "Other" category just as his father's visits to address university commencements on May 13, 1989, were cataloged. However, the George W. Bush trip was clearly related to the series of Katrina visits as was obvious from the date, the location, and the theme of his remarks. Thus this book includes it in the category with other disaster-related presidential visits.

Appendix A

1. *Chicago Tribune*, October 22, 1907, 3.

2. Roosevelt, *Remarks at Tupelo, Mississippi, November 18, 1934*, www.presidency.ucsb.edu.

3. Nixon, *Remarks at the Annual Convention of the Mississippi Economic Council, April 25, 1974*, www.presidency.ucsb.edu.

4. G. W. Bush, *Remarks on Gulf Coast Reconstruction, Bay St. Louis, MS, January 12, 2006*, www.presidency.ucsb.edu.

BIBLIOGRAPHY

Books, Journals, and Online Resources

Allen, Thad. *Thad Allen Named National Incident Commander for Deepwater Horizon Spill.* Marine Log. May 1, 2010. marinelog.com.

Avila, Tomas Alberto. *A Decade of Economic Development Visioning & Execution.* Providence, RI: Milenio Associates, 2007.

Barbour, Haley, and Jere Nash. *America's Great Storm.* Jackson: University Press of Mississippi, 2015.

Bass, Jack, and Walter DeVries. *The Transformation of Southern Politics.* New York: Basic Books, 1976.

Bernard, Shane K., and Paul C. P. McIlhenny. *Tabasco: An Illustrated History.* Avery Island, LA: McIlhenny, 2007.

Boudreaux, Edmond, Jr. *Legends and Lore of the Mississippi Golden Gulf Coast.* Charleston, SC: History Press, 2013.

Boyd, Deanna, and Kendra Chen. *The History and Experience of African Americans in America's Postal Service.* National Postal Museum, 2002. postalmuseum.si.edu.

Brown, Dona. *Back to the Land: The Enduring Dream of Self-Sufficiency in Modern America.* Madison: University of Wisconsin Press, 2011.

Busbee, Walter F., Jr. *Mississippi: A History.* West Sussex, UK: John Wiley & Sons, 2015.

Caemmerer, Richard R. *Preaching for the Church.* St. Louis: Concordia Publishing House, 1959.

CBS News. *Bush Calls for Better Gas Mileage.* April 27, 2006. cbsnews.com.

Clinton, Bill. *Empowering People to Build Better Futures for Themselves, Their Families, and Their Communities.* Letter from President Bill Clinton, Founder, Clinton Foundation, August 22, 2016. clintonfoundation.org.

Clinton Digital Library. *President Clinton's Daily Schedule.* clinton.presidentiallibraries.us.

CNN Money. *Bush Said to Meet with Car Chiefs.* April 27, 2006. money.cnn.com.

CNN Reports [by subject and date]. cnn.com.

Cobb, James Charles. *The Most Southern Place on Earth: The Mississippi Delta and the Roots of Regional Identity.* New York: Oxford University Press, 1992.

Conroy, Scott. *Bush Tours Katrina-Ravaged Areas.* Associated Press. March 1, 2007. cbsnews.com.

C-Span. *Presidential Arrival in Gulfport.* September 20, 2005. c-span.org.

Ellis, Richard J. *Presidential Travel: The Journey from George Washington to George W. Bush.* Lawrence: University Press of Kansas, 2008.

Franklin D. Roosevelt Day by Day. A Project of the Pare Lorentz Center at the FDR Presidential Library. fdrlibrary.marist.edu.

Galston, William A. *Why the 2005 Social Security Initiative Failed and What It Means for the Future.* Washington, DC: Report from the Brookings Institution, September 21, 2007. brookings.edu.

Gatewood, Willard B., Jr. *Theodore Roosevelt and the Art of Controversy: Episodes of the White House Years.* Baton Rouge: Louisiana State University Press, 1970.

Givens, Murphy. *Roosevelt Went Tarpon Fishing Off Port Aransas.* Corpus Christi, TX: The Caller Times, March 26, 2014. caller.com.

Harbaugh, William Henry. *Power and Responsibility: The Life and Times of Theodore Roosevelt.* Revised ed. New York: Octagon Books, 1975.

Hilpert, John M. *American Cyclone: Theodore Roosevelt and His 1900 Whistle-Stop Campaign.* Jackson: University Press of Mississippi, 2015.

House Bill No. 77 (As Approved by the Governor). Regular Session 1936 of the Mississippi Legislature. Mississippi Department of Archives and History.

King, Gilbert. The History of the Teddy Bear: From Wet and Angry to Soft and Cuddly. *Smithsonian Magazine,* December 21, 2012. Smithsonian.com.

King, John, and Suzanne Malveaux. *Bush Gets Ground Tour of Katrina Damage.* CNN, September 12, 2005. cnn.com.

Lakes-to-the-Gulf Deep Waterway Association. *Report on the Fourth Annual Convention, New Orleans, October 30 to November 2, 1909.* St. Louis: Deep Waterway Association, 1910.

Lower Delta Partnership. *Great Delta Bear Affair.* Greatdeltabearaffair.com.

Mississippi Democratic Party. *Bush Overlooking Suffering on Coast.* Official Party Press Release. March 1, 2007. msdemocrats.net.

Montgomery, G. V. "Sonny," Michael B. Ballard, and Craig S. Piper. *Sonny Montgomery: The Veteran's Champion.* Starkville: Mississippi State University Libraries, 2003.

Moore, Glenn. "Richard Nixon: The Southern Strategy and the 1968 Presidential Election." In *Richard Nixon: Politician, President, Administrator,* ed. Leon Friedman and William F. Levantrosser. New York: Greenwood Press, 1991.

Morris, Edmund. *Theodore Rex.* New York: Modern Library, 2001.

Morris, Sara E. "The Rural Electrification of Northeast Mississippi." *Mississippi History Now,* (October 2011). Jackson: Mississippi Department of Archives and History. mshistorynow .mdah.state.ms.us.

Nash, Jere, and Andy Taggart. *Mississippi Politics: The Struggle for Power, 1976–2006.* Jackson: University Press of Mississippi, 2006.

Nixon, Richard. *Presidential Daily Diary September 1–30, 1969.* Entry for September 8, Appendix D. Nixon Presidential Library & Museum. www.nixonlibrary.gov.

Obama, Barack. *Weekly Address on August 29, 2009: Marking the Fourth Anniversary of Hurricane Katrina.* The White House. whitehouse.gov.

Olcott, Charles S. *William McKinley.* Vol. 2. Boston: Houghton Mifflin, 1916.

Peters, Gerhard, and John T. Woolley. *The American Presidency Project.* Comprehensive online resource for presidential speeches, interviews, and various other documents. www.presidency.ucsb.edu.

Pielke, Roger A., Jr., Chantal Simonpietri, and Jennifer Oxelson. *Hurricane Camille Project Report.* July 12, 1999. www.sciencepolicy.colorado.edu.

Roosevelt, Theodore. *Hunting the Grisly and Other Sketches.* New York: G. P. Putnam's Sons, 1893.

Rutherford, Joe. Opinion Piece Recalling Franklin Roosevelt's Visit to Corinth. *Northeast Mississippi Daily Journal,* May 18, 2008.

Sansing, David G. "Charles Clifton Finch: Fifty-Seventh Governor of Mississippi 1976–1980." *Mississippi History Now* (January 2004). Jackson: Mississippi Department of Archives and History. www.mshistorynow.mdah.state.ms.us.

Schultz, Paul. "Camp Shelby, History of Training Camp during WW2 and Today." In *The 85th Division in WW2.* custermen.com.

Smith, Fred C. "The Tupelo Homesteads: New Deal Agrarian Experimentation." *Journal of Mississippi History* (2006): 85–112.

St. Louis Business Men's League. *Down the Mississippi River.* Pamphlet presenting the travel and event agenda for President Taft's flotilla. 1909.

Suarez, Ray. President Bush Visits Gulf Coast for Katrina Anniversary. *PBS News Hour.* August 28, 2006. Transcript of report. pbs.org.

Thompson, Julius E. *The Black Press in Mississippi, 1865–1985.* Gainesville: University Press of Florida, 1994.

WDAM-TV. *President Obama Bypassing Mississippi on His Gulf Coast Visit.* Hattiesburg: Copyrighted by WLOX (Biloxi), 2009. wdam.com.

Wehrum, Kasey. "How I Did It: Hartley Peavey of Peavey Electronics." *Inc. Magazine,* October 2011. inc.com.

White, Daniel. "Obama to Visit New Orleans on Tenth Anniversary of Hurricane Katrina." *Time Magazine,* August 19, 2015. time.com.

White House. *Biography of William J. Clinton.* WhiteHouse.gov.

White House Transition Project. *The President on the Road: International and Domestic Travel, 1977–2005 (Report 2009-05).* WhiteHouseTransitionProject.org.

Widmer, Ted. *Campaigns: A Century of Presidential Races: From the Photo Archives of the New York Times.* New York: DK Publishing, 2001.

Wills, Garry. *Reagan's America: Innocents at Home.* Garden City, NY: Doubleday, 1987.

Witcover, Jules. *Marathon: The Pursuit of the Presidency 1972–1976.* New York: Viking Press, 1977.

WLOX. "Louisiana Flood Victim Surprised by Obama Visit." *Associated Press,* 2016. wlox.com.

Wooten, James. *Dasher: The Roots and Rising of Jimmy Carter.* New York: Summit Books, 1978.

NEWSPAPERS

Aberdeen (MS) Weekly

Amory (MS) Advertiser

Amory (MS) News

Billings (MT) Gazette

Caller Times (Corpus Christi, TX)

Calumet (MI) News

Chicago Tribune

Clarion-Ledger (Jackson, MS)

Clarksdale (MS) Press Register

Columbus (MS) Commercial

Commercial Dispatch (Columbus, MS)

Daily Corinthian (Corinth, MS)

Daily Press (Newport News, VA)

Delta Democrat Times (Greenville, MS)

Deseret News (Salt Lake City, UT)

Evening Star (Washington, DC)

Forest (PA) Republican

Greenville (MS) Times

Hattiesburg (MS) American

Herald and News (Newberry, SC)

Indianapolis Journal
Jackson (MS) Free Press
Kansas Agitator (Garnett, KS)
Los Angeles Times
Macon (MS) Beacon
Minneapolis Journal
Mississippi Press (Pascagoula, MS)
Nashville (TN) Globe
Natchez (MS) Democrat
Neshoba (MS) Democrat
New York Times
New-York Tribune
Northeast Mississippi Daily Journal
    (Tupelo, MS)
Ocean Springs (MS) Record
Okalona (MS) Standard

Pensacola (FL) Journal
Philadelphia Inquirer
Press-Register (Mobile, AL)
Punta Gorda (FL) Herald
Rock Island (IL) Argus
San Francisco Call
St. Louis Republic
Sun (New York)
Sun Herald (Biloxi, MS)
Times Dispatch (Richmond, VA)
Topeka (KS) State Journal
USA Today
Vicksburg (MS) Evening Post
Vicksburg (MS) Post
Washington (DC) Times

INDEX

ABOUT THE AUTHORS

JOHN M. HILPERT spent more than thirty-five years in higher education administration, serving most of two decades of that time as a university president. He retired in 2013. During his career he was elected to three terms as board chair for the Southern Association of Colleges and Schools (SACS) and one term as president of the Mississippi Association of Colleges. John holds a PhD degree from the University of Michigan, where he received the 1985 John S. Brubacher Award for excellence in scholarship on the history of higher education. In 2015 the University Press of Mississippi published his previous book, *American Cyclone: Theodore Roosevelt and His 1900 Whistle-Stop Campaign*. He married Patricia Tucker in 1971; she is an award-winning photographer who spent a thirty-year career as a registered nurse and health care administrator. The couple lives in Sioux Falls, South Dakota.

ZACHARY M. HILPERT is an assistant professor in the Department of Focused Inquiry at Virginia Commonwealth University, where he has taught for six years. Zach holds degrees from four universities, including a PhD in American studies from the College of William and Mary, where his principal research interest was the commercialization of disaster imagery in late nineteenth- and early twentieth-century America—for example, the Great Chicago Fire, the Johnstown Flood, and the San Francisco Earthquake. He has also written on the life and work of American photographer Berenice Abbott. He married Sandy Flemming in 2014; she is a licensed clinical social worker at a state-owned psychiatric hospital. The couple lives in Richmond, Virginia.